Top 20

Top 20

Great Grammar for Great Writing

Keith S. Folse
University of Central Florida

Elena Vestri Solomon
Hillsborough Community College

Barbara Smith-Palinkas
University of South Florida

Houghton Mifflin Company   Boston   New York

Publisher: Patricia A. Coryell
Director of ESL Publishing: Susan Maguire
Senior Development Editor: Kathy Sands-Boehmer
Editorial Assistant: Evangeline Bermas
Senior Project Editor: Tracy Patruno
Manufacturing Manager: Florence Cadran
Marketing Manager: Annamarie Rice

Cover image: © Eyewire

Credits appear on page 303, which is hereby considered an extension of the copyright page.

Printed in the U.S.A.

Library of Congress Control Number: 2001133363

ISBN: 0-618-152997

123456789-DBH-07 06 05 04 03

Contents

Overview

Top 20 offers instruction and review in 20 grammar areas that are essential to good English writing. Because editing of student writing is a primary objective for many courses at this level, a large number of the exercises in *Top 20* deal with editing. In particular, these exercises attempt to draw students' attention to common grammatical errors and then teach students various ways to make corrections. (For good background information for teachers regarding correcting student writing, we recommend *Treatment of Error in Second Language Writing* (Ferris 2002).)

Depending on the class level and the amount of writing and work that are done outside of class, there is enough material in *Top 20* for 70 to 90 classroom hours. However, if time limitations exist, the material could be covered in as little as 45 hours with a faster group, provided that many of the exercises are done as homework.

This book is designed for intermediate to advanced students. However, the passages in many of the exercises are from real textbooks that were written for native speakers. Thus, students will have to understand the grammar points well to be able to apply the skills in the exercises.

For many students, a major obstacle to future educational plans is not being able to write effectively and easily in English. Thus, the quality of any written work that they do is very important. Grammar is often the main problem that keeps them from producing a solid piece of original writing.

Because grammar is such an integral part of good student writing, the exercises in Top 20 focus exclusively on grammar problems that are common in writing. The title *Top 20* refers to the 20 chapters in the book. Each chapter focuses on a common area of difficulty in English grammar, including verb tenses, articles, gerunds and infinitives, noun clauses, modals, sentence matters, subject-verb agreement, word forms, and parallel structure. The topics in the chapters of *Top 20* were selected after surveying many experienced teachers, student writers, textbooks, and course curricula.

You, the teacher, are always the best judge of which chapters should be covered in which order and to what extent. No one knows the language needs of your students better than you do. It is up to you to gauge the needs of your students and then match those needs with the material in the 20 chapters of *Top 20*.

Text Organization

Each of the 20 chapters focuses on one grammar area that affects the quality of student writing. Each chapter is independent of all other chapters and can be taught in any order.

At the back of the book, there are six appendixes. Appendix 1 reviews the parts of speech. Appendix 2 lists irregular verb forms. Appendix 3 is a list of irregular noun plurals. Appendix 4 briefly reviews how to construct comparative and superlative forms of adjectives and adverbs. Appendix 5 presents an overview of the seven steps in the writing process. Finally, Appendix 6 is a list of commonly used editing symbols. You may decide to use these symbols or a modification of them in marking student writing. Many of these symbols can be found on the page that opens each chapter.

Supporting web exercises for *Top 20*, as well as the Answer Key, can be found at: **http://esl.college.hmco.com/instructors** (part of the Houghton Mifflin site).

Contents of a Chapter

Following are the common features and exercise types in each chapter. Not all chapters have every feature or exercise type, but these are the most common chapter components.

Opening Page

The corrected sentence is a student example of a major grammatical error presented and practiced in that chapter. It is important to remember that this is only one kind of error that students may make in the grammar area covered in the chapter. The symbol that is used to edit the student error comes from the list of editing symbols in Appendix 6.

Grammar Reviews and Explanations

The grammar reviews and explanations (set off by a shaded bar) have been written to focus specifically on problems that occur in student writing, not speaking. *Top 20* is not meant to be a complete grammar book; instead, it reviews common problem areas and helps students focus their attention on the gap between what they are writing and what they should be writing.

Exercise Types

Second language acquisition (SLA) research shows the importance of awareness in the second language learning process. Students using this text have had basic grammar instruction, but many continue to make errors. The exercises in *Top 20* are designed to raise students' consciousness of the types of errors that they make in their writing. Additional SLA work has demonstrated the importance of the number of exercises—frequency of practice—in comparison with the nature of the exercise (Folse 1999, Fotos 2002, and Laufer and Hulstijn 1998).

Original Sentences   Some exercises ask students to write original sentences to illustrate a very specific aspect of a given grammar point. We recommend that you have students discuss their answers in groups and possibly write some of their sentences on the board for general class discussion about what is correct, what is not correct, and why a gap between the two exists.

Selecting the Correct Form   This traditional type of exercise usually presents students with two to three answer options, and students must underline or circle the single correct answer. The incorrect answer options are almost always forms that students with various first languages would write. Thus, this kind of exercise is harder than it might appear.

Editing
∧ **Exercise**

Editing of Sentences   Because a paragraph is only as good as the sentences in it, this kind of exercise presents students with sentences one at a time. The sentences are often about a single topic and are related to each other. Students are asked to focus on one specific grammar issue, for example, verb tenses, and check for that specific grammar point in each of the sentences.

Editing
∧ **Exercise**

Editing of Paragraphs   In this kind of exercise, students are given a real paragraph written for native speakers. Common sources are business books, history books, education texts, speech books, sociology texts, the Internet, and newspapers. Students are not told where the errors are, but they are always told 1) how many errors to look for or 2) what type of errors there are.

These two points are important in helping students practice looking for, finding, and correcting *specific* errors that they are likely to be making. Since the teaching goal is to enable students to edit for specific kinds of errors, it makes sense to tell them what errors to look for. For example, if we want students to check for subject-verb agreement and word endings, then teachers and materials should train students to look for these specific mistakes. Instead of the more typical directions that ask students to find "the errors" in a given piece of writing, the most effective exercises direct students to find, for example, two subject-verb errors and three word ending errors, or to find five errors.

Multiple Choice   This kind of exercise follows the traditional multiple-choice format. Four choices are offered with only one choice being correct. This style will be familiar to students who have had experience with TOEFL.

Locating the Error   In this kind of exercise, students must read single sentences that have four underlined parts. Students circle the one underlined area that has a grammatical error and write their edited answer above the error. Again, this exercise type is consistent with the structure section of TOEFL. Error identification exercises are helpful in the overall SLA process because they can raise learners' consciousness of a linguistic feature by requiring learners to focus their attention on the gap between the incorrect form and the correct form (Schmidt, 2001).

Original Writing   In order to achieve the goal of connecting both the grammar instruction and focused review in student writing, each chapter of Top 20 ends with an exercise called Original Writing. Students are given a prompt to which they are asked to respond by writing a paragraph, two paragraphs, or an essay. (It is up to each teacher to establish the writing length parameters of any exercise.) We believe that students should not be writing extensively but rather intensively when the goal is improving writing accuracy. Thus, this activity asks students to write a short piece, but the grammar demands are high. Students are told to practice certain aspects of the grammar in that chapter, to underline their original examples, and to check their correctness with a partner. Underlining key linguistic features has been shown to aid in student noticing and learning of new material.

More about the Exercises in *Top 20*

Teachers have long noticed that students may do well in a grammar class where the focus is on one grammatical form in one type of exercise, but these same students may experience writing problems when trying to transfer or apply this knowledge to original writing. For some reason, students do not transfer the material that they were just taught to their writing. As a result, the majority of the exercises in *Top 20* deal with language in a context. This includes language in a series of related sentences, in a whole paragraph, or even in a short essay. Our experience has shown that students can improve their editing for a specific kind of grammatical error when they review the grammar issue and then practice their editing skills in sentences, in whole paragraphs, and in essays. The 227 exercises in *Top 20* and the additional web activities offer more than enough material to satisfy all students' written grammar needs.

Though a wide array of exercise types is included (see the previous section, Contents of a Chapter), the three exercises most commonly used are fill-in-the-blank, error correction (editing), and original student writing of paragraphs. The most important objectives of *Top 20* are to enable students to feel more comfortable with ESL grammar and to produce better writing by improving their editing skills. Consequently, the number and variety of exercises that students cover are crucial to the success of *Top 20*.

References

Ferris, D. *Treatment of Error in Second Language Writing*. Ann Arbor: University of Michigan Press, 2002.

Folse, K. "The Effect of Type of Written Practice Activity on Second Language Vocabulary Retention." Ph.D. diss., University of South Florida, 1999.

Fotos, S. "Structure-based interactive tasks for the EFL grammar learner." In *New Perspectives on Grammar Teaching in Second Language Classrooms*, edited by E. Hinkel and S. Fotos, 135–154. Mahwah, New Jersey: Lawrence Erlbaum Associates, 2002.

Laufer, B. and J. Hulstijn. "What leads to better incidental vocabulary learning: Comprehensible input or comprehensible output?" Paper presented at the Pacific Second Language Research Forum (PacSLRF), Tokyo, March 1998.

Jourdenais, R., et al. "Does textual enhancement promote noticing: A think-aloud protocol analysis." In *Attention and awareness in foreign language learning*, edited by R. Schmidt, 183–216. University of Hawaii at Manoa, Second Language Teaching and Curriculum Center: Technical Report #9, 1995.

Schmidt, R. "Attention." In *Cognition and second language instruction*, edited by P. Robinson, 3–32. Cambridge: Cambridge University Press, 2001.

For the answer key, additional exercises, and other instructor resources, visit the Top 20 instructor website at
http://esl.college.hmco.com/instructors

Additional exercises for each chapter are available to students on the Top 20 student website at
http://esl.college.hmco.com/students

Acknowledgments

Top 20 is the result of the planning, input, and encouragement of a great many people. We are especially grateful to our editors at Houghton Mifflin, Susan Maguire and Kathy Sands-Boehmer, who have been there for us time and time again as this book was born, grew, and finally came of age.

We wish to express our immense gratitude to Kathy Smith, our developmental editor, who so diligently helped us implement reviewers' and teachers' suggestions into the intermediate and then this, the final product. Without her contributions, *Top 20* would most certainly not be *Top 20*.

Special thanks go to Rachel Koch for her contributions to Chapter 3 and her work in the initial phase of this book.

We would also like to thank the following people involved with the M.A. TESOL Program at the University of Central Florida who offered their insightful ideas for improving this work, namely Suzanne Ball, Cathy Barbano, Patricia Burrows, Pamela Castro, Karina Clemmons, Ann Conrad, Luke Cousineau, Adriana Darido, Linda Dodson, Debbie Dougherty, Nancy Fahnestock, Kimberly Fox, Xhuljeta Gjini, Carole Gonzalez, Rachel Levee, Maria Lopez-Albistur, Susan Lowell, Andrew Macri, Yolanda McAuliff, April McDonald, Judith McCloskey, Jacqueline McFarland, Veronica McGowan, Arleen Mindis, Amal Muhaisen, Amani Nasseraldin, Jan Petrino, Jan Pilcher, Rebekah Richey, Willie Rivers, Sarah Rosser, Carolina Ryan, Wells Rutland, Milagros Salazar, Beth Savitsky, Janet Selitto, Karen Shelley, Vlasta Stofova, Wei-Chun Sun, Peggy Sunvold, and Lucja Wasowska.

In addition, we thank the academic assistants at the Hillsborough Community College Writing Center, Dale Mabry Campus, in Tampa, Florida.

Thanks to the members of TESL-L, an invaluable means of communicating with ESL and EFL professionals all over the globe, who offered their ideas on the use of context in practicing grammar through writing.

Finally, we thank these reviewers whose comments were instrumental in the development of Top 20: Susan Bresee, *University of Maryland;* Vincent Crampton, *Valencia Community College;* Lynn Davis, *Southern Illinois University;* Janet Eveler, *El Paso Community College;* Janet Goldstein, *Bramson ORT College;* David Ross, *Houston Community College;* Joe Starr, *Houston Community College;* and Hoda Zaki, *Camden County College.*

Keith S. Folse
Elena Vestri Solomon
Barbara Smith-Palinkas

In 1848, gold was discovered in California. Two years later, California joins the United States. VT

1

Verb Tense Review

This chapter reviews the verb tenses in English. In Chapter 2, you will work with specific problems that many writers have with verb tenses.

1.1 Verb Tenses in English

The following chart gives you an overview of the twelve verb tenses in English. Then each tense is treated separately with examples of form and the most common uses, followed by practice exercises.

	with REGULAR VERB	with IRREGULAR VERB
Present:	I paint	I eat
Present progressive:	I am painting	I am eating
Present perfect:	I have painted	I have eaten
Present perfect progressive:	I have been painting	I have been eating
Past:	I painted	I ate
Past progressive:	I was painting	I was eating
Past perfect:	I had painted	I had eaten
Past perfect progressive:	I had been painting	I had been eating
Future:	I will paint	I will eat
Future progressive:	I will be painting	I will be eating
Future perfect:	I will have painted	I will have eaten
Future perfect progressive:	I will have been painting	I will have been eating

1.2 Present Tense

The present tense takes the form:

> VERB or VERB + -s   I eat. He eats.

Uses

1. For facts that are not limited to a specific time and for general truths

   Water **boils** at 100° Celsius.

2. For a repeated, habitual, or usual action

   They **play** tennis every Saturday morning.

3. For information from a book, a poem, research, or other work. (This is often called the literary present.)

   In the play, Romeo and Juliet **love** each other despite their family differences.

4. For a future event (but there should be a future expression, usually an adverb or adverbial phrase)

The flight from Boston to New York **departs** in fifteen minutes.

Exercise 1 Write one sentence for each of the four uses of the present tense.*

Use 1. _____

_____

Use 2. _____

_____

Use 3. _____

_____

Use 4. _____

_____

———————

*For the exercises in this chapter, another option is to find sentences from a real source (for example, a magazine or the Internet).

(1.3) Present Progressive Tense

The present progressive tense takes the form:

     am / is / are + VERB + *-ing*   **I am eating.**

Uses

1. For an action that is happening at this moment and that will have a definite end

    Doctors **are meeting** in Amsterdam to discuss treatments for AIDS.

2. For a longer action that is happening "now"

    "Now" can be a short time such as "at this second" or a longer time such as "today" or "this month / year / decade."

    Kevin **is working** on four projects this month.

3. For a repeated action that causes irritation or problems (often used with *always*)

    Politicians **are** always **discussing** ways of increasing government spending.

4. For an event in the near future (used with adverb indicating future)

Twenty students **are taking** TOEFL next Wednesday.

 Remember that we usually put only action verbs in progressive tenses. Therefore, we can say *I am going, I am eating,* and *I am exercising,* but we do not usually say *I am knowing, I am owning,* or *I am being.*

Exercise 2   Write one sentence for each of the four uses of the present progressive tense.

Use 1. _____

_____

Use 2. _____

_____

Use 3. _____

_____

Use 4. _____

_____

1.4   Present Perfect Tense

The present perfect tense takes the form:

have / has + PAST PARTICIPLE   I **have eaten.**

Uses

1. For an action that started in the past and continues in the present

California **has been** a state since 1850.

2. For an action that has just been completed

We **have** just **finished** unit 7.

3. For a past action that still has an effect on the present

The government **has raised** taxes, and many companies **have laid off** workers.

4. For an action that happened several times (no specific past time) and may happen again

The government **has increased** the sales tax three times.

5. To indicate that you have the experience of doing something (no specific past time)

   Have you ever **read** *Hamlet*?

6. For a change or an accomplishment that has occurred (no specific past time)

   Because of the high demand for oil, the price of gasoline **has increased.**

   Scientists **have cloned** a sheep and a cat.

7. To indicate an uncompleted action that may happen (no specific past time)

The judge **has** not **decided** the fate of the criminal yet.

Exercise 3   Write one sentence for each of the seven uses of the present perfect tense.

Use 1. _____

_____

Use 2. _____

_____

Use 3. _____

_____

Use 4. _____

_____

Use 5. _____

_____

Use 6. _____

_____

Use 7. _____

_____

1.5 Present Perfect Progressive Tense

The present perfect progressive tense takes the form:

have / has + been + VERB + -ing   I **have been eating.**

Uses

1. For an action that started in the past and is continuing in the present for a specific duration, with emphasis on the fact that it is still happening

   The president **has been discussing** this problem for more than two years.

2. For an action that started in the past and is continuing in the present for a non-specific duration, meaning "recently" or "lately"

   Congress and the President **have been discussing** this problem.

Exercise 4   Write one sentence for each use of the present perfect progressive tense.

Use 1. _____

   _____

Use 2. _____

   _____

1.6 Simple Past Tense

The simple past tense takes the form:

VERB + -ed   I **painted.**

or IRREGULAR form   I **ate.**

Uses

1. For an action or condition that was completed in the past

   People **discovered** gold in California in 1848.

2. For a series of finished actions

   Texas **became** a state in 1845, and California **joined** the U.S. in 1850.

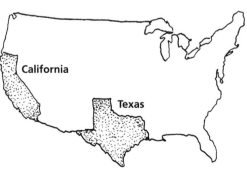

Exercise 5   Write one sentence for each use of the past tense.

Use 1. _____

_____

Use 2. _____

_____

1.6.1   More Expressions for Past Time: *used to* and *would*

In English, *used to* and *would* also express past tense.

Uses

1. For a past habit or action that is no longer true: *used to* OR *would*

     When I was a young boy, I **used to play** tennis after school every day.

     When I was a young boy, I **would play** tennis after school every day.

2. For a past fact that is no longer true: *used to*

     When I was a young boy, my family **used to live** in Pennsylvania.

     NOT When I was a young boy, my family **would live** in Pennsylvania.

3. This is the question form for *used to*:

     "Did you **use to** live in Pennsylvania?"

4. This is the negative form for *used to*:

     "I didn't **use to** like ginger ice cream."   (No "d")

     NOT "I didn't **used to.**"

Exercise 6   For Use 1, write one *used to* sentence and one *would* sentence. For Use 2, write one sentence, one question, and one negative example using *used to*.

Use 1. a. _____

         b. _____

Use 2. _____

Question: _____

Negative: _____

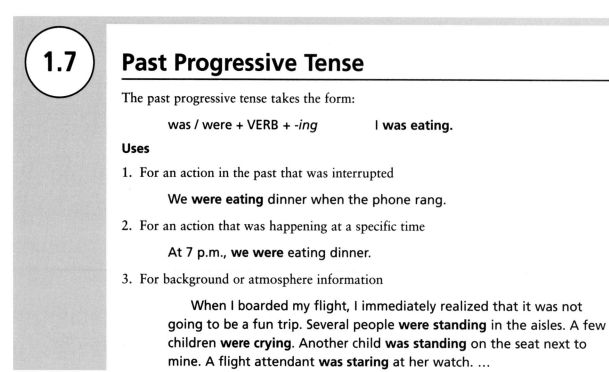

1.7 Past Progressive Tense

The past progressive tense takes the form:

was / were + VERB + -ing   I **was eating.**

Uses

1. For an action in the past that was interrupted

    We **were eating** dinner when the phone rang.

2. For an action that was happening at a specific time

    At 7 p.m., **we were** eating dinner.

3. For background or atmosphere information

    When I boarded my flight, I immediately realized that it was not going to be a fun trip. Several people **were standing** in the aisles. A few children **were crying.** Another child **was standing** on the seat next to mine. A flight attendant **was staring** at her watch. ...

Exercise 7   Write one sentence for Uses 1 and 2. For Use 3, write one longer example using several verbs in the past progressive tense.

Use 1. _____

_____

Use 2. _____

_____

Use 3. _____

_____

_____

_____

_____

_____

1.8 Past Perfect Tense

The past perfect tense takes the form:

had + PAST PARTICIPLE	I **had eaten.**

Uses

1. For a past action or condition that ended before another past action or condition began

    > The man told us that we could not play tennis because it **had rained** too hard.

2. For a past action or past condition that ended before a specific time in the past

    > When Los Angeles became the capital of California in 1845, it **had been** a city for only ten years.

Often the past tense can be used instead of the past perfect tense. When *before* or *after* is used in the sentence, you know which action happened first.

Correct: Kayleen **had taken** French before she took Spanish.

Correct: Kayleen **took** French before she **took** Spanish.

In contrast, expressions such as *by the time that* often require the past perfect tense.

Incorrect: By the time he arrived, the meeting **began.**

Correct: By the time he arrived, the meeting **had begun.**

Exercise 8   Write one sentence for each use of the past perfect tense.

Use 1. _____

_____

Use 2. _____

_____

1.9 Past Perfect Progressive Tense

The past perfect progressive tense takes the form:

had + been + VERB + -*ing*   **I had been eating.**

Use

1. For a continuing action that started in the past before another past action either began or interrupted the first action

    I had been working there for almost five weeks before I received my first check.

Exercise 9   Write a sentence using the past perfect progressive tense.

Use 1. _____

_____

1.10 Future Tense

The future tense takes the forms:

am / is / are + going to + VERB   **I am going to eat.**

will + VERB   **I will eat.**

There are two ways to express the future in English: *be going to* or *will*. Many times you may use either verb without any difference in meaning. However, each form also has its special use, and there are times when only one is correct. In general, there are many more instances for *be going to* than *will*. Unfortunately, many nonnative speakers have been taught that *will* is the "best" or "most correct" future form. For this reason, the most common error with future tense is for nonnative speakers to overuse *will*.

Uses

1. For a future plan: *be going to*

    As a result of his speech, I **am going to support** him in the next election.

    Most of my classmates **are going to go** to Hawaii for New Year's.

2. For a voluntary action: *will* (especially as a request or a response)

    Ben: **Will** you **carry** this bag for me, please?

    Sue: Sure, I **will.**

3. For a promise: *will*

> I **will send** you a postcard when I'm in Paris next week.

4. For a prediction: *will* or *be going to*

> In the next decade, consumers **will spend** more on electronic goods.

> In the next decade, consumers **are going to spend** more on electronic goods.

Exercise 10 Write a sentence for each use of *will* and *be going to*. In Use 4, write two sentences, one using *will* and one using *be going to*.

Use 1. _____

_____

Use 2. _____

_____

Use 3. _____

_____

Use 4. a. _____

_____

b. _____

_____

(1.11) Future Progressive Tense

The future progressive tense takes the form:

will + be + VERB + -*ing*   **I will be eating.**

Uses

1. For an "interrupted" action in the future

    I will be watching TV when you call at eleven tonight.

2. For future atmosphere

    In 2050, families **will be living** in much larger houses. People **will** no longer **be communicating** by telephone. Students **will be learning** from home via the computer and new video machines. ...

Exercise 11   Write one sentence for Use 1. Write a longer example using multiple verbs in the future progressive tense for Use 2.

Use 1. _____

_____

Use 2. _____

_____

_____

(1.12) Future Perfect Tense

The future perfect tense takes the form:

will + have + PAST PARTICIPLE   **I will have eaten.**

Uses

1. For a future action that is completed before another future action

    I will have worked here for more than five years when I get my promotion.

2. For a future action that is completed before a certain point of time in the future

    I will have worked here for more than five years by the year 2008.

Exercise 12   Write a sentence for each use of the future perfect tense.

Use 1. _____

_____

Use 2. _____

_____

(1.13) Future Perfect Progressive Tense

The future perfect progressive tense* takes the form:

will + have + been + VERB + -ing   I **will have been eating.**

Use
For a continuing action that will be finished at a specific time in the future

The pilots **will have been flying** for almost fifteen hours by the time we reach Zurich.

———————

*This tense is seldom used.

Exercise 13   Write a sentence using the future perfect progressive tense.

Use 1. _____

_____

Exercise 14   Fill in the blanks with the correct forms for the verbs shown.

pres	_he works_	_____	_____
pres prog	_____	_they are taking_	_____
pres perf	_____	_____	_____
pres perf prog	_____	_____	_I've been living_
past	_____	_____	_____
past prog	_____	_____	_____
past perf	_____	_____	

past perf prog	_____	_____	_____
future	_____	_____	_____
future prog	_____	_____	_____
future perf	_____	_____	_____
fut perf prog	_____	_____	_____
used to	_____	_____	_____
would	_____	_____	_____

Editing
∧ **Exercise 15** Read this paragraph and look at the seven underlined verbs. Five of them contain an error. Find the errors and correct them. Explain to a partner why the other two are correct.

Strategies for Answering True-False Test Questions

Answering true-false questions on a test is tricky, but there **1** <u>were</u> certain things that you should know about these tests. Most true-false tests **2** <u>are containing</u> more true statements than false statements simply because they are made up by teachers. Since teachers prefer to leave true information in your mind, they usually **3** <u>had stacked</u> the test with true statements. Of course, some teachers will fool you, but after the first test, **4** you<u>'ll know</u> for sure. On a true-false test, it **5** <u>was</u> a good idea to guess at answers that you do not know even if credit is subtracted for wrong answers. According to the laws of probability, you should get fifty percent right when you **6** <u>will guess</u> even if you **7** <u>know</u> nothing about the subject matter. If you are able to make intelligent guesses, you should be able to do much better than that.

Exercise 16   Read this excerpt on the geography of Iran and underline the correct verb tenses in parentheses.

Geography and Resources of Ancient Iran

Iran, "Land of the Aryans," **1** (<u>is</u>, had been, will be) bounded by the Zagros Mountains to the west, the Caucasus Mountains and Caspian Sea to the northwest and north, the Hindu Kush range and the desert of Gedrosia to the east and southeast, and the Persian Gulf to the southwest. The northeast is less protected by natural boundaries, and through that corridor, Iran **2** (is, has been, was) open to attacks by the nomads of Central Asia in earlier times.

With high mountains at the edges, salt deserts in the interior, and mountain streams traversing a sloping plateau and draining into seas or interior salt lakes and marshes, Iran **3** (is, will be, will have been) a harsh land. To survive, humans **4** (had, had had, will have had) to find ways to exploit limited water resources. Unlike the valleys of the Nile, Tigris-Euphrates, Ganges, and Yellow Rivers, ancient Iran never **5** (has, had, has had) a dense population. In Iran, the best-watered and the most populous parts of the country **6** (are, were, had been) to the north and west; aridity increases and population decreases as one moves south and east. On the interior plateau, oasis settlements **7** (spring, will be springing, sprang) up beside streams or springs. The Great Salt Desert, which **8** (is covering, covers, will cover) most of eastern Iran, and Gedrosia in the southeast corner, are extremely inhospitable, and the scattered settlements in the narrow plains beside the Persian Gulf are cut off from the interior plateau by mountain barriers.

Exercise 17   Read the whole paragraph. For each pair of blanks, fill in the first blank with the name of the correct verb tense and the second blank with the verb in that tense. For example, you might write:

(go) _____*future*_____ / _____*will go*_____.

Campbell Serves Soup Around the World

Over 125 years ago, the Campbell Soup Company (introduce) _____ /

_____ canned condensed soup and (give) _____ / _____

2

the world its first convenience food. Since then, those well-known red and white labels

and the sigh "Mmmm, mmmm good" (become) _____ / _____

3

icons of American culture. Although sales of the popular brand total $4.3 billion and

Campbell's brands currently (account) _____ / _____ for 80

4

percent of canned soup sold in the United States, the company (face) _____ /

5

_____ declines in domestic sales. Turning to global markets, Campbell

executives (hope) _____ / _____ that in the very near future, more

6

than half of the firm's profits (come) _____ / _____ from foreign

7

sales.

Exercise 18   Read this paragraph and underline the correct verb forms in parentheses.

An Ancestor to Contemporary Fiction: The Traditional Tale

In the history of English, *tale* **1** (<u>is</u>, had been) a close cousin of *tell*; stories **2** (have, will have) a much longer association with the voice than with the pages. Some of the greatest and most familiar tales **3** (are being, were) told for centuries before they **4** (had been, were) written down by folklorists like the Brothers Grimm. When we read them, we notice how much there **5** (has been, is) to hear. The peasants and townspeople who **6** (recite, recited) their tales for the Brothers Grimm **7** (had, will have) memorized them word for word as a magician might memorize a spell (and indeed, in medieval German and English, the word *spell* might mean either a story or an incantation). A story **8** (changes, would change) gradually over decades of telling, but a traditional tale was not to be loosely paraphrased. The telling, that is, the spell, required certain syllables in a certain order. In this respect, the traditional tale is more like a poem or song than it **9** (is, was) like most modern novels, which **10** (will not be, are not) made to be read aloud, let alone memorized.

Exercise 19   In each sentence circle the letter of the correct answer.

1. When the fire broke out, the flight attendants quickly _____ things under control with the aid of a fire extinguisher.
   a. got
   b. had gotten
   c. were getting
   d. would get

2. When I was a young girl, my Aunt Mary _____ let me help her in her flower garden.
   a. was
   b. has
   c. used to
   d. had been

3. Some students who are _____ in many extra activities find it hard to complete their homework.
   a. participating
   b. participate
   c. participated
   d. used to participate

4. It is a fact that every planet _____ a certain number of moons or natural satellites.
   a. have
   b. had had
   c. has
   d. had

5. When the earthquake hit at 4:30 a.m., the children _____ in their beds.
   a. slept
   b. were sleeping
   c. had slept
   d. would sleep

6. Don't disturb your mom! She _____ a nap.
   a. is taking
   b. was taking
   c. take
   d. takes

Exercise 20   Get a copy of a paragraph in English from a magazine, newspaper, or the Internet. Underline the verbs and identify their tenses. Then bring your work to class to check with a partner.

Original Writing

Exercise 21   Write two paragraphs about two people who have been important in your life. Try to use both affirmative and negative verb forms. Underline all of the verbs and be prepared to identify the verb tense for each.

- In the first paragraph, write about someone who is no longer living. Tell who the person was, when he or she was born, where he or she lived, his or her relationship to you, and why this person was important to you.

- In the second paragraph, do the same thing, but write about someone who is still living.

> If you need help with the steps of writing a paragraph, see Appendix 5.
>
> **www** You will find additional exercises for the grammar in this chapter on the Top 20 website at **http://esl.college.hmco.com/students**

WF

Twi used to <u>lived</u> in Turkey,
but now he lives in Australia.
He moved there in 1988 and
hopes to remain there forever.

2

Problems with Verb Tenses

This chapter focuses on three of the most common problems that writers have with verb tenses: (1) incorrect forms, (2) maintaining the same verb tense, and (3) confusing verb tenses. As you study this chapter, you can refer to Chapter 1 for examples of the forms of the verb tenses.

2.1

Problems with Verb Forms

The following five verb tense uses often give writers trouble with the form of the verb. Study these rules, errors, and correct examples. Do you sometimes make these errors in your writing?

2.1.1 Progressive Tense and *-ing*

With a progressive tense, it's easy to forget the *-ing*. The rule is:

> Use *be* + PRESENT PARTICIPLE for a progressive tense.

🎯 Don't forget the *-ing*.

am / is / are / was / were will be / has been have been / had been will have been	+ VERB	+ ing

While passengers on long international overnight flights **are sleeping**, the pilot **is working** hard to keep things going smoothly.

2.1.2 Passive Voice and Past Participle

In passive voice, some writers forget to use the past participle form of the verb. The rule is:

> Use *be* + PAST PARTICIPLE for the passive voice.

am / is / are / was / were will be / has been have been / had been will have been	+ PAST PARTICIPLE

After the exams **have been graded**, they **will be returned** to the students.

2.1.3 Perfect Tenses, Past Participle, and *have*

For perfect tenses, you need to use the past participle with the correct form of *have* (*have, has, had, will have*). The rule is:

Use *have* + PAST PARTICIPLE for perfect tenses.

have / has / had	+ PAST PARTICIPLE

We **had visited** Los Angeles before the last earthquake struck, but we **have not gone** back since then.

2.1.4 *Do* and the Form of the Verb

With *do / does / did*, don't put an *-s* or *-ed* on the verb. The rule is:

Use the base form of the verb with *do / does / did*.

Don't add any endings to a verb following *do / does / did*.

do / does / did	+ SUBJECT	+ VERB

How many people **do** you **expect** to attend the gathering this Saturday evening?

2.1.5 Modals and the Verb

With modals, some writers make the mistake of adding the word *to* before the verb or adding an ending (*-s, -ed, -ing*) to the verb.

The rule is: Use only the base form of the verb after modals. Don't use *to* after modals. Don't add any endings to the verb.

will / would / can / could should / must / may / might had better	+ SIMPLE VERB (base form)

Some scientists **will participate** in the experiment, but others **may refuse** to do so.

Exercise 1   As you read the paragraph, underline the correct verb forms.

The Construction of the Impossible Bridge

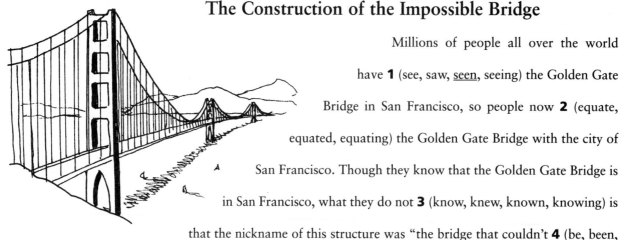

Millions of people all over the world have **1** (see, saw, <u>seen</u>, seeing) the Golden Gate Bridge in San Francisco, so people now **2** (equate, equated, equating) the Golden Gate Bridge with the city of San Francisco. Though they know that the Golden Gate Bridge is in San Francisco, what they do not **3** (know, knew, known, knowing) is that the nickname of this structure was "the bridge that couldn't **4** (be, been, being) **5** (build, built, building)." The idea of the construction of a bridge across San Francisco Bay had **6** (be, been, being) **7** (discuss, discussed, discussing) for years before the construction of the Golden Gate Bridge was actually **8** (start, started, starting) in 1933. This bridge was **9** (consider, considered, considering) impossible to build for a variety of reasons. First of all, the weather in the area—with high winds, rain, and fog—was rarely good. Second, engineers **10** (think, thought, thinking) that the strong ocean currents in the bay meant that the bridge could not **11** (to be, be, been, being) **12** (build, built, building). In addition, they were **13** (concern, concerned, concerning) about how the strong winds in the area would **14** (to affect, affect, affected, affecting) any large structure. Finally, it was the Depression. The poor economy was **15** (cause, caused, causing) people to experience incredible difficulties, so many people thought that it would **16** (to be, be, been, being) foolish to spend such a large amount of money on such an impossible project. Getting the funds to build a bridge of this magnitude was a monumental task. In fact, it took four times as long to collect enough money to build the bridge as it actually took to build the bridge. In spite of all these hindrances, the bridge was **17** (construct, constructed, constructing) in four and a half years at a cost of thirty-six million dollars. The cost was high not only in monetary terms but also in human life; fourteen lives were **18** (lose, lost, losing) during the construction of the Golden Gate Bridge.

Exercise 2   As you read the paragraph, fill in each blank with the correct form of the verb in parentheses.

Americans and Their Political Parties

In every presidential election since 1952, voters across the nation (have) _have_
1

(be) ____been____ (ask) ____asked____, "Generally speaking, do you usually (think)
2   **3**

_____ of yourself as a Republican, a Democrat, an independent, or what?"
4

Most voters (think) _____ of themselves as either Republicans or Democrats,
5

but the proportion of those who think of themselves as independents has (increase)

_____ over time. The size of the Democratic Party's majority has also (shrink)
6

_____. Nevertheless, most Americans today still (identify) _____
7   **8**

with one of the two major parties, and Democrats still (outnumber) _____
9

Republicans. The question on many politicians' minds is whether this situation will

(continue) _____ or not.
10

Maintaining the Same Verb Tense

In a nutshell, this is the rule for being consistent with verb tenses: Don't change verb tense in a paragraph unless you have a specific reason for doing so.

A common error made by all writers (both nonnative and native) is an incorrect shift in verb tense. If your paragraph is about the history of a country, most of the verbs will be in the past tense. If your paragraph tells how a machine works, most of the verbs should be in the present tense.

2.2.1   When a Tense Shift Is Correct

Sometimes a shift in verb tense is necessary, but it is important to consider the time of the action of the verb and its relationship to other actions or events in the paragraph. You may want to state a present fact such as

> Nuclear reactors **are** a huge threat to our well-being.

Then explain why you believe this by supporting it with a past historical fact:

> The horrible nuclear accident at Chernobyl in 1986 **killed** almost three thousand people in the immediate and surrounding areas as well as in faraway lands.

This shift from present tense to past tense is logical because the historical event occurred in the past (but nuclear reactors still exist).

2.2.2 Switching Between Present Tense and Past Tense

Shifting between the present and past tense of a verb is the most common shift error.

Error 1: You might begin a narrative paragraph in the past tense, shift to present tense, and then shift back to past tense.

Error 2: You might be explaining something in the present tense and unexpectedly shift to past tense.

The solution to this problem is to *think* about the time of each action that you are writing about and to *proofread* your work carefully with this time in mind.

Editing
∧ **Exercise 3**   As you read the paragraph, find and correct ten errors in shifting verb tenses. Be sure to take into account the time of the action.

Buying a Used Car

One of the worst experiences that I have ever gone through was buying a used car. I had heard many things—both good and bad—about buying a used car, but I never think anything bad would happen to me. I respond to an advertisement in the local newspaper. After I was calling the person and I made arrangements to see the car with him, I went to the owner's house and take the car for a test drive. The car seemed fine, but of course I took it to a car repair shop to have a professional mechanic look it over. Once he tells me that the car seems okay to him, I paid $2,900 cash for the car. The owner assured me that everything in the car was working fine. Unfortunately, less than a month after I buy the car, the engine started making noises. Soon after, the car stopped running completely. I called the owner, but legally, he did not have any obligation to me. I quickly learn the meaning of the phrase "as is." In the end, I have to pay an additional two thousand dollars to have a new engine installed. Therefore, my used car ends up costing me almost five thousand dollars. In hindsight, I could have used that sum as a hefty down-payment on a brand-new car.

Editing
∧ **Exercise 4**   As you read the paragraph, find and correct seven errors in shifting verb tenses. Be sure to take into account the time of the action.

Censoring Music

One of the basic rights that we enjoy is freedom of speech, and this includes our right to listen to any kind of music that appealed to us. However, some of the music that is currently being played on the radio is obscene and should be banned. I don't have any children, but I do have* a seven-year-old niece. While I was driving her to school the other day, we were talking and listening to the radio. One of the songs on the radio is about sex and had some foul language in it. My niece asks me what one of the words meant. Clearly, what children heard has an influence on them. While I agree with the concept of free speech, I also thought that everyone had an obligation to set limits and not cross those lines. When songs deal with sex and use foul language, I think that the limit will be breached. This is not censoring; it is common sense.

———————
*Do / does / did + VERB is the emphatic form: I **do have** a car. I **did study** the material.

∧ **Exercise 5**   As you read the paragraph, find and correct twelve errors in shifting verb tenses. Be sure to take into account the time of the action.

The Tough Job of a Server

Everyone has eaten in a restaurant, but I wonder how many people really know how hard a server's job is. I have been a server for almost five years. At first, it was a part-time job, but now it is my main job. I worked at a small upscale restaurant called the White Wolf Café. The restaurant served dinner from 5 p.m. to 10 p.m., but my shift runs from 4 p.m. to midnight. I get to work a few minutes before 4. After I have clocked in, I start folding napkins. Sometimes I had to help set silverware on the tables, but sometimes someone else takes care of that task. Though we open at 5, hardly any customers showed up till around 5:30 or 6. For the rest of the evening, my job entailed greeting customers who are sitting in my section, which consisted of six tables. I explain things on the menu, take people's drink orders, take their food orders, and made sure that customers have what they need. I think that I am a good server because I am good at anticipating what people needed before they ask for it and customers appreciated my service. The work is hard, but I enjoy working with people. The only negative aspect of this job is dealing with rude or difficult customers, but this was part of every job that deals with the public. We stopped serving anything from the kitchen after 10, but some customers did not leave until 11. I have to stay until midnight to clean up and then organize some things for the next day. My job as a server is not an easy one, but I love this job and would not trade it for any other.

Exercise 6   **Analyze Real Language for Verb Tenses**   Select a paragraph that you find interesting from an article or website. Underline all of the verbs in the excerpt. Work with a partner to give a reason for the tense of each verb. Remember that some verb tense shifts are correct, for example, in moving from a present fact to the past history of how that fact came about. In your excerpt, can you find examples of verb tense shifts? Explain why the writer made these shifts.

2.3 Confusing Verb Tenses

In English, there are twelve verb tenses. (See Chapter 1.) Some tenses are easy to use; others are more difficult. A few verb tenses are easily confused with others. Most of the confusion centers around four verb tenses, all of which have a connection to past time.

2.3.1 Past Tense

- Use the past tense when you are referring to an action that is finished:

   Lincoln governed the United States during a difficult period.

Common errors that happen when you mean to use past tense:

Past progressive: **Lincoln was governing** ...   (indicates a longer action that was interrupted)

Past perfect: **Lincoln had governed** ...   (indicates that one past action happened before another past action)

2.3.2 Present Perfect Tense

- Use the present perfect tense when you are referring to an action that began in the past and continues now:

   The U.N. has solved world problems for five decades.

- Use the present perfect tense when you are referring to an action that is important now:

   The government has reformed the tax system.

- Use the present perfect tense when you are referring to a past action with an indefinite time, especially an accomplishment:

   Scientists have discovered how aspirin works.

Common errors that happen when you mean to use present perfect tense:

Present progressive: **The U.N. is solving** ...   (indicates an action that is continuing right now)

Past tense: **Scientists discovered** ...   (indicates an action that is finished, with no relationship to the present; often used with a date)

> Present perfect is often used for a past action when that action is relevant or important to the new information being presented. Consider this example from a conversation:
>
> Ann: It's hot in here!
>
> Pedro: I know, but **I've turned on** the air conditioner, so we have to wait a few minutes.
>
> The action of turning on the air conditioner is clearly a past action, but we use present perfect tense to show that it has a relationship to Ann's first statement "It's hot in here."

2.3.3 Past Progressive Tense

- Use the past progressive tense when you want to set the scene or atmosphere in prose:

    What a scene! A mother **was trying** to quiet her children.

- Use the past progressive tense when you are referring to a longer action that was interrupted:

    The cashier **was studying** a receipt when the phone rang.

    The flight **was going** smoothly when the pilot received a radio message about possible bad weather.

Common errors that happen when you mean to use past progressive tense:

Present tense: The cashier **is studying** … (There is no need to switch to present tense.)

Past tense: The flight **went smoothly** … (Indicates that you are talking about one event and then another.)

2.3.4 Past Perfect Tense

- Use the past perfect tense when you are referring to a past action that happened before another action:

    I **had** never **lived** abroad before, so living in Malaysia was difficult.

Common errors that happen when you mean to use past perfect tense:

Past tense: I never **lived** abroad … (Indicates that you are talking about one event that was not necessarily completed before the second event.)

Exercise 7   Read the paragraph and underline the correct verb tenses. Distinguish between using the past tense and the present perfect tense. Be sure to take into account the time of the action.

My ESL Teaching Experiences

My name is Carl Davids, and I am an ESL teacher. I **1** (was, <u>have been</u>, had been) an ESL teacher since 1985. I **2** (taught, was teaching, have taught) English in the United States and several foreign countries. In fact, I **3** (had, have had, was having) more teaching jobs overseas than here in the United States. In 1985, I **4** (started, have started) teaching in a large English program at a big university. Most of my students then **5** (were, have been, had been) Spanish speakers or Arabic speakers. After that, I **6** (moved, was moving, had moved) to a smaller city in a different state and **7** (got, was getting, had gotten) a teaching position at a small college. I **8** (worked, have worked, had worked) there for five years. In 1992, I **9** (was deciding, decided, have decided) to accept a job in Saudi Arabia. I **10** (have never worked, had never worked, never worked) in a foreign country before, so this **11** (had been, was, has been) a big shock in many ways. I **12** (stayed, have stayed) there for one year. I **13** (taught, have taught) English to officers in a military program. The following year I **14** (moved, have moved) to Malaysia to work at a brand-new English program just outside Kuala Lumpur. For many reasons, it **15** (was, has been) the best teaching experience that I (had, have had) in my life. I **16** (stayed, have stayed) in Malaysia for three years. After Malaysia, I **17** (took, have taken) a job in Japan. In late 1997, I finally **18** (came, have come) back to the United States. In early 1998, I **19** (was finding, found, have found) a great teaching job at a university in California where I **20** (was, have been, had been) since then. I have great memories of my years overseas. In fact, I **21** (went, was going, have gone) back to Malaysia and Japan twice and hope to be able to go back again next summer. When I first chose this career years ago, I was not so sure that it was the right career for me, but I **22** (was enjoying, had enjoyed, enjoyed, have enjoyed) my years of ESL tremendously and am certain that I made the right choice.

Exercise 8 Read each mystery and then answer the questions. Be sure to identify the verb tenses in your answer and explain what they mean.

1. Karen was writing a book in 1995. Lynn wrote a book in 1997. One of these books was published in 1998. Whose book was it? _Lynn's_ How do you know?
The past tense verb "wrote" shows that the book was completed, while _the past progressive tense verb "was writing" shows that the writing_ _continued and may still continue._

2. Tom has been ill since last week. Jerry was sick last week. Which person is probably not ill now? _____ How do you know? _____

_____

3. Mohammed lived in Pakistan for twelve years. Twi has lived in Turkey since 1999. Hussein used to live in Syria. Which of these people might live in the U.S. now? _____ How do you know? _____

_____

4. When the lights went out last night, Kevin was studying. Jack had studied. Who is probably better prepared to take the test today? _____ How do you know? _____

_____

5. Luke, Kyle, and Rick share an apartment. At 9:15 last night, the phone rang. Luke had taken a shower, Kyle was going to take a shower, and Rick was taking a shower. Which one could not answer the phone? _____ How do you know? _____

_____

BONUS   6. Explain the differences in meaning in these sentences:

    a. When the phone rang, I was eating. _____

    b. When the phone rang, I ate. _____

    c. When the phone rang, I had eaten. _____

    d. When the phone rang, I was going to eat. (More common: When the phone rang,

       I was about to eat.) _____

    e. When the phone rang, I had been eating. _____

Exercise 9   Circle the letter of the correct choice.

1. At the present time, hundreds of animal
   species _____ in danger of becoming extinct.
   - a. are
   - b. were
   - c. have been
   - d. will be

2. Since 1973, the U.S. government _____ to implement programs to save endangered
   species.
   - a. attempted
   - b. was attempting
   - c. has attempted
   - d. had attempted

3. The good news is that some endangered animals such as the bald eagle _____.
   - a. saved
   - b. were saving
   - c. have saved
   - d. have been saved

4. Other animals on the endangered list _____ the mountain gorilla *(Gorilla beringei)*
   and the snow leopard *(Panthera uncia)*.
   - a. are including
   - b. are included
   - c. included
   - d. include

5. The bad news is that by the time the Endangered Species Act was finally approved
   in 1973, many species _____ already.
   - a. have died
   - b. had died
   - c. died
   - d. were dying

6. For example, the last sighting of the Oahu Thrush and the Laysan Millerbird in
   Hawaii _____ in 1824 and 1923, respectively.
   - a. is
   - b. was
   - c. has been
   - d. had been

Original Writing

Exercise 10   Write a paragraph about either (1) an important current event or (2) an important recent problem.

- Tell what the current situation is, why or how this event or problem happened (including when it began), and what is going to happen next.

- Use both affirmative and negative forms.

Try not to confuse any tenses. Underline all of the verbs. Exchange paragraphs with a partner and check each other's work for correct verb tenses.

> If you need help with the steps of writing a paragraph, see Appendix 5.
>
> **www** You will find additional exercises for the grammar in this chapter on the Top 20 website at **http://esl.college.hmco.com/students**

> At Hercules Corporation and other
> similar companies, all new
> [#] employee receive a booklet with advices [WF]
> about operating the equipments. [WF]

3

Nouns

In this chapter you will review the forms and characteristics of nouns and the words that go with them. The two main groupings of nouns are *count nouns* and *noncount nouns*. Briefly, count nouns name things that can be counted, such as *car* and *computer*. Noncount nouns name things that cannot be counted, such as *freedom* and *happiness*.

3.1 Count Nouns

Nouns that can be counted are called count nouns. They can be singular or plural in form.

Singular:	one subject	a problem	one reason	a child
Plural:	five subjects	two problems	three reasons	eight children

3.1.1 Singular Count Nouns

Singular count nouns, together with any descriptive adjectives, have an article (*a, an, the*) or other determiner before them (*my, your, this, one, every, each*).

> an exam, a long exam   my brother, my oldest brother

Don't use a singular count noun without an article or other determiner:

Incorrect:	~~house~~	~~new house~~	~~car~~	~~old car~~
Correct:	a house	their new house	my car	our old car

However, there is an important exception to this rule: In some idiomatic expressions, no article is used:

> have dinner   in school   at home   at work
>
> by bus (*by* + transportation)   by phone (*by* + communication)

Exercise 1 Underline the sixteen singular count nouns and circle their articles or determiners.

By (the) end of the twentieth century, almost every person in the country owned at least one telephone and one television set. Most homes also had a washing machine, and many possessed a microwave oven. Since the beginning of the new millennium, the cellular phone has become commonplace, and most households now have a computer. The times have certainly changed. They have changed so much that most people cannot even imagine an evening at home without a computer or some other appliance.

3.1.2 Plural Count Nouns

Plural count nouns are sometimes preceded by the definite article *the* or by another determiner, or they may appear alone. Plural count nouns are NOT preceded by *a* or *an*.

Incorrect: ~~a houses~~   ~~an expensive houses~~

Correct: the houses   some houses   big houses   some big houses

Regular Plurals

Most count nouns form their plural by adding -*s* to the singular noun.

    cat / cats   tree / trees   taxi / taxis

Irregular Plurals

A few common count nouns have an irregular plural form.

    man / men   woman / women   child / children   mouse / mice
    fish / fish   tooth / teeth   foot / feet   person / people

Special Spellings of Plurals

A few types of count nouns form their plurals in a slightly different manner. Nouns ending in a CONSONANT + *y* form their plurals by changing the -*y* to -*i* and adding -*es*.

    baby / babies   lady / ladies   copy / copies

 This rule does *not* apply to nouns that end in a VOWEL + y.

    monkey / monkeys   donkey / donkeys   boy / boys

Nouns ending in -*s*—or in a sound similar to -*s* (-*sh*, -*ch*, -*x*, *and* -*z*) add -*es* to form the plural.

    class / classes   bush / bushes   box / boxes

Editing
∧ **Exercise 2**   Five of the ten underlined phrases in this paragraph contain an error. Circle the errors and write the corrections above.

    All economic indicators are up. People are building **1** <u>new houses</u> at a very high rate. They are also buying **2** <u>a new cars</u>. Among consumer products that are selling well are cellular telephones, **3** <u>computer</u>, and big-screen **4** <u>TV sets</u>. Unemployment is low—**5** <u>jobs</u> are not difficult to find, but **6** <u>a good employees</u> are. **7** <u>Some firms</u> are offering bonuses or stock options to attract **8** <u>capable workers</u>. **9** <u>An interest rates</u> are at a comfortable level, resulting in heavy sales of **10** <u>a consumer items</u>.

Exercise 3 Change the noun phrases so that the nouns are plural. Note that you will drop the *a* and *an* in most cases when you make the noun plural.

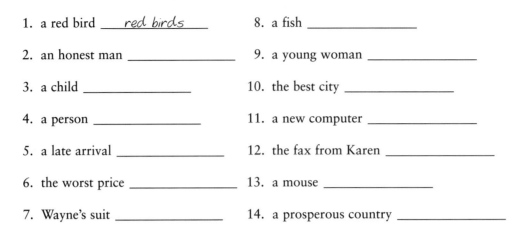

1. a red bird ___red birds___

2. an honest man _____

3. a child _____

4. a person _____

5. a late arrival _____

6. the worst price _____

7. Wayne's suit _____

8. a fish _____

9. a young woman _____

10. the best city _____

11. a new computer _____

12. the fax from Karen _____

13. a mouse _____

14. a prosperous country _____

3.2 Noncount Nouns

Nouns that cannot be counted are called noncount or mass nouns.

- Noncount nouns are often liquids or gases:

    water   air   oil   oxygen

- Noncount nouns often refer to a whole or a mass made up of small particles or items.

    sugar   salt   white sand
    new furniture   homework   good news

- Noncount nouns are often weather phenomena, fields of study, raw materials, or abstractions.

    rain   economics   gold   happiness
    hot weather   psychology   hard coal   luck

The following noncount nouns are often mistakenly used as plural count nouns:

    furnitures̶   advices̶   homeworks̶   equipments̶

Exercise 4 Read the paragraph and underline the seventeen count nouns. Draw a circle around the twelve noncount nouns.

It is a commonly known <u>fact</u> that dairy products such as (milk) yogurt, and cheese are rich sources of calcium, but how many people know that these food products are also loaded with protein? This is the reason that dietitians recommend that people consume two to four servings of this group each day. A glass of milk or a cup of yogurt has high-quality protein that is equivalent to an ounce of meat or cheese or to one egg. These food items are certainly good for your health. Whenever possible, however, you should opt for items that are not so high in fat.

3.2.1 Comparing Noncount and Count Nouns

Noncount nouns are like count nouns in certain ways.

1. Noncount nouns act like singular and plural count nouns

   - Like singular and plural count nouns, noncount nouns may have certain determiners in front of them, such as the definite article *the* or the possessive adjectives *my* and *your*.

   - Possessive adjectives have the same forms in front of all three types of nouns: singular count nouns, plural count nouns, and noncount nouns.

   - You can use *this* and *that* with singular count nouns and noncount nouns; *these* and *those* can appear in front of plural count nouns.

Singular Count Nouns		Plural Count Nouns		Noncount Nouns	
Determiner	**Example of noun**	**Determiner**	**Example of noun**	**Determiner**	**Example of noun**
the	car	**the**	cars	**the**	traffic
an	apple	—	apples	—	fruit
my, your	vegetable	**my, your**	vegetables	**my, your**	rice
his, her, its	job	**his, her, its**	jobs	**his, her, its**	work
our, their	job	**our, their**	jobs	**our, their**	work
this, that	cat	**these, those**	cats		

2. Noncount nouns act like plural count nouns

Noncount nouns, just like plural count nouns, may be preceded by determiners and certain expressions of quantity, or they may appear alone.

In the chart below, the determiners before plural count nouns and noncount nouns are the same.

Singular Count Nouns		Plural Count Nouns		Noncount Nouns	
Determiner	Example of noun	Determiner	Example of noun	Determiner	Example of noun
a	taxi	∅	taxis	∅	traffic
the	taxi	the	taxis	the	traffic
one	taxi	some	taxis	some	traffic
		a lot of	taxis	a lot of	traffic
		enough	taxis	enough	traffic
		plenty of	taxis	plenty of	traffic
Incorrect: Let's get taxi. *Correct:* Let's get **a taxi.** Remember that singular count nouns must have an article or determiner.		**Some taxis** have air conditioning. There aren't **enough taxis** in this city. **Taxis** are more comfortable than buses.		There will be **some traffic** on the highway tonight. There is **plenty of traffic** on that narrow road. **Traffic** is always heavy on weekends.	

In the following chart, the determiners—certain expressions of quantity—before plural count nouns and noncount nouns are different.

Singular Count Nouns		Plural Count Nouns		Noncount Nouns	
Determiner	Example of noun	Determiner	Example of noun	Determiner	Example of noun
a	taxi	many	taxis	much	traffic
the	taxi	a few	taxis	a little	traffic
one	taxi	several	taxis	a great deal of	traffic
		two, six, ten	taxis		

Exercise 5   Underline the correct noun form(s) in each sentence.

1. Dr. Rachel Lindstrom is studying a special aspect of (a biology / <u>biology</u>).

2. She's is doing (research / a research) on (a certain plant / certain plants) and their products that countries export.

3. For example, Dr. Lindstrom has found that (some plants / a plants) contain substances that can fight (a diseases / a lot of diseases).

4. She and her colleagues now have (an information / plenty of information) to write (book / a book) about their investigations.

5. Specifically, this new volume will examine the consequences that can result from a country's (export / exports).

6. For example, does the fact that Colombia exports (several / a great deal of) coffee have any negative impact on Colombia?

7. In Ecuador, (many / much) types of bananas can be found all over. They are harvested and sent worldwide.

8. In the United States, bananas grow in only (a few / a little) places, so the fact that Ecuador exports its bananas is a good thing for the United States. However, is there any negative effect of this exportation on Ecuador?

9. Likewise, Chile exports (much / many) kinds of fruit—grapes, peaches, and cherries, for example—to countries in the Northern Hemisphere during their winter months.

10. In addition, until recently, (many / a lot of) beautiful wood used to come from the forests of Brazil; now, however, Brazil exports less wood as it attempts to save its forests.

Exercise 6   Read each sentence and underline the correct choices in parentheses.

1. Henry is studying at Harvard University; he's going to become (lawyer / <u>a lawyer</u>).

2. (A law / Law) is a difficult subject.

3. It requires (a concentration / a lot of concentration).

4. (A lawyer / Lawyers) study in law school for three years.

5. After law school, the graduates have to take (a difficult / difficult) examination.

6. (Some graduates / Some graduate) pass this examination, but others don't.

7. (A little graduates / A few graduates) take the examination a second or even a third time.

8. (Some people / A people) say that there aren't (enough good lawyer / enough good lawyers).

9. Others say that there aren't (many good lawyers / many good lawyer).

10. (Some lawyers / A lawyers) feel satisfied with (a work / their work).

11. (This lawyers / These lawyers) have clearly chosen the right profession.

12. (Satisfaction / Satisfactions) with one's work is extremely important.

Exercise 7   Put a check mark (✓) beside each expression that could be used correctly before the noun in each sentence.

Let's take _____ taxi.	I heard _____ police cars last night.	There's _____ traffic in this town on weekends.
Ø _____	Ø _____	Ø _____
a __✓__	a _____	a _____
some _____	some _____	some _____
many _____	much _____	not much _____
much _____	a lot of _____	a lot of _____
a lot of _____	a few _____	many _____
a few _____	a little _____	a little _____
three _____	two _____	four _____

Exercise 8   Put a check mark (✓) beside each of the expressions that could be used correctly before each noun.

_____ new student in our class didn't pass the test.	_____ students failed the test.	The students said that they had _____ information, but it was not enough.
Ø _____	Ø _____	Ø _____
A ✓	A _____	an _____
The _____	Some _____	some _____
That _____	Much _____	the _____
These _____	A lot of _____	enough _____
Some _____	A few _____	a lot of _____
Many _____	A little _____	many _____
Much _____	Enough _____	a few _____
Enough _____	Several _____	a little _____
A lot of _____	One _____	ten _____
A few _____	Four _____	one _____
Two _____	Those _____	those _____
One _____	This _____	that _____
Plenty of _____	Plenty of _____	plenty of _____
A great deal of _____	A great deal of _____	a great deal of _____

∧ **Exercise 9**   In eleven of the underlined noun phrases, the quantifiers are used incorrectly. Find the errors and make the corrections. More than one option may be correct. Use ∅ to indicate that no article or other quantifier is needed.

Rainforest Island has been kindly treated by <u>nature</u>. It has <u>much dense forests</u>, which produce <u>beautiful wood</u>. On the north side of the island it has <u>mountains</u> where <u>a coffee</u> is grown. In the southern area, there are thousands of acres of <u>bananas</u> and <u>one sugar</u> there as well. The island exports <u>a lot of wood, coffee, bananas, and sugar.</u> There are other resources to be developed, too. The eastern shore has <u>a beautiful beaches</u> and would be ideal for tourism; so far, however, tourism has not brought <u>many money</u>. There are only <u>a little hotels</u> on the island, and these are not in good condition. There is <u>a good news</u>, though; the Islands Hotel Investment Group is planning to invest heavily in the area. This will result in <u>much excellent facilities</u> and will provide <u>many work</u> for the inhabitants of the island. Even more importantly, at the end of the twentieth century, <u>a few oil</u> was discovered just off the northern shore. Since then, scientists have found that there is <u>many oil</u> underneath the island. Until now, Rainforest Island has depended on agriculture, but in the future—with <u>oil and tourism</u> about to be developed—it is likely that there will be <u>some changes</u> in the character of the island.

Exercise 10   Read each sentence and circle the letter of the correct answer.

1. We need to buy _____ for the living room.
   a. a new furniture
   b. new furniture
   c. new furnitures
   d. a few new furnitures

2. I heard _____ wonderful news today!
   a. a
   b. some
   c. a few
   d. those

3. Before my interview, I have to get _____ information about the company.
   a. an
   b. a few
   c. some
   d. one

4. My son spends too _____ watching television.
   a. much time
   b. much times
   c. many time
   d. many times

5. Doctor, can you give me _____ about vitamins?
   a. an advice
   c. some advices
   b. some advice
   d. advices

6. Since she moved to California, my sister has _____ friends and _____ money, so she's OK.
   a. a little / a few
   b. a few / a little
   c. a little / a little
   d. a few / a few

7. Carol: What time do you want to _____?
   David: Not too late. We have to come home _____, remember.
   a. have dinner / by a bus
   b. have a dinner / by bus
   b. have dinner / by bus
   d. have a dinner / by a bus

8. I hope Professor Gibbs doesn't give us _____ tonight. There's _____ important basketball game!
   a. homeworks / a very
   b. homework / very
   c. homeworks / very
   d. homework / a very

Original Writing

Exercise 11 Write a paragraph about some products or crops that come from the area you are in. Name at least five products. Include the following expressions in your essay: *a, some, several, many, a lot of, much, a little, a few, a great deal of, plenty of,* and *enough*. Then underline all the count and noncount nouns and have a partner check to see if the articles and determiners are correct.

If you need help with the steps of writing a paragraph, see Appendix 5.

www You will find additional exercises for the grammar in this chapter on the Top 20 website at **http://esl.college.hmco.com/students**

*Many schools are famous for certain fields of study, so a **POSS** university that is famous for their business program might not be a good choice for people who want English literature to be their field of study.*

4

Pronouns

Pronouns are similar to nouns because they often take the place of subjects, objects, or objects of prepositions. In this chapter you will review many important kinds of pronouns.

4.1 Common Pronouns

These are the most common English pronouns.

Subject pronouns: I you he / she / it we you they who

Object pronouns: me you him / her / it us you them whom

In general, don't use a pronoun if you have yet to mention the noun. The word that the pronoun refers to is called the *antecedent* (coming before).

I don't like to eat it.   (object pronoun; We have no idea what *it* is; there is no antecedent.)

My mother is making *lasagna.* I don't like to eat it.   (In the first sentence, *lasagna* is the antecedent of the pronoun *it.*)

Exercise 1 Read the following sentences. Change the underlined nouns to pronouns. Use the subject and object pronouns from the list above.

1. My sister Sheila is in medical school. *She* <u>Sheila</u> is one of the busiest people I know.

2. My brothers, on the other hand, want to become famous athletes, so <u>my brothers</u> spend a lot of time practicing to become better at sports.

3. I myself am busy studying literature with Dr. Smithson. He's a great professor, but his lectures are repetitive. I'm tired of <u>Dr. Smithson's</u> lectures.

4. When my sister comes home on weekends, she often goes to the cineplex with <u>my brothers and me</u>.

5. Everyone in my family is usually too busy to do things together. However, my family is planning a trip to Spain next year. <u>My family and I</u> have never been to Spain, so we're very excited about seeing <u>Spain</u>.

6. Madrid and Barcelona are two of the most famous cities in Spain. <u>These cities</u> offer many things to do, and thousands of tourists travel to them every year.

7. If everything goes well, we will all take a break from our busy lives and have a great vacation. I'm really looking forward to <u>this vacation.</u>

4.2 Object Pronouns Used After Prepositions

Use the object pronoun in prepositional phrases, even if the prepositional phrase comes at the beginning of the sentence.

> According to **them,** it's not easy to get into that field.
>
> Besides **me,** a lot of people are signing up for Dr. Winston's class.
>
> I will never forget our trip to France and the Eiffel Tower standing grandly in front of **us.**

Exercise 2 As you read the following sentences, put an object or a subject pronoun in the blanks.

1. Bob is late for Ex-Co's meeting again, but __*he*__ will probably show up by 10:30.

2. Ex-Co's CEO, Miguel Rodriguez, ran the meeting. According to _____, the company's stock prices will lose 20 percent of their value this quarter.

3. This loss will affect the merchants. These merchants bargained for the sale of Ex-Co's goods, but _____ weren't successful at maintaining their target prices.

4. Most of Ex-Co's employees, however, blamed the company's losses on Julie Lee, the company's financial analyst. Because of _____, the proposed increases in salary didn't go through.

5. The bureaucracy in certain corporations is staggering. However, with a new restructuring plan, _____ should decrease as time goes by.

6. Ex-Co's employees don't have much confidence in this new plan. _____ want to organize a walkout if the changes aren't implemented smoothly.

7. All these problems are not surprising. With the economy so sluggish, it's no surprise that employees are unhappy with the current situation. _____ don't see a happy ending for themselves or for Ex-Co.

4.3 Possessive Pronouns versus Possessive Adjectives

It's easy to confuse possessive pronouns with possessive adjectives. Remember that possessive adjectives, like all adjectives, describe something. They are always used with a noun. Their function is to show property—*who* does the object belong to?

> Did you get **your *car*** repaired today?

Compare possessive adjectives with possessive pronouns, which take the place of nouns and are used alone. Nouns do not follow possessive pronouns.

> I just got **my *car*** repaired. When will you get **yours** repaired?

This chart compares possessive adjectives with possessive pronouns.

Possessive Adjectives	Possessive Pronouns
my + NOUN	mine
your + NOUN	yours
his, her, its + NOUN	his, hers
our + NOUN	ours
your + NOUN	yours
their + NOUN	theirs

Exercise 3   Read the paragraph and fill in the blanks with the correct possessive adjective or the correct possessive pronoun.

Choosing a university is not an easy task. First, you must decide what _your_ major
                                                                                                                    1

is going to be. Why is this important? Many schools are famous for certain fields of study,

so a university that is famous for _____ business program might not be a good choice
                                                                2

for people who want English literature to be _____ field of study. A friend of _____,
                                                                                      3   **4**

James, decided to study at the University of Michigan because it has an excellent language

program. _____ parents wanted him to stay in California and go to UCLA, but for the
                       5

program he was interested in, going to a school in Michigan made more sense. Another

important factor is tuition. For example, my brother, who worked part-time throughout

high school, was able to get into a private university. The cost of _____ university is
                                                                                                    6

much higher than _____, which, as a public university, costs me 70 percent less per year.
                                     7

_____ choice was purely economic. The bottom line is this: Whatever university you
8

decide on, make the best of _____ choice and take advantage of everything the university
                                                9

has to offer. It can be one of the most important decisions of _____ life.
                                                                                                    10

4.2.1 Possessive Pronouns and Antecedent Agreement

Make sure that possessive pronouns always agree with their antecedents in number (singular or plural), and in gender.

The **boys** always ride to school on **their** bikes.

The possessive adjective *their* (plural) agrees with the noun *boys* (plural).

Britney usually calls **her** friends after school.

The possessive adjective *her* agrees with the noun *Britney* (singular, feminine).

Incorrect: Each **person** in this class should have **their** own textbook.

The possessive adjective *their* is plural, but the subject of the sentence, *person*, is singular. There are two ways to correct this error:

1. Change the possessive pronoun to the singular *his* or *her*.

   Each **person** in this class should have **his or her** own textbook.

2. Make the subject plural: *people*.

   People in this class should have **their** own textbook.

Editing
∧ **Exercise 4**   The following paragraph contains seven pronoun or possessive adjective errors. Underline the errors and write a correction above each one.

Irrigation management is an interesting field, especially in places where water supplies are low. Irrigation experts have various tasks such as taking soil samples, checking existing water tables, and projecting the amount of rain for the future. These people usually get his degrees from irrigation institutes. Them study many years in order to become familiar with the various tasks involved in her profession. For some of they, a job with local water authorities is a good place to begin his career. Others prefer to find jobs as contractors, working independently to aid farmers with our irrigation needs. Whatever the job, irrigation experts are becoming increasingly important. Water is a precious commodity, and they cannot be taken for granted.

Reflexive Pronouns

You can use a reflexive pronoun when both the subject and the object refer to the same person or thing—the reflexive pronoun refers to the noun. Here are the reflexive pronouns:

myself	yourself	himself	herself	itself
ourselves	yourselves	themselves		

The **children** saw **themselves** on the television monitor.

The **skier** hurt **himself** when he veered off the main ski slope.

Do not use a reflexive pronoun after a preposition unless the pronoun is the same as the subject.

Incorrect: My **sisters** laughed at **myself** when I dyed my hair.

Correct: My **sisters** laughed at **me** when I dyed my hair.

Correct: **I** laughed at **myself** when I dyed my hair.   (The subject pronoun *I* and the object of the preposition pronoun *myself* are the same person.)

● Reflexive pronouns are never used as subjects.

● The following are NOT grammatically correct English words:

hisself   ourselfs   theirselves   themself

Editing
∧ **Exercise 5**   Read each sentence. If it is correct, put a C in the blank. If there is a pronoun error, put an X in the blank and make the correction above the error.

_____ 1. The defendant looked around and silently asked herself how the jury felt about her.

_____ 2. At the same time, the members of the jury were probably asking theirselves how they got chosen to participate in the trial.

_____ 3. The prosecuting attorney questioned the defendant as to whether she had incriminated herselves by not answering a previous question.

_____ 4. During closing remarks, the jury wondered how many times the defense attorney listened to himself practice that speech.

_____ 5. Since the trial ended up taking longer than expected, the judge asked the jury members to be sequestered in a hotel, without any access to outside information. This event put themselves in a difficult position.

_____ 6. With no access to newspapers, television, etc., the members of the jury had to find other ways of entertaining themselves while they were sequestered in the hotel.

_____ 7. The jury foreman promised hisself that he would remain calm during deliberations.

_____ 8. After the trial, one of the jury members said, "We certainly didn't enjoy ourselfs during this time."

4.4.1 Using Reflexive Pronouns for Emphasis

You may hear reflexive pronouns used to emphasize a point. In this case, the reflexive pronoun means the same thing as the noun or pronoun it refers to or reflects.

> I don't know what *you* want to do, but I **myself** want to go to the park.

> It was he **himself** who built the tree house in the backyard.

> We enjoyed the play **itself** but not the musical score.

However, note the difference between:

> Lisa painted **herself** green for the Halloween party. (Lisa painted her body.)

> Lisa painted by **herself**. (Lisa painted alone; we don't know what she painted.)

Exercise 6 Fill in the blanks in this paragraph with reflexive pronouns (alone) or prepositions (for example, *for, at, of,* and *by*) and reflexive pronouns.

John is an ambitious young man. He never asks for help from anyone although he

lives __*by himself*__ . He is also an accomplished painter. In fact, he has recently painted
      1

a self-portrait. He never officially studied art, but he _____ says that there is
                                                       2

nothing a person cannot learn by practicing. When he first started painting, the results

were not so good. John, always a good sport, just laughed _____ and tried
                                                         3

again. He doesn't feel sorry _____ when he makes a mistake. He learns from
                                             4

his mistakes and goes on. Last week, one of his paintings sold for over $1,000! He was

very proud _____! The buyers _____ were surprised that John was
                      5   **6**

a novice painter. John _____ was not; he knows how much he can accomplish
                              7

in his life.

4.5 *You, one,* and *they* Used as Indefinite Pronouns

You can use the indefinite pronouns *you, one,* and *they* in general terms.

> Credit card companies can harass **you** if **you** don't pay your bill on time. (*You* refers to any person. This use is considered informal.)

> **One** never knows what can happen during a long trip. (*One* refers to any person. This use is more formal than *you*.)

> **They** ski in the Alps, but I'd be afraid to. (*They* refers to people in general. Do not use in formal speech or writing.)

Exercise 7 Read the following dialogue. Above the underlined indefinite pronouns, write the person or people these pronouns refer to.

Joanne: Hi, Gina. What's new?

Gina: Don't ask! I'm mad!

Joanne: Why? Who are you mad at?

Gina: A travel agency. <u>They</u> never get anything right.
People who work in travel agencies

Joanne: What happened?

Gina: I booked a flight and cruise to Mexico for Spring Break.

Joanne: And?

Gina: You know the saying "<u>You</u> should always double check everything"?

---

54 Chapter 4 Pronouns

Joanne: Sure. <u>You</u> never know the kinds of mistakes people will make.

Gina: Well, I should've listened to that advice. I bought my tickets and thought everything was fine until I noticed that the dates were all wrong! And my tickets are non-refundable. Now it's too late to change the tickets.

Joanne: Can you talk to someone at the agency? Complain maybe?

Gina: You know how <u>they</u> are … everything's about contracts and reading the fine print. I'm stuck with these tickets, and the travel dates, unfortunately, fall during final exams this semester.

Joanne: Hmm. Maybe you could talk to your professors about changing the exam dates. <u>One</u> should never underestimate the flexibility of some instructors.

Gina: Maybe you're right. <u>You</u> never know! I'll give it a try.

Exercise 8   Circle the letter of the correct answer.

1. According to _____, there was no proof of plagiarism in the research paper.
   a. them   c. they
   b. themselves   d. theirs

2. The president _____ came to the awards ceremony!
   a. he   c. herself
   b. by himself   d. hisself

3. Don't go to the art exhibit at the Forum. _____ awful!
   a. They are   c. It
   b. She is   d. It is

4. _____ never knows what can happen after buying a lottery ticket.
   a. You   c. One
   b. They   d. It

5. _____ style of life is much more advanced than mine.
   a. His   c. Hers
   b. Him   d. Himself

6. Whose new car do you prefer? His or _____?
   a. herselves   c. my
   b. hers   d. its

Editing

∧ **Exercise 9**   In each item, one of the four underlined words or phrases is not correct. Circle the letter of the error and write the correction above the error.

1. Mike flew to Toronto to be with her sister. It had been over two years since they
                                                  A   **B**   **C**

   had seen each other.
                D

2. Everyone in the building moved quickly out of their offices except the people who
                     A   **B**

   were in the basement at the time.
     C   **D**

3. I took so many suitcases with me on vacation. I even brought my laptop, seven
            A   **B**   **C**

   paperbacks, and mine sister's CD player.
               D

4. It was the teachers' union that worked to give their members a new deal
                             A   **B**

   including more sick leave, a higher salary, better benefits for teachers and their
                                                              C

   families, and a more solid pension plan.
    D

Original Writing

Exercise 10   Write a paragraph about your best friend from childhood.

- Recall some specific characteristics about this person and his or her family.
- Think about some memories that you share.
- Identify the reasons that this person was or continues to be special to you.

Be sure to include as many pronouns as you can. Exchange paragraphs with a partner and underline the pronouns. Are they all correct?

If you need help with the steps of writing a paragraph, see Appendix 5.

WWW You will find additional exercises for the grammar in this chapter on the Top 20 website at **http://esl.college.hmco.com/students**

To this end, the mayor recently appointed several prominent citizens as members of a committee on city development. The Committee leaders of the development project
s/v
is working on a new proposal for expansion.

5

Subject-Verb Agreement

This chapter covers subject-verb agreement, including these important categories:

- basic subject-verb agreement

- subjects separated from verbs

- indefinite pronouns as subjects

- quantity words as subjects

- plural words that take singular verbs

5.1 Basic Subject-Verb Agreement

In general, subjects and verbs must agree when the verb is in the present tense, in the present perfect tense, in the passive voice, or combined with a phrase using "be going to."

This is the main rule to remember: A subject must agree with its verb in number (singular or plural). Read these examples and notice how the verb changes to plural when the subject is plural.

1. In present tense, the verb must contain an -s ending for a singular subject. The plural verb does not end in -s.

   Singular: Andrea's sister **lives** in New South Wales.   (present)

   Plural: My mother and father **live** in Spokane, Washington.   (present)

2. These examples show subject-verb agreement for the irregular verb *be*.

   Singular: I **am going to walk** to the park this afternoon.   (be going to)

   Singular: She **is going to walk** to the park this afternoon.   (be going to)

   Plural: They **are going to walk** to the park this afternoon.   (be going to)

3. In these examples, the auxiliary verb *have* must agree with each subject.

   Singular: Harold **has bought** a new car.   (present perfect)

   Plural: Harold and Joanne **have bought** a new car.   (present perfect)

The main verb *bought* is the same for these two examples. However, the auxiliary verb *have* must agree with the plural subject *Harold and Joanne*.

Exercise 1 Read the following paragraphs. Underline the subjects and draw a box around the verbs in each sentence.

1. In order to attract more visitors to our area, the <u>city council</u> has a rather interesting plan. To be successful, this plan calls for the development of a new amusement park. This new amusement park is going to open next year. According to a report in yesterday's newspaper, the park will feature more than 50 rides and other attractions. The brainchild of a local millionaire, the park could add more than 2,000 jobs to the local economy in the next two years.

2. How much should an item of clothing cost? What is reasonable? A pair of jeans can cost anywhere from $15 to $115. T-shirts range in price, too, but not nearly as much as jeans. A nice T-shirt might cost between $15 and $25. Sweaters can be a different story. Made of wool, my new sweaters cost more than $200 dollars each! Perhaps the most expensive item is shoes. Depending on their quality and country of origin, new shoes can cost very little or very much.

3. Linda and her family are driving to New Orleans for Mardi Gras tomorrow. This will be their first trip to New Orleans, the home of Mardi Gras. Each year thousands of people visit New Orleans. Because of its unique history and geography, New Orleans offers something for many different kinds of tourists. For example, historians can appreciate the early years of New Orleans. A combination of French, Spanish, and African cultures, Louisiana draws millions of tourists such as Linda and her family every year.

5.2 Subjects That Are Separated from the Verb

You may find it more difficult to see the connection between the subject and the verb if there is extra information between them. The extra information can be a prepositional phrase, an adjective clause, or a reduced clause.

> The little *girl in the light blue jumper and matching tennis shoes* **is crying.**   (prepositional phrase)

> The new board *members who decided to vote down the proposed stock split* **are renegotiating** their positions.   (adjective clause)

> The *thundershowers pounding the coastline* **have caused** some damage to the sand dunes.   (reduced adjective clause)

Exercise 2   Read the following paragraphs. Underline the subjects and draw a box around the verbs in each sentence.

1. The <u>members</u> of the U.S. Naval Academy in Maryland are going to have their commencement ceremony at the end of the month. This commencement ceremony recognizes the achievements of all the men and women in this year's graduating class. Graduates of the U.S. Naval Academy have accomplished no simple feat. According to many different sources, both military and nonmilitary, this Maryland institution offers one of the most demanding programs around.

2. As usual, the house is a mess. In the bedroom, the wool pants that John wore two days ago are still lying on the bed. Another pair of pants is lying on the red armchair. Shoes of all kinds are strewn across the floor. In the living room, there is a bag of chips lying between the couch and the window. A sports magazine is on the floor in front of the TV. Not surprisingly, all of the advertisements that were in the magazine litter the floor. Perhaps worst of all is the kitchen. Dishes fill the sink, and dirty plates and a saucer or two hide the top of the table. Who was responsible for making this mess? Who is responsible for cleaning it up?

3.   The city faces a quandary. The causes of the problem are evident; the solutions, unfortunately, are not. Tourism is down. Fewer and fewer people are traveling very far from their homes these days. Due to this recent downturn in area tourism, the city now needs to seek an alternative source of revenue. To this end, the mayor recently appointed seven prominent citizens as members of a committee to look into city development. The committee leaders of the development project are working on a new proposal for expansion. Help is needed now, but the proposal will not be realized until the end of the year at the very earliest.

5.3 Indefinite Pronouns as Subjects

The list below shows common indefinite pronouns. Though these pronouns often refer to more than one person or thing, they take a singular verb when they act as the subject.

	every-	some-	any-	no-
-one	everyone	someone	anyone	no one
-body	everybody	somebody	anybody	nobody
-thing	everything	something	anything	nothing

Is *anyone* coming to the party tomorrow night?

***Something* has** to be done about the increasing crime rate!

If you believe in yourself, ***nothing* is** impossible.

Exercise 3   As you read the following paragraph, fill in each blank with the correct form of the verb in parentheses. Be sure the verbs agree with their subjects.

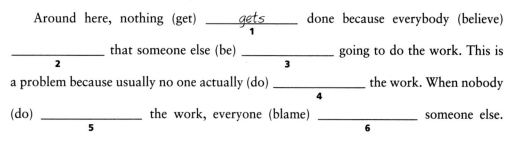

Around here, nothing (get) _____*gets*_____ done because everybody (believe)
                                        1
_____ that someone else (be) _____ going to do the work. This is
        2   **3**
a problem because usually no one actually (do) _____ the work. When nobody
                                                        4
(do) _____ the work, everyone (blame) _____ someone else.
        5   **6**

No one (want) _____ to take responsibility. Anyone who can't

              7

recognize this paradox probably (have [negative]) _____ much

                                            8

experience in the real work world.

(5.4) Expressions of Quantity

Quantity expressions can be troublesome when it comes to subject-verb agreement. The rules below govern quantity expressions with both singular and plural verbs.

- When a quantity word is followed by a prepositional phrase, the verb usually agrees with the quantity word.

  One of the presidential candidates **is** in town today.

  Three of my classes **were** canceled yesterday!

- Some expressions of quantity can take either a singular or a plural verb depending on whether the noun in the prepositional phrase is singular or plural.

	Singular	**Plural**
All of the....	All of the **restaurant was** full.	All of the **restaurants were** full.
A lot of ...	A lot of the **money was** torn.	A lot of the **bills were** torn.
Some of the ...	Some of the **pizza has** been eaten.	Some of the **pizzas have** been eaten.
One half (third, quarter) of the ...	One half of the **population is** going to vote.	One half of the **people are** going to vote.

- The quantity word *none* takes a singular verb.

  I looked at all the paintings. **None is** interesting to me.

  None of the **paintings is** interesting to me.　(formal)

Informal use only: In spoken English, most people use a plural verb when a plural noun follows *none*.

  None of the **paintings are** interesting to me.

Exercise 4   Look around your classroom as you complete these sentences. Be sure to consider quantity when choosing a verb.

1. One of my classmates _____ *is sleeping in class* _____ .

2. None of my friends _____ .

3. Some of the people in class _____ .

4. Everyone _____ .

5. Some of the desks _____ .

6. No one in the class _____ .

7. One half of the class _____ .

8. One half of the students _____ .

When you use the following quantity words alone as subjects, without objects of prepositions after them, they take the verbs indicated below.

Singular	Plural
One **is / makes**	A few **are / have**
A little **is / falls**	Both **are / take**
Each **is / needs**	

Exercise 5   As you read the paragraph, fill in each blank with the correct form of the verb in parentheses.

The number of people choosing a career in information technology (increase) _*is increasing*_ year by year. This decision is a smart one, for most companies now
1

(need) _____ someone with advanced computer knowledge. Web design,
2

computer graphics, and software development (be) _____ just some of
3

the areas that (be) _____ in demand. Anyone with the skill to manipulate
4

a keyboard and be creative (have) _____ the opportunity to find
5

an excellent employer. For those who (be, not) _____ happy working
6

for someone, other opportunities (exist) _____ . Consulting (be)
7

_____ an excellent way to make a good living but not be tied down to
                8
one job. People who like to make their own hours, choose their contracts, and decide how

much they are willing to work (thrive) _____ on consulting work.
                                              9
Overall, a career in information technology, one of the most booming sectors that (have

developed) _____ over the last ten years, (be) _____ a
                   10   11
very smart choice.

Connecting Words and Phrases and Subject-Verb Agreement

The next two sections show some common connecting words and phrases. The agreement of the verb depends on the particular connecting word or phrase.

- With the connecting words *both + and* and *either + or*, the verb must agree with the subject that is closest to the verb.

    Both the professor and her **students are** in the library.

    Both the students and the **professor is** in the library.

    Either my mother or my **uncles are taking** a vacation next week.

    Either my uncles or my **mother is taking** a vacation next week.

- With the connecting phrases *along with* and *together with*, the verb must agree with the first noun mentioned.

    The **professor,** along with her students, **is** in the library.

    The **students,** along with their professor, **are** in the library.

    The anatomy **books,** together with the corresponding instructor's guide, **look** brand new.

    The instructor's **guide,** together with the corresponding anatomy books, **looks** brand new.

Exercise 6   The phrases in the first column are subjects, and the phrases in the second column are verbs plus objects. Match the verb phrases with their corresponding subjects.

_c_ 1. The committee members, along with the company president,

_____ 2. Some of the more recent history books

_____ 3. None of the storm victims

_____ 4. Either the romantic comedies or the action film

_____ 5. Everyone in the modern dance class

_____ 6. Two-thirds of the band members

_____ 7. Anyone born in the United States

_____ 8. Half of the class

a. want to change musical style.

b. is eligible to become president.

c. are evaluating the annual report.

d. is excited about the performance.

e. discuss oppression of Native Americans.

f. are going to win the movie award.

g. is going to get government aid.

h. is scheduled to be shown on TV tonight.

i. isn't ready for the exam.

5.6   *A number of* versus *the number of*

The phrases *a number of* and *the number of* have different subject-verb agreement rules:

- The quantity phrase *a number of* always takes the plural form of the verb.
- *The number of* takes the singular verb ending.

> **A number of** consulting firm addresses **were** left to me by my old boss.
>
> **The number of** consulting firm addresses in the directory **is** extremely short.

 A number of literally means "quite a few" or many while *the number of* refers to the actual number of items.

5.7 Some Plural Nouns That Take a Singular Verb

Some miscellaneous rules about subject-verb agreement may seem illogical, but you must learn them. Here are few about plural nouns and singular verbs.

1. Names of areas of study usually take a singular verb even when the noun has an *-s* ending.

   ***Mathematics* is** not an easy subject for many people, including myself.

2. Country names with the plural *-s* ending take the singular verb form.

   ***The Netherlands* is** also known as Holland.

3. Expressions of money, time, and distance take the singular verb form.

   Fifty hours a week **seems** like too much time to spend in an office.

Editing

∧ **Exercise 7** The following paragraph contains six errors in subject-verb agreement. Read the paragraph and correct the errors.

Kim, along with three of her friends, ~~are~~ *is* going to move to New York City next summer. They are all very excited about the move, but they are having some problems. One of the biggest problems are the amount of money they have to spend on rent. There are four of them, and a two-room apartment in Manhattan cost almost $3,000. Three thousand dollars are a lot of money to spend every month. Because of this, the friends has been saving money for the past three years. Kim's money, together with the others' funds, is probably going to be enough to pay for half a year. In this way, they don't have to worry too much about finding jobs right away. Kim and her friends wants to be stage performers on Broadway, but they will have to work hard to make it.

Exercise 8   Read each sentence and circle the letter of the correct answer.

1. The United States _____ established in the eighteenth century.
   a. were   c. ∅
   b. was   d. is

2. A lot of the information we requested _____ available through the Internet.
   a. aren't   c. wasn't
   b. not   d. have been

3. The number of people it takes to build a house _____ depending on the type of structure that is being built.
   a. vary   c. are varied
   b. varies   d. various

4. The House of Representatives Subcommittee on campaign finance reform _____ in session all next week.
   a. are going to be   c. was
   b. were   d. is going to be

5. _____ physics your best subject in school?
   a. ∅   c. Are
   b. Is   d. Is it

6. Two-thirds of the students _____ going to be housed on campus next year.
   a. is   c. are
   b. will   d. ∅

Editing
∧ **Exercise 9**   In each sentence, one of the four underlined words or phrases is not correct. Circle the letter of the error and write the correction above the error.

1. The members <u>of the</u> swim team <u>was disqualified</u> for <u>having had</u> too <u>many false</u>
            A   **B**   **C**   **D**
   starts during the last state competition.

2. My landlord, <u>together with</u> the other <u>owners</u> of our apartment building, <u>is getting</u>
                A   **B**   **C**
   ready to set up a renovation contract, so the apartments <u>is going to</u> look much
                                                                      D
   better.

3. Many of the TV <u>shows</u> that <u>are aired</u> these days are reality-type shows; the <u>general</u>
   A   B   C

   public, however, <u>are not so</u> happy with the content.
                    D

4. Everyone who <u>was present</u> in class yesterday <u>was</u> surprised by the <u>instructor's</u> pop
                 A   B   C

   quiz. A lot of <u>the student</u> were unprepared for the quiz.
                  D

Original Writing

Exercise 10   Write a paragraph about a career that you're interested in. Discuss the background necessary for getting into this line of work and the job opportunities. Use at least five quantity words or connecting phrases such as:

no one	everyone	together with	a number of
most of	some	either … or …	both … and …

Exchange paragraphs with a partner and check each other's work for correct subject-verb agreement.

If you need help with the steps of writing a paragraph, see Appendix 5.

www   You will find additional exercises for the grammar in this chapter on the Top 20 website at **http://esl.college.hmco.com/students**

Employees are expected to think hard for [PREP] their role in the new company. Furthermore, they must contribute toward achieve [WF] the company's mission.

6

Prepositions

In this chapter, you will review and practice the most commonly used prepositions in English. Prepositions come in two basic types: single-word prepositions, such as *in* and *by*, and multi-word prepositions, such as *in front of*. Their use can be literal, such as *on the table*, or idiomatic, such as *on the contrary*.

6.1 Common Prepositions

We can group many prepositions into categories such as time, location, or direction. Some prepositions, such as *at*, are in all three of these categories. Other prepositions need to be memorized and are used with specific nouns, verbs, or adjectives. The exercises in this chapter will offer you practice with different kinds of prepositions. Here is a chart of the most common English prepositions. How many do you recognize?

about	beside	inside	past
above	besides	in spite of	since
across	between	into	through
after	beyond	instead of	throughout
against	but	like	till
ahead of	by	near	to
along	close to	next to	toward(s)
among	despite	of	under
around	down	off	underneath
as	during	on	unlike
at	except	onto	until
back to / from	far from	on top of	up
before	for	opposite	upon
behind	from	out	with
below	in	outside	within
beneath	in back / front of	over	without

6.2 A Few Basic Rules

These few basic rules about prepositions will help you as you work through this chapter.

1. A preposition is a word that shows the relationship between a noun (or a noun equivalent, such as a noun phrase, a clause, or a gerund phrase) and another word in a sentence.

> The girls' soccer team played **on** the new field. (*On* shows the relationship of the noun *field* to the verb *played*.)

2. A preposition always has an object. The object can be a noun, a pronoun, or a noun-equivalent (a noun phrase, a clause, or a gerund phrase). Together they form what is called a *prepositional phrase*.

In the following examples, the preposition is bold and the object is in a box.

> They received a notice **from** Mr. Taft. (object = noun)

> They received a notice **from** him. (object = pronoun)

> They received a notice **from** a young lawyer. (object = noun phrase)

They received a notice **from** a young lawyer who works downtown.
(object = noun phrase + clause)

They received a notice **about** cleaning up their yard.
(object = gerund phrase)

3. Some prepositions may be used as adverbs or as particles. Their meanings can be either literal or idiomatic.

He walked **up** the stairs.   (preposition; literal meaning)

Stand **up.**   (adverb)

Look **up** the rule.   (particle; used with the verb to form one unit of meaning, which is idiomatic)

6.3) Prepositions of Time

Prepositions of time can be about a specific time, a general time, or a length of time.

6.3.1 Specific Time

Here is a list of prepositions of specific time:

after	during	past
at	for	since
before	from	till
between	in	to
by	on	until

Use these prepositions when you know the specific time, such as *at 6:00* or *before noon.* Here are more examples:

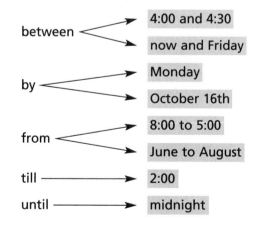

Expressions of Specific Time

It's 10 to / till 3.	It's ten minutes **to** 3:00.
It's 20 after / past 7.	It's twenty minutes **after** 7 o'clock.
in time	They arrived **in time** to see the opening act. (not too late)
on time	They arrived **on time** for the meeting. (at the required time)
out of time	That's it. We're **out of time**. (allotted time is over)
at the end of	The report is due **at the end of** the day. (time the work day ends)

Exercise 1 On a separate sheet of paper, write a short paragraph about how you spend a typical day. Use at least six prepositions and expressions of specific time. Underline the prepositions.

6.3.2 General Time

Use prepositions of general time—*at, by, in, on*—when you refer to the time of day, a day of the week, a month, a season, or a year.

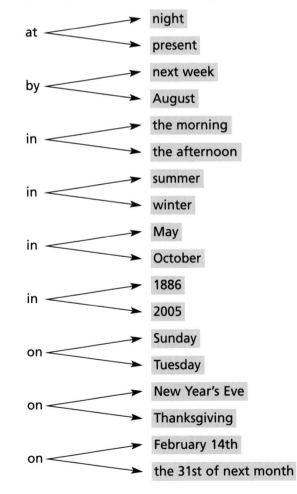

at → night
at → present

by → next week
by → August

in → the morning
in → the afternoon

in → summer
in → winter

in → May
in → October

in → 1886
in → 2005

on → Sunday
on → Tuesday

on → New Year's Eve
on → Thanksgiving

on → February 14th
on → the 31st of next month

Exercise 2 Write six sentences about how you spend your evenings or weekends, how you have celebrated holidays, or what you will do in the future. Use each of these prepositions of general time at least once: *at, by, in,* and *on.* Underline the prepositions.

1. _____

_____

2. _____

_____

3. _____

_____

4. _____

_____

5. _____

_____

6. _____

_____

6.3.3 Length of Time

The prepositions *at, for, during, since,* and *through* indicate a span of time rather than one specific time or a general time.

at	the end of a week
	this time
during	the day
	the rainy season
since	yesterday afternoon
	August 1974
through	the end of this year
	Saturday
for	25 minutes
	two and a half weeks

 In English "a half" comes *after* the number as in "two and a half weeks," not "two weeks and a half."

Exercise 3 Fill in the blanks with the correct preposition of specific time, general time, or length of time.

The Bureau of Citizenship and Immigration Services (BCIS) office is open _from_
1

9:00 a.m. _____ 5:00 p.m. Monday _____ Friday. It is closed
2   3

_____ an hour _____ 12:00 and 1:00 p.m. for lunch. Applications
4   5

to become a permanent resident are accepted _____ 4:30 p.m. every day. No
6

applications will be accepted _____ 4:30.
7

Please keep in mind that the BCIS office is especially busy _____ the
8

morning. If you wait _____ 3:00 p.m. to come to the office, chances are you
9

will not be served. You will be told _____ the end _____ the day to
10   11

return again the following day.

It is critical to arrive _____ time for any and all scheduled appointments.
12

_____ present, there is a backlog of applications, and new appointments are
13

being scheduled for the month _____ next. It is not uncommon for applicants
14

to have to wait _____ three months for an appointment. Applicants for
15

citizenship who submit all required paperwork and complete the interview process

_____ March of any year should receive notification of approval of citizenship
16

_____ time to vote in any fall election.
17

6.4 | # Prepositions of Location

Prepositions of location tell where something is. Here are the most common ones:

above	behind	close to	near	throughout
across	below	far from	next to	under
across from	beneath	in	on	underneath
ahead of	beside	in back of*	opposite	
among	between	in front of*	outside	
at	by	inside	over	

*Pay careful attention to the word *the* in these expressions with prepositions of location:

in back of

The cat is sleeping **in back of the car.**   (behind the car)

in the back of

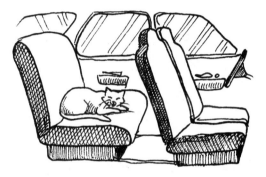

The cat is **in the back of** the car. (inside the back part of the car)

in front of

There is a snake **in front of the car.**   (before the car)

in the front of

There is a snake **in the front of the car.**   (inside the front part of the car)

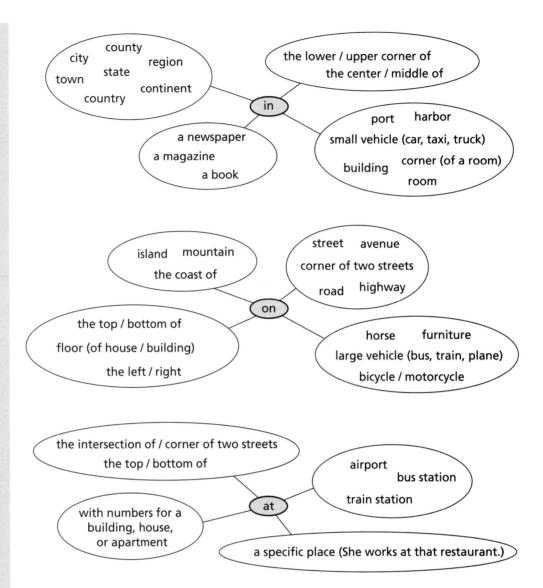

Use the preposition *between* with two people or things.

> **Between** you and me, I'm really getting tired of this place.

Use *among* for three or more people or things:

> **Among** all my friends, Joan is the hardest-working one.

6.4.1 Idiomatic Expressions with Prepositions of Location

Here are some idiomatic uses of prepositions of location that you may need to memorize:

in bed (sleeping)   on the bed (sitting)
at home   at work
at / in school   at / in church   at / in the office
at the hospital (visiting, working)   in the hospital (a patient)

Exercise 4   As you read the paragraph, choose the correct preposition from the two in parentheses and underline it.

Susana was **1** (in, <u>at</u>) home on Tuesday, standing **2** (in front of, in the front of) the window **3** (in, on) her living room **4** (at, on) the 18th floor of Ocean Towers, her apartment building. As she gazed out the window, she saw the marina **5** (behind, below) her.

Scattered **6** (outside, throughout) the marina were small boats, some tied to the docks and others sitting **7** (between, among) the many buoys **8** (at, in) the harbor. **9** (On, In) her left, Susana saw a cruise ship sailing into port. She watched as the tugboat **10** (beneath, behind) the ship guided it to its berth. Passengers **11** (in, on) the ship were **12** (over, outside) standing **13** (at, on) the decks and waving to people **14** (at the bottom of, below) them.

Susana wished she could take a cruise. It had always been her dream. She imagined herself **15** (at, on) an island, surrounded **16** (by, close to) deep blue water and **17** (across from, far from) everyone and everything.

Suddenly, Susana heard the intercom **18** (in front of, near) the front door ring. It was the doorman, buzzing to let her know that the taxi she had called for had arrived. In a couple of hours, she would be **19** (on, at) the airport, sitting **20** (on, at) a plane headed for the Arctic Circle, **21** (in the top of, at the top of) the world. The Arctic Circle was as **22** (far to, far from) a tropical island as a person could get, she thought. Susanna shivered as she closed the door to her apartment and waited **23** (near to, next to) the elevator. She'd really rather be headed for a vacation **24** (on, beside) that island!

6.5 Prepositions of Direction or Movement

These prepositions indicate a specific direction or a movement in a direction.

across	back to / from	in / into	past
along	by	off	through
around	down	onto	to
at	for	out of	towards
away from	from	over	up

Here are some examples:

If you go **across** the road, you'll see the entrance to the trail.
(*across* applies to a flat area, such as a road, a parking lot, or a bridge)

You'll have to go **over** a hill before you see the pond.   (*over* refers to an up/down movement, such as over a hill, a fence, or a bridge)

When you go **through** the Miller's garden, you'll know it's the end of the trail.   (*through* indicates something having two sides or entrance/exit, such as a window, a garden, or a city)

6.5.1 Expressions with Prepositions of Direction or Movement

arrive **in** a city, state, country

> I arrived **in** Dallas yesterday.

arrive **at** other places   (restaurant, school, or work)

> I arrived **at** the bank late.

go **to** or leave **for** a place

> I left **for** the airport at noon.

go **from** a place **to** another place

> I went **from** Miami **to** New York.

∧ **Exercise 5**   Read the following directions for the treasure map. Underline the 13 prepositions that show *direction* or *movement*; correct the four that are wrong.

    First, climb <u>out of</u> the boat. Walk along the pier out of the shore. When you get to the shore, turn east and go past the palm trees. Near the palm trees are some huge boulders. Climb by the boulders and head for the tower. Walk around the tower and through the bushes that run into the stream. Go across the stream, away from the tower. Soon you will see a flag on a pole. Dig until you find the box buried beneath the pole. Head back from your boat at the dock.

Original Writing

Exercise 6   Write a paragraph describing a trip that you have taken or would like to take. Use at least eight direction/movement prepositions in your paragraph. Be sure to underline them.

Prepositions in Combination

Some prepositions occur in combination with nouns, verbs, and adjectives.

6.6.1 Prepositions with Nouns

Prepositions in combination with nouns may come either before or after the noun. You must learn these combinations as a unit. There is no rule to explain when to use a certain preposition with a specific noun. NOUNS + PREPOSITIONS are commonly followed by gerunds (nouns with an *-ing* ending).

PREPOSITION + NOUN

at	on	out of	in
odds	hold	control	a hurry
risk	sale	order	control
war	vacation	time	danger
work			debt
			luck
			love
			shape
			trouble
			pain
			person
			public
			private

NOUN + PREPOSITION

confusion about	answer for	take advantage of
question about	concern for	understanding of
	excuse for	
experience in	fondness for	experience with
interest in	need for	
	question for	
answer to	reason for	
	something for	

Exercise 7   Fill in the correct preposition with the noun. Then write an original sentence using each phrase. Underline these phrases in your sentences.

1. show a need <u>*for*</u> : <u>*The census statistics show a need for more*</u>

<u>*elementary schools in Los Angeles and Houston.*</u>

2. have a question _____ : _____

_____

3. develop a special interest _____ : _____

_____

4. take advantage _____ : _____

_____

5. be no excuse _____ : _____

_____

6. have experience _____ : _____

_____

Exercise 8   Assign each noun from the word bank to one of these prepositions: *at, in,* or *on.* Then write a sentence using each NOUN + PREPOSITION combination.

a hurry	hold	person	sale	war
debt	odds	public	vacation	work

in a hurry   1. <u>We were in a hurry to get to the movie.</u> _____

_____   2. _____

_____   3. _____

_____   4. _____

_____   5. _____

_____   6. _____

_____   7. _____

_____   8. _____

_____   9. _____

_____   10. _____

6.6.2 Prepositions with Verbs

As with PREPOSITION + NOUN combinations, prepositions that are combined with verbs must be learned as a unit. Below are some of the most common combinations, grouped by preposition.

Verbs + *about*	Verbs + *of*	Verbs + *to*	Verbs + *with*
ask	complain	agree	agree
complain	die (also *die from*)	be used	argue
dream	get rid	belong	break up
forget		explain	compete
talk	**Verbs + *off***	introduce	cooperate
think	break	listen	disagree
worry	call	object	fill
	cut	pay attention	get along
Verbs + *at*	fall	relate	help
guess	jump	reply	finish
laugh	keep	say	work
look	live	speak	
smile	take		
stare	turn	**Verbs + *toward***	
yell		contribute	
	Verbs + *on*	head	
Verbs + *for*	count	turn	
apologize	have	walk	
ask	keep	work	
buy	pick		
do	put		
look	rely		
make	take		
pay	wait		
study	work		
thank			

Editing
∧ Exercise 9 Read the following paragraphs with underlined VERB + PREPOSITION combinations. Find and correct the three mistakes in the combinations.

One of the most sought-after qualities in an employee is the ability to **1** <u>get along with</u> others. In today's world, and especially in the world of business, employees are seen as team members. They are expected to **2** <u>relate with</u> all other members of the team and to **3** <u>work toward</u> a common goal, company success.

Similarly, employees are also expected to **4** <u>think about</u> and **5** <u>contribute toward</u> achieving the company's mission. Although at times employees may not **6** <u>agree about</u> a specific company policy, they are expected to support and follow it. At times they may even have to temporarily **7** <u>forget about</u> their personal goals and desires in order to

accomplish the goals of the company.

Employees who cannot or will not **8** <u>cooperate with</u> others on the team often find

they no longer **9** <u>belong to</u> the "inner circle" and begin to **10** <u>worry for</u> keeping their jobs.

In many cases, they leave the company in search of another that better suits their work

style and personality.

Exercise 10   Fill in the correct preposition for each verb listed in the first column. Then draw lines
to match the VERB + PREPOSITION combinations in the first column with the correct
phrases in the second column. Finally, write a sentence using each VERB + PREPOSITION
and phrase combination.

1. guess __*at*__   a. running my own business

2. apologize _____   b. a college entrance exam

3. listen _____   c. three others on an economics project

4. study _____   d. several answers on a test

5. work _____   e. other people's points of view

6. dream _____   f. calling you so late

1. _____

_____

2. _____

_____

3. _____

_____

4. _____

_____

5. _____

_____

6. _____

_____

6.6.3 Prepositions with Adjectives

Certain adjectives can be combined with prepositions. These, too, function as one unit and must be learned together. Listed below are some of the most common combinations.

to be ...

angry about / at	afraid of
concerned about	fond of
excited about	guilty of
happy about / with	in favor of
sorry about / for	proud of
unhappy about / with	sure of
worried about	tired of
	unsure of
bored by / with	
embarrassed by	boring to
frustrated by / with	committed to
	confusing to
bad for	important to
good for	married to
ready for	opposed to
necessary for	pleasing to
	related to
different from	similar to
divorced from	unimportant to
isolated from	
	familiar with
disappointed in / with	impressed with
interested in	pleased with
	satisfied with

Exercise 11   Circle the letter of the correct answer.

1. The students are so excited _____ graduation that they can't concentrate on anything during class.
   a. to
   b. of
   c. about
   d. in

2. I know him! He's married _____ the account manager of Trace Financial Services.
   a. with
   b. to
   c. from
   d. ∅

3. She made an appointment to see her student advisor. She's _____ studying for her MBA.
   a. interesting in
   b. interested for
   c. interested about
   d. interested in

4. Let's go north on vacation this year. I'm tired _____ visiting Florida beaches every year.
   a. for
   b. to
   c. about
   d. of

5. When there is a lot of lightning, it's important _____ stay indoors.
   a. to
   b. among
   c. for
   d. about

6. Do you really feel it's necessary _____ everyone in the family to have a flu shot this year?
   a. for
   b. to
   c. of
   d. by

7. Maggie was so _____ her SAT test scores.
   a. pleasing to
   b. pleased to
   c. pleased with
   d. pleased of

8. The would-be car thieves were so _____ the anti-theft wheel locks that they gave up trying to steal the car.
   a. frustrating to
   b. frustrated by
   c. frustrated to
   d. frustrating by

Exercise 12 Finish each sentence with a prepositional phrase (PREPOSITION + NOUN / NOUN equivalent).

1. We're all in favor (*of*) *changing the channel.*

2. I believe that it's good (   )

3. They are not at all familiar (   )

4. Were you unhappy (   ) ?

5. What's most confusing (   ) ?

6. Most parents are worried (   )

7. The little girl was embarrassed (   )

8. Studying prepositions is similar (   )

9. People who live in the country are isolated (   )

10. Are they satisfied (   ) ?

Editing

∧ Exercise 13   Find the seven errors in ADJECTIVE + PREPOSITION usage and correct them.

Young people are often unsure with themselves in social situations. During adolescence, teens are especially concerned in what others think of them. It's important to them that their peers like them. Surprisingly, some teens often act as if they don't care what others think on them. Although this conflict is normal, many adolescents are often frustrated at these feelings they experience.

As they mature, adolescents are ready for more responsibility, and yet oftentimes they are angry for their parents for making them accountable of their actions. Some teens are afraid of their growing independence while others are proud for it.

Original Writing

Exercise 14   Write a paragraph describing a specific event you attended or an experience you had. Be sure to identify when and where the event or experience occurred. Include how you reacted, how you felt, what you thought, and what you did. Before you begin, make a list of the prepositions or noun, verb, and adjective + preposition combinations from this chapter you will try to use. In your paragraph, underline the ones from the list you were able to use. Exchange paragraphs with a partner and check each other's work for correct use of prepositions.

> If you need help with the steps of writing a paragraph, see Appendix 5.
>
> **www**   You will find additional exercises for the grammar in this chapter on the Top 20 website at **http://esl.college.hmco.com/students**

If you are a little late in sending your birthday wishes, **ART** *there's still a chance to send the last-minute gift that will warm the heart.*

7

Articles:

a, an, the

Articles—those little words that can be so difficult to use correctly—introduce and identify nouns. There are two kinds of articles in English: indefinite *(a, an)* and definite *(the)*. Articles occur before nouns *(the* book) and before ADJECTIVE + NOUN combinations *(a* big book).

Article Basics

This chart gives you the basic uses of articles in English. (For a review of count and noncount nouns, see Chapter 3.)

Articles	Count Nouns		Noncount Nouns
indefinite articles (a, an)	a cat an ugly cat an answer	cats ugly cats answers	money
definite article (the)	the cat	the cats	the money

7.1.1 Three Rules for Avoiding Common Article Mistakes

These three rules, repeated later in the chapter, are grouped here because they are the main rules that will help you avoid the most common mistakes with articles.

1. Use *a, an,* or *the* (or another word such as *my* or *this*) in front of a singular count noun.

Incorrect: Jefferson was certainly important president in U.S. history.

Correct: Jefferson was certainly **an** important president in U.S. history.

2. Use *the* with specific noun references.

Incorrect: Questions on yesterday's grammar test were difficult.

Correct: **The** questions on yesterday's grammar test were difficult.

3. Do not use *the* with general noun references.

Incorrect: Our government should spend more money on the education.

Correct: Our government should spend more money on ~~the~~ education.

Exercise 1 As you read the paragraph, fill in each blank with *a, an, the,* or ∅. Be prepared to explain your answer choice using information from one of the three rules discussed in Section 7.1.1.

___*A*___ Magic Trick with ___∅___ Numbers
1   2

Here is _____ trick with _____ numbers that will amaze your friends. Have
3   4

_____ friend think of _____ number between one and ten. However, tell _____ friend
5   6   7

not to say _____ number aloud. Ask your friend to double _____ number. Next,
8   9

_____ person should add eight. _____ answer that your friend will have now is
10   11

_____ even number. Ask your friend to divide _____ number in half. Have your friend
12   13

subtract _____ original number that was used in _____ first step. Regardless of which
14   15

number your friend chose in step one, _____ final answer is always four. There is
16

_____ mathematical explanation for this trick, but your friends will think it is _____
17   18

magic.

7.2 Indefinite Articles

The indefinite articles are *a* and *an*. Use *a* and *an* with singular count nouns. Here are the four main rules for indefinite articles.

Uses

1. Use *a* and *an* to introduce a singular count noun.

   There is **an excellent** show on TV tonight.

2. Use *a* and *an* to define or classify something.

   Jambalaya is **a rice** dish that is native to south Louisiana.

3. Use *a* and *an* to show that you are talking about one (of the item).

   Excuse me. Do you have **a pencil** that I could borrow?

(Do not use *one* interchangeably to mean *a.* "Do you have one pencil?" emphasizes the *number,* not the *pencil.*)

4. Use *a* and *an* for a general truth about a singular count noun.

   A piano has 96 keys.   *or*   Pianos have 96 keys.

We do not usually use an article with a noncount noun.

   Time is (no article) **money.**

Exercise 2   Write an original sentence for each of the four uses of indefinite articles.

1. _____

2. _____

3. _____

4. _____

(7.3) The Definite Article

The definite article is *the*. Use *the* with singular, plural, and noncount nouns. Use *the* to indicate that you are referring to something specific. Here are five main rules for definite articles.

Uses

1. Use *the* to refer to a specific thing or person.

> **The** window has been closed all day.

> **The** pilots who work for that airline will go on strike at midnight.

2. Use *the* for the second and all subsequent references to the same item. Note that sometimes different nouns are used to refer to the same thing.

> A **deadly car crash** (noun A—first reference) involving **three vehicles** (noun B—first reference) occurred on Highway 62 last night. Police said that **the wreck** (noun A—second reference) happened just after midnight and may have been due to bad weather. Though damage to **the three cars** (noun B—second reference) appeared to be minimal, we now know that **the accident** (noun A—third reference) claimed two lives.

Notice how *crash* becomes *wreck* and then becomes *accident*. *Vehicles* becomes *cars*. Although a different word is used each time, each word still refers to the same original thing. When this is the case, the article changes from indefinite (*a*) to definite (*the*).

3. Use *the* with a superlative or with ranking.

> **The** third part of any joke is usually the punch line.

> Many sports offer good exercise, but tennis is **the** best sport for people of all ages.

4. Use *the* with the parts of something.

> I like this watch. **The** minute hand is blue, and **the** hour hand is red.

Do not use *the* with body parts. Use a possessive adjective.

> **My** stomach hurts!

However, we use *the* to talk about a body part in a more formal way, for example, in a science or health discussion.

> **The** stomach contains special liquids to help with digestion.

5. Use *the* when the item is known to both the writer and the reader (or to the speaker and the listener).

> Rick: Where's your phone?
>
> Cara: It's next to **the** refrigerator.

6. Use *the* in general statements about a whole species (kind) or category.

> **The** Apple computer was not developed by Bill Gates.
>
> **The** green sea turtle is on the threatened and endangered list.
>
> More medicine is needed for **the** sick.   (*the sick* = sick people)

The use of *the* + SINGULAR NOUN is more formal than the more conversational style of using **plural** + no article.

> **The tiger** is native to India.   (formal)
>
> **Tigers** are native to India.   (less formal)

Exercise 3   Write an original sentence for each of the six uses of the definite article. In each sentence, underline the article and be prepared to explain why you used it.

1. _____

_____

2. _____

_____

3. _____

_____

4. _____

_____

5. _____

_____

6. _____

_____

7.4 No Article (∅)

In English, articles are not always needed. Here are ten main rules indicating when no article is needed.

Uses

1. No article is needed when you are referring to the whole group or whole class.

> Most people agree that more tax money should be spent on **education.** (NOT *the* education)

> **Tigers** are native to India. (NOT *The* tigers)

2. No article is needed when you are referring to a thing in general, rather than to a specific member of a group.

> The most popular subjects are **English, math,** and **world history.**
> (NOT *the* English, *the* math, and *the* world history)

> Exception: Use an article when you refer to a specific kind within a general thing.

> I understand English well, but I sometimes have difficulty understanding **the** English spoken by young children.

3. No article is needed with names of cities, states, and countries. Exceptions include place names that include the words *united, union,* or *republic of,* as well as plural names.

No article: New York Tokyo Florida California France Argentina

Article: **the** United States **the** Soviet Union **the** Republic of Colombia **the** Philippines **the** Hawaiian Islands

4. No article is needed with a (single) lake, but use *the* with all other bodies of water.

No article: Lake Michigan Lake Tikal

Article: **the** Great Lakes **the** Caribbean Sea **the** Pacific Ocean **the** Mississippi River

5. No article is needed with directions, but use *the* with areas identified by direction words.

> Go **north** on the highway. (NOT *the* north)

> He lives in **the** South. (the southern part of the U.S.)

6. No article is needed with diseases, but use *a* with injuries, symptoms, and other non-diseases.

No article: HIV AIDS cancer cholera

> Exception: *the* flu

Article: **a** cold **a** headache **a** heart attack **a** broken leg

7. No article is needed with *in back of* or *in front of*.

> The cat is **in back of** the car.

 Exception: Use *the* to mean inside the container or vehicle.

> The cat is **in the back of** the car.

(See Chapter 6, p. 75, for more information about prepositions of location.)

8. No article is needed with people's names.

> Dr. Jenk's office is next to Brenda's office. (NOT *The* Dr. Jenk's office / *the* Brenda's office)

 Exception: With a title that has no proper name, use the article.

> This is **the** President.

9. No article is needed with months, dates, days, or holidays.

> Christmas is December 25th. (NOT *the* December 25th)

> My birthday is January 23rd. (NOT *the* January 23rd)

 Exception: Use *the* with dates in this phrase:

> **the** 12th of August

10. No article is needed with commonplace words in certain idiomatic expressions.

> He is **at home** now. (NOT at *the* home)

> He's **at work**. (NOT at *the* work)

> Marguerite is still **in bed**. (NOT in *the* bed) .

> They're **on vacation**. (NOT on *the* vacation)

Exercise 4   Write an original sentence for each of the ten rules when no article is needed, including any exceptions to the rule. In each sentence, underline the place where writers might mistakenly put an article and be prepared to explain your choice.

1. _____

_____

2. _____

_____

3. _____

_____

4. _____

_____

5. _____

_____

6. _____

_____

7. _____

_____

8. _____

_____

9. _____

_____

10. _____

_____

Exercise 5   As you read the paragraph, fill in each blank with *the* or ∅.

_∅_ Women's Rights and _the_ Struggle
1   2
for ____ Social Justice
3

During _____ second half of _____ 19th century, progress toward equality
                4   5

between _____ men and _____ women in _____ Western Hemisphere was slow. No
                6   7   8

woman was able to receive a medical degree in _____ Canada until _____ 1895, so
                                                          9   10

_____ Canada's first women doctors were forced to train in _____ United States. Full
   11   12

enfranchisement occurred in Canada in _____ 20th century, but _____ Canadian
                                                   13   14

women had gained _____ right to vote in some provincial and municipal elections before
                          15

1900. Like women in the United States, Canadian women provided leadership in

temperance, child welfare, and labor reform movements. _____ Argentina and _____
                                                                    16   17

Uruguay were among _____ first Latin American nations to provide _____ public
                            18   19

education for _____ women. Both nations introduced _____ coeducation in _____
20 ... 21 ... 22

1870s. In _____ same decade, Chilean women gained access to some professional
23

careers. In _____ Argentina, _____ first woman doctor graduated from medical school
24 ... 25

in 1899. In _____ Brazil, where many women were active in the abolitionist movement,
26

_____ four women had graduated in _____ medicine by 1882. More rapid progress
27 ... 28

was achieved in lower-status careers that less directly threatened _____ male economic
29

power. By _____ end of _____ century, women dominated _____ elementary school
30 ... 31 ... 32

teaching throughout _____ Western Hemisphere.
33

Editing

∧ Exercise 6   Each of these proverbs contains one article error. Edit the proverb and then explain what it means.

Proverb 1: The time is money.

Meaning: _____

_____

Proverb 2: Don't judge book by its cover.

Meaning: _____

_____

Proverb 3: Where there is a will, there is way.

Meaning: _____

_____

Proverb 4: There's no time like present.

Meaning: _____

_____

Proverb 5: While the cat's away, mice will play.

Meaning: _____

_____

Exercise 7 Read each sentence and fill in the blanks with the correct article: *a, an, the,* or ∅. Then answer the question in the blank on the left.

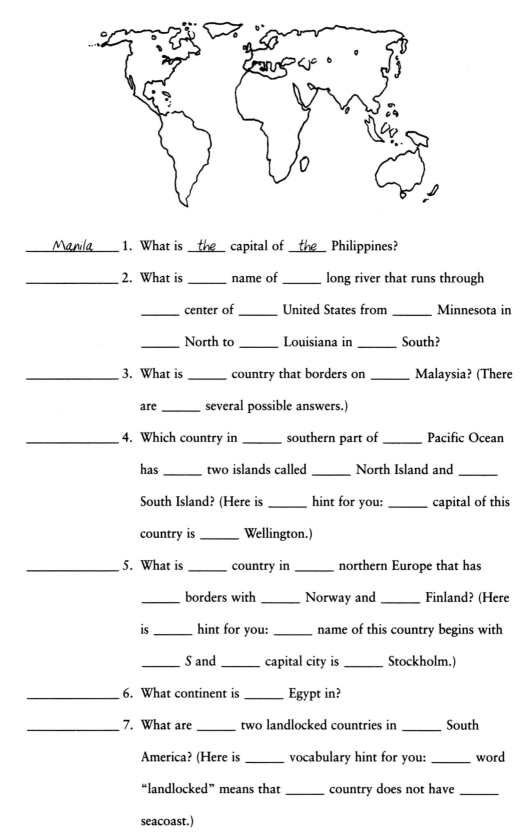

_____Manila_____ 1. What is __the__ capital of __the__ Philippines?

_____ 2. What is _____ name of _____ long river that runs through

_____ center of _____ United States from _____ Minnesota in

_____ North to _____ Louisiana in _____ South?

_____ 3. What is _____ country that borders on _____ Malaysia? (There

are _____ several possible answers.)

_____ 4. Which country in _____ southern part of _____ Pacific Ocean

has _____ two islands called _____ North Island and _____

South Island? (Here is _____ hint for you: _____ capital of this

country is _____ Wellington.)

_____ 5. What is _____ country in _____ northern Europe that has

_____ borders with _____ Norway and _____ Finland? (Here

is _____ hint for you: _____ name of this country begins with

_____ S and _____ capital city is _____ Stockholm.)

_____ 6. What continent is _____ Egypt in?

_____ 7. What are _____ two landlocked countries in _____ South

America? (Here is _____ vocabulary hint for you: _____ word

"landlocked" means that _____ country does not have _____

seacoast.)

_____ 8. What are _____ three continents that have _____ shores on

_____ Mediterranean Sea?

Exercise 8 Consult the Internet or a reference book for international geography information. Use the information to create five geography questions like those in Exercise 7. In groups, take turns asking your geography questions. Correct each other's use of articles in the questions and answers.

1. _____

2. _____

3. _____

4. _____

5. _____

Exercise 9 Circle the letter of the correct answer.

1. According to the student, there was no proof of _____.
   a. plagiarism in research paper
   b. the plagiarism in the research paper
   c. the plagiarism in research paper
   d. plagiarism in the research paper

2. _____ eventually caused flooding in the valley below.
   a. The bad weather in the mountains
   b. The bad weather in mountains
   c. The weather in the mountains was bad
   d. The bad weather was in the mountains

3. In order to make _____, it's important to start with good ingredients.
   a. a pie apples well
   b. an apples pie well
   c. a well apple pie
   d. an apple pie well

4. You never know what can happen after buying a lottery ticket. _____ for many people.
   a. Unknown is attraction
   b. Unknown are the attraction
   c. The unknown is attraction
   d. The unknown is the attraction

5. Included in this database are more than 1,500 commercial airline accident records, large and small, covering _____.
   a. 1970 through present
   b. the 1970 through present
   c. the 1970 through present
   d. 1970 through the present

6. (From a travel advertisement) "You can book rooms for as low as $42 per _____ participating hotels and inns in the U.S. and Canada."
   a. night at
   b. the night at
   c. night on
   d. the night on

∧ **Exercise 10** In each numbered item, one of the four underlined words or phrases is not correct. Circle the letter of the error and write the correction above the error.

1. If <u>you are</u> looking for <u>the</u> tennis racket, <u>the</u> best advice you'll ever get is to try out
       A   **B**   **C**

   <u>as many different ones as you can</u>.
             D

2. If <u>you are a little late in sending</u> your <u>good</u> wishes, there's <u>still a</u> chance to
          A   **B**   **C**

   <u>send last-minute gift</u> that will warm the heart.
          D

3. <u>The</u> bat, <u>the only</u> mammal that can <u>fly, modified</u> hands and arms that serve
     A   **B**   **C**

   <u>as wings</u> that enable this animal to fly.
       D

4. <u>When freshly fallen snow</u>, perhaps <u>the</u> finest material in the world, is compressed,
          A   **B**

   this material <u>can be compared</u> to <u>the</u> light concrete.
           C   **D**

⊙riginal Writing

Exercise 11 Write a paragraph about an important event in history. Identify the event, when it happened, why it happened, why it was important, who was involved, and so on. In your concluding sentence, write your opinion regarding this event or the importance of this event. Exchange paragraphs with a partner. Circle all the articles on your partner's paper and check for their correct use.

> If you need help with the steps of writing a paragraph, see Appendix 5.
>
> **WWW** You will find additional exercises for the grammar in this chapter on the Top 20 website at **http://esl.college.hmco.com/students**

WF

Louise's childly behavior got her into trouble at work. If there is another incident, she will most definitely be fired.

8

Word Forms

In this chapter you will find charts with different word forms for the major parts of speech: nouns, adjectives, adverbs, and verbs. Study the charts before you do the exercises that follow them.

8.1　Adjective Endings

Following is a list of commonly-used endings for adjectives. Refer to them as you complete Exercise 1.

Ending	Meaning	Examples
-able	able to	enjoy**able**, wash**able**
-al	having the quality of	crimin**al**, gener**al**, music**al**
-ant	having the quality of	reluct**ant**, defi**ant**
-ar / -ary	related to	spectacul**ar**, ordin**ary**
-ative	having the quality of	talk**ative**, primi**tive**
-ed	past participle	bor**ed**, interest**ed**
-en	made of	gold**en**, wood**en**
-ent	having the quality of	consist**ent**, depend**ent**
-esque	in the style of	pictur**esque**, grot**esque**
-ful	full of	beauti**ful**, joy**ful**
-ible	able to	ed**ible**, vis**ible**
-ic / -ical	related to	hero**ic**, con**ical**
-ine	having the nature of	femin**ine**
-ing	present participle	bor**ing**, interest**ing**
-ive	tending to	act**ive**, explos**ive**
-lent	full of	succu**lent**, viru**lent**
-less	without	harm**less**, child**less**
-like	like, similar to	child**like**, lady**like**
-ly	having the qualities of	matron**ly**, world**ly**
-ory	related to	mandat**ory**, obligat**ory**
-ous / -ious	full of	contemptu**ous**, grac**ious**
-proof	protected from	fool**proof**, child**proof**
-y	related to	cream**y**, unhealth**y**

Exercise 1 Read the paragraph and underline the 25 adjectives. Many of them contain endings from the list on the previous page.

Central Asia offers possibilities for imaginative travelers to experience new horizons. The many cities available to travelers include the pristine mountains of Kyrgystan, the historical cities found in Uzbekistan, and the picturesque countrysides of Kazakstan. The relatively unknown areas offer alternative venues to the more popular areas of Europe, South America, and Asia. As the local economies are growing slowly, Central Asian prices are relatively cheap. Visitors can witness not only natural beauty but also towns and cities rich in history. Opulent mosques and palaces can be seen in the regional capitals of Central Asia. For a truly unforgettable experience, Central Asia has numerous venues of interest for the brave traveler.

Noun Endings

This list gives commonly-used noun endings. Refer to them as you complete Exercise 2 below.

Ending	Meaning	Examples
-acy	condition	demo**cracy**, fall**acy**
-age	action, state	marri**age**, us**age**
-an / -ian	person related to	Morocc**an**, librar**ian**
-ance / -ence	condition, state	attend**ance**, excell**ence**
-ant / -ent	person who	particip**ant**, stud**ent**
-ar	person who	li**ar**, schol**ar**
-ation	action, state	inaugur**ation**, explor**ation**
-ee	person who receives something	grant**ee**, refug**ee**
-er / -or	person who does	danc**er**, employ**er**, profess**or**
-ery	action	brib**ery**, slav**ery**, robb**ery**
-ese	belonging to	Vietnam**ese**, Chin**ese**
-hood	state of	brother**hood**, child**hood**
-ics	science, art, or practice	mathemat**ics**, academ**ics**
-ing	gerund (action)	swimm**ing**, bowl**ing**
-ion / -sion / -tion	action, state, result	opin**ion**, occa**sion**, recep**tion**
-ism	belief, practice	social**ism**, skeptic**ism**
-ist	person who believes or does	capital**ist**, terror**ist**
-ment	result of action	argu**ment**, achieve**ment**
-mony	action or result	cere**mony**, hege**mony**
-ness	quality, state	dark**ness**, polite**ness**
-or	activity, quality, or state	behavi**or**, demean**or**
-ship	condition, quality	partner**ship**, scholar**ship**
-ty / -ity	quality, condition	eligibil**ity**, commun**ity**

Exercise 2   In each sentence, write the correct noun ending.

1. The inaugur _ation_ of the new university president was quite an event.

2. Memb_____ of the media were present to film the occa_____.

3. Current stud_____ were also on hand to witness the cere_____.

4. The university president spoke of the import_____ of academic excell_____.

5. She also mentioned strengthening the partner_____ between the university and the commun_____.

6. After the ceremony, a recep_____ was held in the University Center.

Verb Endings

Here are some commonly used endings for verbs. Refer to them as you complete Exercise 3 below.

Ending	Meaning	Examples
-ate	cause, make	graduate, complicate
-en	made of, make	blacken, ripen, widen
-ify	make	beautify, simplify
-ize	make	criticize, symbolize

Exercise 3   As you read the paragraph, fill in the missing verbs using the clues in parentheses.

Many Americans have trouble understanding the difficult tax forms they need to fill out every year. The Internal Revenue Service should (make simple) _____

these forms. Taxpayers often (give criticism) _____ the IRS for

continuing to use these forms. The highly advanced legal language on these tax forms

(gives complications) _____ the process of answering the questions

correctly. If taxpayer resentment (becomes wider) _____, perhaps the IRS

will really think about paperwork reduction and reform.

8.4   Adverb Endings

Most words ending in -ly are adverbs. They answer the question "how?"

Ending	Meaning	Example
-ly	manner of	happi**ly**, strange**ly**

Some adverbs have irregular forms that you have to memorize.

    well   hard   worse   late   fast

Editing

∧ **Exercise 4**   Read the dialogue and look for 10 word form errors in the underlined phrases. Write a correction above each error.

Mario: Hi, Ian. I haven't seen you in <u>a while</u>!

Ian: I know. I've <u>been ~~real~~ busy with</u> school and other things.
                           really

Mario: What other things? Did <u>you get a job</u>?

Ian: Of course not! You know <u>my opinionate</u>: always concentrate <u>on academize</u>

       <u>subjects</u>.

Mario: That's right. So … what's been keeping you <u>so actively</u>?

Ian: Well, it's related to <u>my professorship</u>, Dr. Cleaver.

Mario: What about her? Are you helping her out <u>with research</u>?

Ian: Actually, it's about <u>my scholar</u>. I must put in at least 20 hours per week in the

       research lab to maintain <u>my eligible</u>. It's <u>mandatory</u>.

Mario: I see <u>what you mean</u>. It must be tough to keep up with <u>all that work</u>. Are you

       getting paid, at least?

Ian: A little. That's the <u>good news</u>, I guess. With my own pocket money, I don't

       have to be so <u>dependence on my parents</u>.

Mario: Well, <u>you've only got</u> one more year till you <u>graduation</u>. I think you should

       look on the bright side.

Ian: I guess you're right. Boy, things really have changed since <u>our childlike</u>, huh?

Mario: You can say *that* again.

Word Forms Across Parts of Speech

This chart gives you the forms a word takes in different parts of speech. Refer to this information as you complete Exercise 5 below.

Noun	Verb	Adjective	Adverb
description	describe	descriptive	descriptively
desire	desire	desirable	—
finance	finance	financial	financially
development	develop	developed / developing	—
time	time	timely	—
information	inform	informative	—
preference	prefer	preferential / preferred	—
fear	fear	fearful	fearfully
benefit	benefit	beneficial	beneficially
lead/leader	lead	leading	—
strength	strengthen	strong	strongly

Exercise 5 Write eight sentences using at least two words from the chart above in each sentence. Circle those words.

1. The (leader) of the trade union offered a (beneficial) package to the members.

2. _____

_____

3. _____

_____

4. _____

_____

5. _____

_____

6. _____

_____

7. _____

_____

8. _____

_____

Exercise 6   Read the paragraph. From the following list choose the correct word form to insert in each blank.

produce production   class classy classic
involved involvement involve   poor poorly
excellence (excellent)   popularity popularly popular
China Chinese   newness new newly

A new action film was released last Friday by Tri-Moon Pictures. Titled "Unlikely Avenger," this movie opened in Los Angeles to ___*excellent*___ reviews. It stars the
                                                                                    1
_____ action hero Xin-Yeo in his first U.S. _____. The plot of the
        2   **3**
film is not _____. It is the _____ good versus evil idea that has been
              4   **5**
so _____ in the past decade, especially with U.S. audiences. Mr. Xin-Yeo plays
        6
a _____ young man who gets involved in a series of seemingly unrelated
      7
incidents. His _____, however, ruins the plans of the enemy. "Unlikely
                    8
Avenger" will open nationwide next month.

Exercise 7 Rewrite each sentence, changing the underlined word or words to the word form indicated in parentheses. You may have to make other changes to the sentence.

1. The king's robe was made of <u>gold</u>. (change to adjective)

   The king's robe was golden.

2. Valerie likes to <u>talk a lot</u>! (change to adjective)

   _____

   _____

3. Shelby believes in the <u>democratic</u> system. (change to noun)

   _____

   _____

4. Why does Victor always want to make things more <u>complicated</u>? (change to verb)

   _____

   _____

5. The Emancipation Proclamation gave freedom to <u>slaves</u>. (change to another noun form)

   _____

   _____

6. This meat is too tough. I can't <u>eat</u> it! (change to adjective)

   _____

   _____

7. Lisa always <u>argues</u> with her sister. (change to noun)

   _____

   _____

8. The white flag can be a <u>symbol</u> of peace or surrender. (change to verb)

_____

_____

9. The exam was <u>easy</u>. I finished it in under an hour. (change to adverb)

_____

_____

10. Greta works in the <u>library</u>. (change to another noun form)

_____

_____

11. The <u>violence</u> on TV shows seems to be increasing. (change to adjective)

_____

_____

12. This math problem is too complicated. I wish it were more <u>simple</u>. (change to verb)

_____

_____

Exercise 8   Use a dictionary to find as many word forms as you can for each word. Be sure to include a notation for the part of speech of the variations you list (n = noun; v = verb; adj = adjective; adv = adverb).

1. (v) marry: _____

2. (adj) popular: _____

3. (n) problem: _____

4. (n) immediacy: _____

5. (adj) current: _____

6. (v) labor: _____

7. (v) sympathize: _____

8. (n) president: _____

Exercise 9   Circle the letter of the correct answer.

1. Louise's _____ behavior got her into trouble at work.
   a. childly   c. child
   b. children   d. childish   (d circled)

2. The party was wonderful, including its _____ host.
   a. gracious   c. grace
   b. graciously   d. gracing

3. Henry doesn't _____ for a school loan because his parents make too much money.
   a. qualification   c. qualified
   b. qualificate   d. qualify

4. The new zoning regulations for the airport are _____ for the people living in that area.
   a. problematic   c. problematically
   b. problem   d. problemed

5. Many young people are still _____ on their parents because they can't find jobs.
   a. dependence   c. dependently
   b. dependent   d. depend

6. Lorna sings _____. She should consider becoming a _____ singer.
   a. beautifully / professional   c. beautiful / professional
   b. beautifully / professionally   d. beautiful / professionally

Editing

∧ **Exercise 10**   In each item, one of the four underlined words or phrases is not correct. Circle the letter of the error and write the correction above the error.

1. The <u>argumentative</u> presented by the <u>prosecuting</u> attorney were not
       A   **B**

   <u>accepted</u> by the judge in last week's murder <u>case</u>.
       C   **D**

2. I would <u>classificate</u> my <u>childhood</u> as being <u>ordinary</u> and <u>simple</u>. Nothing exciting
          A   **B**   **C**   **D**

   ever happened to me.

3. If Karen <u>stated</u> that she was <u>interested</u> in soccer, she was lying. Everyone
          A   **B**

   knows for a <u>fact</u> that her <u>actually</u> interest lies in baseball.
              C   **D**

4. The <u>unhealthsome</u> food being served in the cafeteria is <u>inedible</u>. Some of the
          A   **B**

   students should <u>protest</u> to the principal. She needs to have <u>sympathy</u> for her
                  C   **D**

   students!

Original Writing

Exercise 11   Write a paragraph or short essay about a current event. You may use a topic featured on television news, in the newspaper, or at your school. Give a short background of the issue. Describe the problem, when it happened, why it exists, and who is involved. Pay close attention to word forms as you write. Exchange paragraphs with a partner and check each other's work for correct word forms.

If you need help with the steps of writing a paragraph, see Appendix 5.

www You will find additional exercises for the grammar in this chapter on the Top 20 website at **http://esl.college.hmco.com/students**

Please let us know if you would to prefer the basic or deluxe version. With the deluxe version, you will be able ∧ enjoy the benefits for even more years to come than with the basic version.

9

Modals:
Present and Future

In English, modals—or modal auxiliaries—are words used with verbs to express many different meanings, such as the speaker's attitude or point of view about an action, additional meaning, and certainty. Modals include *can, could, might, have to, must,* and *supposed to.* This chapter covers both present tense and future tense modals. (Past tense modals are covered in Chapter 10.) The exercises will offer you practice with modals in their various contexts.

Modals

Modals can show:

- permission and requests (9.3)
- possibility and probability (9.4)
- ability (9.5)
- preference and desire (9.6)
- necessity, prohibition, and lack of necessity (9.7)
- advisability and suggestion (9.8)
- prediction, intention, and expectation (9.9)

Here are a few examples of how modals are combined with verbs:

- In the verb phrase You **should go**, the modal *should* expresses the speaker's advice.
- Modals give additional meaning to a verb, for example: She **can go** (versus She *goes*), which adds the meaning of "able to" to the verb *go*.
- Modals may also express how sure or certain the speaker feels about something: It **could rain** versus It **will rain**, which changes the meaning from less certain to more certain.
- Some modals have multiple meanings: He **may come** means either *It is possible that he will come* or *He has permission to come.*

Following is a list of common modals in present tense and future tense. The same form is used in both tenses for most forms.

Modal Auxiliaries	
Single-Word Modals	**Phrasal Modals**
can	be able to
could	be supposed to
may	be going to
might	had better
must	have to
ought to	have got to
should	
would	
shall	
will	

9.2 **A Few Basic Rules**

These few basic rules about modals will help you as you work through this chapter.

1. The verb following the modal is the base or simple form.

   > I **must speak** to him as soon as possible.

    Do not use *to* between the modal and the verb, as in this error:

   > I must ~~to~~ speak to him.

2. Use only one single-word modal with a verb.

   > I **may come.**   (NOT I *may can come.*)

   It is sometimes possible to use a single-word modal with a phrasal modal:

   > I **may be able to come.**

3. Modal auxiliaries do NOT require these verb endings:
   - final *-s* for third-person singular
   - *-ing*
   - *-ed*

4. Negative modals are formed in this order: MODAL + *not* + VERB

   > She **should not be** here.

5. Questions with modals are formed in this order: MODAL + SUBJECT + VERB

   > **Could** you please **answer** the phone?

6. In short answers, use this order: *Yes / No* + SUBJECT + SINGLE-WORD MODAL

   > (**Can** you go?) **Yes, I can.**

   or this order: *Yes / No* + SUBJECT + AUXILIARY

   > (Do you **have to** go?) **No, I don't.**

7. Both present tense and future tense modals are expressed in one form.

   > You **may see** the doctor now.   (present)

   > It **may rain** tomorrow.   (future)

8. Modals can be used with the progressive forms (verb ending in *-ing*):

   > We **must be going.**

   > I **should be studying** for tomorrow's exam.

   > The plane **will be leaving** in a few minutes.

9. Some modals are used in their contracted form to express a negative:

can / can't	should / shouldn't	will / won't
could / couldn't	must / mustn't	would / wouldn't

(9.3) Modals for Permission and Requests

can	may	could	might	will	would

One of the most common uses of modals is to ask for or give permission or to make a request. Choosing the proper modal depends on how formal the situation is and how well the speaker knows the listener. It is common to add *please* to requests.

can (permission or request—informal)

> You **can give** your presentation in the class today.
>
> **Can** I please **borrow** your class notes?

may (permission—formal; polite request)

> You **may leave** as soon as you've finished the exam.
>
> **May** I **make** an appointment to see you on Wednesday?

could (polite request)

> **Could** you please **sign** the purchase order for me?

might (polite request—formal; not commonly used)

> **Might** I **ask** why you did not approve my car loan?

will (polite request)

> **Will** you **hold,** please?

would (polite request)

> **Would** you **get** the door for me, please?

would (permission)

> **Would** you **mind** if I asked you your age?

Pay careful attention to the response for questions with *would you mind*:

> Yes, I **would.** = Yes, I do mind. Do not ask me; it's unacceptable to ask me.
>
> No, I **wouldn't.** = No, I don't mind. You may ask me; it's acceptable to ask me.

Exercise 1   Fill in each blank with one of these modals: *can, may, could, might, will,* or *would.* Consider the level of formality and politeness required by the situation. Be prepared to explain the reason for your choice.

Situation 1   A college professor and her student

A: Excuse me, Dr. Conners. _____May_____ I speak to you for just a minute?
        1

B: Certainly. What _____ I help you with?
                    2

A: Well, I'm a bit confused about the last assignment you gave us. _____ you
                                                                      3

mind explaining it once more?

B: No, of course not. For this assignment, you _____ choose either to interview
                                                4

a recent immigrant about his or her experiences adapting to life here or to write a

short paper describing the stages of cultural adaptation most immigrants go through.

A: _____ I interview my grandfather? He's not a recent immigrant, but ...
      5

B: Well, the person should be a recent immigrant.

A: _____ I ask why it has to be a recent immigrant?
      6

B: Well, a recent immigrant is usually better able to recall specific instances of cultural

conflict and the techniques used to resolve or adapt to such a conflict. I'll tell you

what, try to find a recent immigrant, but if you absolutely can't get anyone, then

you _____ use your grandfather for the interview.
         7

A: Thank you, Dr. Conners.

Situation 2   Two co-workers in an office

A: Lorie, _____ you order some supplies for me?
           8

B: Sure, what do you need?

A: Well, is there a limit? And _____ I also order a new desk chair? Mine's
                               9

broken.

B: The policy is each employee _____ order supplies totaling no more than
                                10

$50. You _____ only order more than that with the boss's approval.
         11

A: _____ you talk to the boss about ordering a new chair?
      12

B: Sure, no problem.

A: And _____ you please not tell her it's for me? We're not on the best of
13
terms these days.

B: I'll see what I can do. _____ I ask what happened between you two?
14

A: Well, you see, last week at work I was writing this e-mail to my sister and ...

(9.4) Modals of Possibility and Probability

| can | may | could | might | should | must | has / have to |

Another common use of modals is to express possibility and probability. The degree of possibility or probability depends on how certain the speaker is that the situation exists or will exist. Similarly, the choice of a modal may depend on a conclusion the speaker has drawn, using earlier information or knowledge.

can   (possibility—certain)

> You **can swim** in the Gulf of Mexico in the winter.   (often combined with ability)

> You **can see** the Gulf of Mexico from my bedroom window.

> This **can't be** wrong! I followed the directions to the letter. (impossibility—certain)

may   (possibility—less certain)

> I **may get** a raise. I'll find out tomorrow.

> She **may not know** you, but I'm sure she's read your book.

could   (possibility—less certain)

> He **could be** the one I spoke to, but his voice doesn't sound familiar.

might   (possibility—less certain)

> We **might cancel** our plane reservations and go to Canada by car instead.

should   (probability or logical conclusion—more certain)

> I exercise regularly, so I **should do** well on the physical fitness exam.

> You **shouldn't have** a problem at the border because all your papers are in order.

must   (probability or logical conclusion—more certain)

> It's so dark outside. It **must be** after 8:00.

> You put in so many extra hours at work. You **must like** your job a lot!

has / have to (probability or logical conclusion—more certain)

The invitation says 526 Hudson. This **has to be** the place.

They **have to know** how to fix it. After all, they wrote the software.

Exercise 2 Match the situation (Column A) with the appropriate response (Column B).

Column A

__f__ 1. Where are my car keys? I've looked everywhere for them.

_____ 2. Evan just rented a top-floor apartment with no A/C in Sunspot, New Mexico.

_____ 3. They were honored for the restoration work they did on their 1927 bungalow.

_____ 4. Be sure to go on the "Duck Tour" when you visit Tampa next week.

_____ 5. I know you hate going to museums, but you really have to visit this one.

_____ 6. When is she coming?

_____ 7. She sat in on a psychology class with a friend last week and loved it.

_____ 8. You have such talent. I love your charcoal sketches.

Column B

a. If it's that good, it might change my mind about art.

b. We plan to. We can get a view of the city from both land and water that way.

c. If she really enjoyed it, she may change her major.

d. I hope you're right. If so, then my artwork should sell easily.

e. He must be crazy!

f. They could still be in the car.

g. They have to feel great about that.

h. She may not even show up.

Modals of Possibility and Probability   **117**

Modals of Ability

can   be able to

The modals in this group express various kinds of ability: general, physical, or mental. *Can* and *be able to* express ability in the present or future. (The modals *could* and *was / were able to* express ability in the past and are covered in Chapter 10.)

can

I **can handle** most home-repair problems myself.   (general ability)

Donna **can change** a flat tire in under six minutes.   (physical ability)

Ryo **can solve** complicated math problems in his head.   (mental ability)

be able to

I'm **able to write** with either hand.

Used with other modals:

She **might be able to** help you with that form.

You **should be able to** access the Internet from here.

Exercise 3   Read the following paragraph about Bev. Then write sentences to describe her abilities. Write both affirmative and negative sentences with *can* and *be able to*. Possible verbs to use with the modals include: *play, reach, teach, fit, sit, buy, laugh,* and *wear*.

Bev is 6' 8" tall and is definitely into sports. On weekends, she plays for a local women's basketball team, and during the summer she coaches children's softball and T-ball teams. Her height is often an advantage. For example, whenever she visits her mother, who is only 4' 11" tall, Bev is often asked to dust the top of doorframes and to clean the ceiling fan blades. She changes light bulbs without using a ladder, and she knows what's on every top shelf in all the closets!

Sometimes being so tall has its disadvantages. Bev usually drives her own car everywhere because she's too tall to ride comfortably in her best friend's small VW. She has to order specially made sheets for her extra-long bed. She doesn't shop at local clothing stores either because the clothes aren't long enough.

Nevertheless, Bev is happy-go-lucky and always ready with a smile or a joke about the weather "up there."

1. *Bev can play basketball because she is so tall.*

2. _____

   _____

3. _____

   _____

4. _____

   _____

5. _____

   _____

9.6 — Modals of Preference and Desire

would rather / would rather ... than   would like
would prefer to / would prefer

The modal *would* combines with *rather, prefer,* and *like* to express the speaker's preferences or wants. Use *would* in questions to offer choices or invitations.

would rather + VERB; would rather + VERB ... than VERB (preference)

> **Would** you **rather read** a novel or a short story?

> They **would rather eat** bees **than listen to** his lecture!

> I'**d rather** not **pay** with cash.   (*I'd* = I would)

would prefer to + VERB; would prefer + VERB + -*ing* . . . to (preference)

> **Would** you **prefer to go to** the mall or the plaza?

> Most students **would prefer taking** a multiple-choice test **to** an essay exam.

> I'**d prefer reading** a novel **to watching** a movie.

would like + INFINITIVE / NOUN (want or desire; offer; invitation)

> I'**d like to try on** these jeans, please.

> I'**d like** cream with my coffee, please.

> **Would** you **like to come** shopping with us tomorrow?

> **Would** you **like** fries with your sandwich?

! It is common to use *would* alone with a verb in the result clause of conditional sentences or in sentences with *wish*:

If you saw this movie, you **would love** it.

I wish he **would leave.**

Editing
∧ **Exercise 4** Read the letter below. Underline the sixteen modals you studied in Sections 9.3 through 9.6. Then find and correct the six errors in modal choice.

Dear Current Resident:

You <u>might</u> not realize it, but you could be the first one in your neighborhood to own a revolutionary new mental-image creator. This incredible product may create hours of nonstop entertainment for you and your family. Take a moment to stop and think.

Will you rather spend hundreds of dollars a year on movies and video rentals or enjoy free interactive, self-produced entertainment within your own four walls? This letter from me could turn out to be the opportunity of a lifetime for you and your family. Couldn't you like to be the envy of your neighbors by being the first on your block to have one of these amazing products?

If you act soon, we should can have one of these marvelous inventions in your home up and working by next week. When you call, please let us know if you would prefer the basic or deluxe version. With the deluxe version, you will be able to enjoy the benefits for even more years to come than with the basic version. That fact alone must make you want to reach for the phone right now!

However, you should still have doubts about ordering our product sight unseen. If so, perhaps you would prefer to try out our product for one full week—at no cost to you, of course. Would you mind if one of our representatives stopped by to demonstrate this easy-to-use wonder? We'll call you back to confirm your appointment.

Chapter 9   Modals: Present and Future

In closing, would I take this opportunity to congratulate you on your wise decision to purchase this soon-to-be popular method of entertainment. Your purchase is guaranteed to bring you and your family hours of enjoyment and satisfaction.

Sincerely,

Rita Booke

9.7 Modals of Necessity, Prohibition, and Lack of Necessity

must	have to	have got to

Use these modals when you want to say that something is necessary or not necessary or when you want to say that something is prohibited—not allowed.

must

> You **must have** a visa to enter the country.   (necessity / obligation)
>
> You **must not overstay** your visa.   (prohibition / no choice)
>
> **Must** we **finish** this report tonight?   (questioning necessity / obligation)

- *Must* is used for present and future situations. In order to express a necessity or obligation in the past, use *had to* instead of *must*.

  Rosa had to finish her term paper last night.

- *Must* is not commonly used to make questions; use *do / does* + *have to* instead.

  Do we **have to keep** a journal in this class?

- When *must* is used in questions, it is sometimes interpreted as a complaint.

Must you **slam** that door every time you walk in?

have to

> Neil **has to pass** his final exams in order to graduate next week.
> (necessity / obligation in present and future)

> He **doesn't have to attend** the graduation ceremony, but he will.
> (choice / optional action)

have got to   (not used in negatives)

> Jeanine **has got to get** her car fixed. I can't keep driving her everywhere.

> **Have** we **got to go** there tonight? Can't we just stay home?   (complaint)

Exercise 5   Fill in the blanks with the correct form of *must, have to,* or *have got to.*

1. Come on, you guys. It's getting late. We ____*have to*____ go.

2. They _____ stop playing their music so loudly this late at night. They're going to be evicted if they're not careful.

3. _____ she _____ write up the annual report this year, or do you?

4. You _____ skip any doses of this antibiotic. You _____ take all the pills.

5. I _____ take classes this summer, but I might.

6. You _____ pack items such as nail clippers, tweezers, or pocketknives in your carry-on luggage. If you do, you won't be allowed to board.

7. We _____ go out for dinner tonight, but we can if you're too tired to cook.

8. _____ you always tell the same joke at every party we go to?

9. The sign read "All cellular phones _____ be turned off while you are in the building."

10. I _____ do some laundry tonight. I'm running short of clean clothes.

9.8 Modals of Advisability and Suggestion

should	ought to	had better	shall	can	could	might

We use these modals to give advice, make suggestions, and express strong meanings. The modals in this group imply that the advice or suggestion is a good idea but that it is only the speaker's opinion.

should   (advice; strong suggestion)

> Ella **should pay** more attention to her studies than she does.

> You **shouldn't watch** so much TV.

> **Should** we **get** the sofa re-upholstered or **buy** a new one?

ought to   (advice; strong suggestion; not commonly used in negatives or questions)

> You and I need to lose weight. We **ought to try** ballroom dancing.

had better   (advice; very strong suggestion that implies that something bad will happen if the advice is not taken)

> He**'d better finish** that report by 9:00 tomorrow morning (or he'll be in trouble).

> I**'d better not** order dessert (or I'll feel uncomfortable from being too full).

shall   (suggestion; polite offer of help; used mainly in questions with *we* and *I*)

> **Shall** we **get** the wood blinds or the metal ones?

> I can see you're busy. **Shall** I **answer** the phone for you?

can   (advice or suggestion; speaker feels listener may take advice; used in affirmative sentences)

> Let's go see that movie. We **can** always **order** some takeout if we don't feel like cooking after we get home.

could   (offer advice or suggestion; speaker is unsure if listener may take advice; used in affirmative sentences)

> If you're unhappy, just quit. You **could start** your own business, you know.

might   (indirect suggestion)

> We **might consider** hiring someone to help Mom with the cleaning.

> Katie **might not want** to quit her job just yet—the unemployment rate went up again last month.

Exercise 6   Read the situation and the advice or suggestion. Then rewrite the advice or suggestion using *should, ought to, had better, shall, can, could,* or *might*. More than one modal may be correct.

1. a. My hands are so dry that they actually hurt.
   b. You need to wear gloves when you wash dishes.

   You should / ought to wear gloves when you wash dishes.

2. a. I've had a toothache for three days. It doesn't seem to be going away.
   b. You must see the dentist before it gets worse.

   _____

   _____

3. a. She has a lovely speaking voice.
   b. That's nothing. You have to hear her sing.

   _____

   _____

4. a. Let's clear off the table.
   b. Can I go ahead and put these dishes in the dishwasher for you?

   _____

   _____

5. a. I wonder what I should make for dinner when my in-laws come.
   b. You have to make something with fish.

   _____

   _____

6. a. I brought home a ton of brochures to help us decide where to go on vacation this year.
   b. Will we go to New Orleans?

   _____

   _____

7. a. What will we do if our home loan isn't approved?
   b. Well, we will continue to rent and apply again next year.

   _____

   _____

9.9 Modals of Prediction, Intention, and Expectation

will	be going to	be supposed to	should	ought to

With this group of modals, you can express strong certainty about an action or a situation.

will

> I think he**'ll get** the scholarship he applied for.   (prediction)
>
> We**'ll meet** you at Gate 3 at 8:45 p.m.   (agreement)
>
> I**'ll return** your hedge clippers as soon as I'm done with them.   (promise)
>
> She**'ll be** at the party with Jason.   (expectation)

 Although you can use *shall* for a future action, it's more common to use *will*. Using *shall* often adds emphasis to the sentence in very formal English:

> We **shall work** hard to change the law.

be going to

> Look at the sky. It**'s going to rain.**   (prediction)
>
> You**'re going to miss** the bus if you don't leave now.   (prediction)
>
> I**'m not going to go** to class this afternoon.   (intention)

be supposed to   (expresses what has been planned or arranged; conveys expectation)

> The movie **is supposed to be** on Channel 8 at 10:00 p.m.   (expectation)
>
> We**'re supposed to go** bowling Saturday morning.   (planned)

> I**'m supposed to be** on my way to work right now.   (planned)

should (strong certainty)

> He left at 6:00. He **should be** here by now.   (expectation)

ought to (strong certainty)

> If we leave before rush hour, we **ought to get** there before the movie starts.   (expectation)

Exercise 7 Fill in each blank with the correct form of the modals. Choose from *will, be going to, be supposed to, should,* or *ought to.*

A: The party _is supposed to_ start about 7:00. What time is it now?
    ₁

B: It's a little after 7:00, so it _____ be starting right about now.
    ₂

A: How long do you think it will go?

B: I imagine it _____ last till the food runs out.
    ₃

A: With Ken's friends, that _____ only take a couple of hours. They
    ₄

    _____ park themselves in front of the buffet table and eat till
    ₅

    everything's gone.

B: What kind of entertainment _____ there _____ be?
    _{6A}   _{6B}

A: I think Ken hired a D.J. who _____ play from 8:00 to midnight.
    ₇

B: The D.J. _____ be setting up for that now.
    ₈

A: Well, let's get going. We _____ be late if we don't leave soon. We
    ₉

    _____ be there to help Ken greet his guests.
    ₁₀

Exercise 8 Multiple choice. Circle the letter of the best answer.

1. Mom, _____ I sleep over at Nicole's tonight? Please, _____ you let me?
   a. may, might   c. can, will
   b. can, may   d. might, can

2. Joyce told me the company _____ sell off one of its divisions. If that's true,
   Human Resources _____ know who's going to be laid off.
   a. might, must already   c. may, can't
   b. should, could already   d. might, doesn't have to

3. Many people _____ to travel around the world. To do so without major problems, a person _____ to adapt quickly to a country's culture and customs.
   a. would like, might be able
   b. would like, should
   c. would prefer, can be able
   d. would like, should be able

4. Would you mind closing the window? I would rather use the A/C. _____
   a. Yes, I would. I like it closed.
   b. No, I wouldn't. I like it open.
   c. Yes, I would. I prefer A/C, too.
   d. No, I wouldn't. I prefer A/C, too.

5. What's the hurry? We _____ be there for another hour. You _____ to learn to relax.
   a. must not, have
   b. don't have to, have got
   c. have to, don't have
   d. don't have to, must

6. The doctor told him he _____ exercise at least 30 minutes a day and _____ start watching his fat intake. He's at risk for heart disease.
   a. could, should
   b. should, had better
   c. should, might
   d. had better, shall

7. Sally, _____ I tell you what I think? You _____ put your house on the market for six months. You _____ always change your mind, you know.
   a. shall, should, can
   b. shall, had better, can
   c. should, shall, can
   d. shall, had better, might

8. You call this art? What _____ it _____ to be? If this is truly art, I _____ eat the museum program!
   a. is / going , will
   b. is / supposed, should
   c. is / supposed, will
   d. is / supposed, am going to

Original Writing

Exercise 9   Write a dialogue between two people who are seeking and giving advice, for example:

- between a veterinarian and a customer with a sick pet

- between an academic advisor and a student

- between a career planner and a laid-off worker

   Before you begin, make a list of your target modals from this chapter. Underline the ones that you are able to use in your dialogue. Exchange dialogues with a partner and check each other's work for correct present and future modals.

If you need help with the steps of writing a paragraph, see Appendix 5.

www   You will find additional exercises for the grammar in this chapter on the Top 20 website at **http://esl.college.hmco.com/students**

MODAL

It should have been around 6 or 7 o'clock because it was getting a little dark.

Past Modals

This chapter reviews the meaning and use of verbs with past modals. Past modals consist of three parts: (1) the *modal,* (2) the word *have,* and (3) the *past participle* of the verb. It is the past participle that makes the whole verb past tense.

10.1 Form of Past Modals

The form of past modals is MODAL + *have* + PAST PARTICIPLE. The following sentences give an example of each past modal covered in this chapter.

> I **should have cooked** more burgers. Now we don't have enough.

> Sam **must have gone** to the beach yesterday. He has a sunburn today.

> They **could have driven** their car, but they decided to walk instead.

> She **might have left** her keys on the table, but she's not sure.

> It **may have rained** last night. Look, the grass looks wet.

> You **would have won** the contest for sure if you had entered it.

 With past modal constructions, you must always use the past participle of the verb after MODAL + *have*.

Incorrect: She must have **take** the 7 p.m. flight to New York.

Correct: She must have **taken** the 7 p.m. flight to New York.

10.2 The Modal *should*

Use *should* + *have* + PAST PARTICIPLE to form the past modal.

1. We use *should have* + PAST PARTICIPLE when the action (of the verb) did not happen and someone is sorry (regrets) that the action did not happen.

> I failed the test. I **should have** *studied* last night.   (The speaker did not study. The speaker regrets not studying last night.)

2. We use the negative form, *should not have* + PAST PARTICIPLE, when the action (of the verb) happened and someone is sorry (regrets) that the action happened.

> My stomach hurts! I **shouldn't have** *eaten* those four doughnuts.   (The speaker ate four doughnuts. The speaker regrets eating them.)

Exercise 1 Underline the *should have* + PAST PARTICIPLE construction in each sentence. Then put a check mark (✓) beside all of the sentences underneath that are true.

1. She <u>should have cooked</u> the beans and the rice in separate pots.

___✓___ a. She cooked the beans and rice in the same pot.

_____ b. She cooked the beans and rice in two pots.

2. Tom is sure that he shouldn't have traveled to Taiwan in the summer.

_____ a. Tom traveled to Taiwan.

_____ b. Tom regrets traveling to Taiwan.

3. You should have told me this news sooner.

_____ a. The speaker now knows the news.

_____ b. The speaker still doesn't know the news.

4. I'm sorry for not inviting you to my party. I should have sent you an invitation.

_____ a. The speaker invited the person to the party.

_____ b. The speaker did not invite the person to the party.

5. Many people think that the U.S. shouldn't have dropped atomic bombs on Japan.

_____ a. Many people agree with the use of atomic bombs in World War II.

_____ b. Many people disagree with the use of atomic bombs in World War II.

6. Mark should have studied more for today's exam.

_____ a. Mark didn't study enough for today's exam.

_____ b. Mark didn't perform well on the exam today.

7. The boys shouldn't have climbed up that tree.

_____ a. They climbed up the tree.

_____ b. They didn't climb up the tree.

8. That shirt shouldn't have faded after just one washing.

_____ a. The shirt lost some color when it was washed.

_____ b. The shirt looked better after it was washed.

9. Dinner last night certainly should have cost less than $40.

_____ a. The bill was $40 or more.

_____ b. The speaker expected to pay less than $40.

10. Venus should have been visible last night.

_____ a. The speaker expected to be able to see Venus last night.

_____ b. It was not possible to see Venus last night.

Exercise 2   Write a sentence that uses *should have* or *should not have* + PAST PARTICIPLE to express the same idea.

1. Joe bought a used car. He regrets buying it.

   Joe should not have bought a used car.

2. You did not get a new umbrella. You are sorry about this.

   _____

   _____

3. Instead of taking a taxi, we took a bus from the airport. Taking a bus took much longer and was not as good as taking a taxi.

   _____

   _____

4. Toshio regrets quitting his job today.

   _____

   _____

5. Last night I went to bed after midnight. I regret doing this.

   _____

   _____

(10.3) The Modal *must*

Use *must* + *have* + PAST PARTICIPLE to form the past modal.

1. Use *must have* + PAST PARTICIPLE when you are almost certain that the action happened. Based on the facts or current situation, you conclude that the action happened.

   Joe looks really tired today. He must have *gone* to bed late last night.
   (The speaker thinks that Joe went to bed very late last night.)

2. Use the negative form, *must not have* + PAST PARTICIPLE, when you are almost certain that the action did not happen.

   Irene failed her spelling test. She must not have *studied* very much.
   (The speaker does not think that Irene studied very much.)

Exercise 3   To complete these sentences, write the correct construction using *must (not) have* + PAST PARTICIPLE with the verb in parentheses.

1. No one ordered any dessert after dinner. Everyone (be) __*must have been*__ full.

2. When I saw Ben this morning, he didn't know who had won the football match last night. He (watch) _____ it on TV.

3. Paula's French is outstanding. I know she's a good language learner, but she (have) _____ a great French teacher, too.

4. Ellen returned four of the five dresses that she bought yesterday. They (fit) _____ her very well.

5. Rick didn't follow the teacher's directions for this assignment. He (understand) _____ the directions clearly.

6. Look at the decorations on these cakes! They're so elaborate! It (take) _____ a long time to make them!

The Modal *could*

Use *could have* + PAST PARTICIPLE to form the past modal.

1. Use *could have* + PAST PARTICIPLE when the speaker had the opportunity to do something, but you are not sure he did it. You can also use it when the action was possible but you are not sure if it really happened.

> After dinner, I felt really sick. It **could have *been*** the fish. It tasted a little strange.   (The speaker thinks that one possible reason for being sick was the fish.)

2. Use the negative form, *could not have* + PAST PARTICIPLE, when you are almost positive that the action did not happen. This form implies that it was impossible for the action to have occurred.

> The woman **couldn't have *killed*** her husband because she was traveling in a different country when he was killed.   (According to the speaker, it was impossible for the woman to have killed the man.)

Editing

∧ **Exercise 4**   Write a correction above the errors in the underlined parts of the sentences.

1. If you missed eight of the ten questions on the test, you <u>could have passed</u> it.

2. No one believes that the man <u>could have kill</u> his boss.

3. My late grandfather was extremely <u>poor</u>. He didn't own a BMW, but he could have easily bought one or more of them.

4. I <u>could visit</u> many more places in Paris if I had had more time.

5. I <u>could have lent</u> you my car yesterday because I needed it all day.

6. I could have lent you my car because I <u>needed</u> it all day yesterday.

7. When we went to France last year, we could <u>have fly</u> on the Concorde.

8. It <u>couldn't rain</u> this morning. I would have noticed!

(10.5) The Modal *might*

Use *might have* + PAST PARTICIPLE to form the past modal.

1. Use *might have* + PAST PARTICIPLE when the action was possible, but you are not sure if it happened. (This is the same meaning as *may have* or *could have* + PAST PARTICIPLE.)

   After dinner, I felt really sick. It **might have *been*** the fish. It tasted a little strange.   (The speaker thinks that one possible reason for being sick was the fish.)

2. *Might have* + PAST PARTICIPLE has a second meaning. It can be a suggestion about a past event, like *could have*. Sometimes it is a form of complaint.

   Mother: The train trip took us several hours. I don't know why we came by train.

   Ana: We **might have *flown*.** It would have been so much faster.

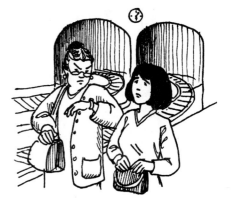

3. The negative form, *might not have* + PAST PARTICIPLE is used when the negative situation was possible, but you are not sure if it happened. (This is the same meaning as *may not have* + PAST PARTICIPLE.)

   The teacher believes that Joe **might not have *written*** his paper by himself. (The teacher believes it is possible that someone helped Joe write his paper.)

Exercise 5   Read each sentence. Then write a sentence that means the same as the first sentence. Use *might have* or *might not have* + PAST PARTICIPLE.

1. It is possible that it rained last night. I'm not sure.

   It might have rained last night.

2. When you called last night, maybe David wasn't home then.

   _____

3. Why did Hector leave the party? Maybe he didn't feel well.

   _____

The Modal *might*   **135**

4. The student's answers are all wrong. Maybe he didn't understand the directions.

_____

5. Perhaps the doctor prescribed the wrong medicine.

_____

6. Why did the accident happen? Maybe the pilot turned onto the wrong runway.

_____

10.6 The Modal *may*

Use *may have* + PAST PARTICIPLE to form the past modal.

1. Use *may have* + PAST PARTICIPLE when the action was possible, but you are not sure if it happened.

   After dinner, I felt really sick. It **may have _been_** the fish. It tasted a little strange.   (The speaker thinks that one possible reason for being sick was the fish.)

2. The negative form *may not have* + PAST PARTICIPLE is used when the negative situation was possible, but you are not sure if it happened.

   The teacher believes that Joe **may not have _written_** his paper by himself. (The teacher believes it is possible that someone helped Joe write his paper.)

Exercise 6   Read each sentence. Then write a sentence that means the same as the first sentence. Use *may have* or *may not have* + PAST PARTICIPLE.

1. Perhaps Jennifer went to her cousin's house.

   Jennifer may have gone to her cousin's house.

2. It's possible that Ned didn't like the gift that Linda gave him.

   _____

   _____

3. Maybe some passengers survived the plane crash.

   _____

   _____

4. Maybe he didn't hear the announcement.

_____

_____

5. It's possible that the secretary has already received the documents.

_____

_____

6. Perhaps it was too late for Alan to buy a cheap ticket for the flight.

_____

_____

(10.7) The Modal *would*

Use *would have* + PAST PARTICIPLE to form the past modal.

1. Use *would have* + PAST PARTICIPLE when the action did not happen. This meaning is for the main clause in conditional sentences: another condition was missing, and that's why the second action did not happen.

> The young couple **would have *purchased*** the house if it had had two bathrooms.   (The house did not have two bathrooms, so the young couple didn't purchase it.)

2. The negative form *would not have* + PAST PARTICIPLE is used when the action actually happened, but it would not have happened if something else had occurred first.

> The pie **wouldn't have *tasted*** so sweet if I had added the correct amount of sugar.   (The pie tasted too sweet because speaker added the wrong amount of sugar.)

Exercise 7 Fill in the blanks with *would have* + PAST PARTICIPLE of the verbs in parentheses.

1. (start, [negative]) If Lincoln had not become the 16th president, the Civil War

   ___would not have started___ in 1861.

2. (like) People _____ the party better if you had had good

   music.

3. (be, [negative]) The spaghetti _____ crunchy if you had cooked it a little longer.

4. (win) If Kostov had done better in the second set, perhaps he _____ _____ the match.

5. (be) The outcome of the election _____ the same if people had voted on computers instead of using the old methods.

6. (have, [negative]) If you had taken the medicine correctly, you _____ _____ any problems with your stomach.

Exercise 8 Underline all of the six past modal forms in this paragraph and explain their meanings to a partner.

My Oldest Memory

My oldest memory is of a time when I was a very young child. I couldn't have been more than five years old. In fact, I might have been as young as three. I remember that I was with a woman who was our neighbor. It must have been around 6 or 7 o'clock because it was getting a little dark. The woman told me that we were going to walk to the store on the corner to get an ice cream cone. Just as we left the front steps of our house, the light above the store went out. They had just closed. We should have left earlier. If we had left the house a few minutes earlier, then we might have gotten to the store in time. If we had done that, then I could have had some ice cream. To this day, I cannot remember who the woman was exactly, but I certainly remember the day that I didn't get any ice cream.

Exercise 9   Circle the letter of the correct answer. Be prepared to explain your answer to a partner.

1. Why did the alarm go off? Someone may _____ one of the emergency doors by mistake.
   a. open
   b. have open
   c. have opened
   d. had opened

2. No one knows why the car stopped. There may have _____ a problem with the battery.
   a. be
   b. been
   c. was
   d. being

3. The cook _____ so much salt to the soup. We could hardly eat it.
   a. should have added
   b. should add
   c. shouldn't have added
   d. shouldn't add

4. I can't believe that no one was able to give you a hand with this work. You _____ have told me, and I would have helped you at once.
   a. should
   b. must
   c. may
   d. can

5. Ann: Mark says that he had a Mazda Miata in 1975.
   Ben: Are you sure that that's what he said? He _____ a Mazda Miata then because they weren't produced until 1982.
   a. might not have had
   b. could not have had
   c. must not have had
   d. should not have had

6. Why didn't the waiter give you a receipt? He _____ you a receipt.
   a. must have given
   b. couldn't have given
   c. might have given
   d. should have given

Exercise 10   Fill in the blanks with a correct past modal form of the verb in parentheses. More than one answer may be possible.

Kevin: Hey, Bob, how did your golf game turn out?

Bob: Excellent. In fact, it (be) _____ couldn't have been _____ better!
                                                        1

Kevin: That's great news. What was your score?

Bob: 71. That's my best game ever.

Kevin: Wow, you (play) _____ really well.
                              2

Bob: I had a very good day, but I almost didn't get to play.

Kevin: Really? What do you mean?

Bob: I got up late. I (get) _____ up at six, but I forgot to
                              3

        set my alarm clock and didn't wake up till seven!

Kevin: So what happened?

Bob: I arrived thirty minutes late. As a result, they put me with another group of players. If I had arrived on time, I (play) _____ in the same group as Jack Nickson, the famous pro.
4

Kevin: Wow, that's too bad! But, hey, you played well and you had a great score!

Bob: Well, I (oversleep) _____, but you're right. The end result was great!
5

Editing

∧ Exercise 11 Five of the eight underlined sentence parts have an error. Find the errors and make a correction above them.

1. Officials at NASA <u>should have decided</u> to send humans to the moon much earlier than they actually did. If NASA had started earlier, perhaps they <u>must have sent</u> a human to Mars by now.

2. According to the police, the driver of the red car <u>might not have seen</u> the white truck in time to stop. The slippery roads <u>couldn't have contributed</u> to the accident, too.

3. All of the students agreed that they <u>must have studied</u> harder for the test. If they had studied harder, they <u>must have passed</u> the test.

4. Why did a 747 suddenly fly into a mountain? Many things <u>may cause</u> the crash of that jumbo jet in Malaysia. In fact, we <u>may never know</u> the true answer to this mystery.

◎riginal Writing

Exercise 12 Write a paragraph about an important event in history or in your life. Tell what happened and why it happened. Tell how it could have been different. Consider what should have been done to make it different (if it was something negative). Use at least five of the past modals in this chapter. Use both affirmative and negative forms. Exchange paragraphs with a partner. Circle all the past modals on your partner's paper and check for his or her correct use.

> If you need help with the steps of writing a paragraph, see Appendix 5.
>
> **www** You will find additional exercises for the grammar in this chapter on the Top 20 website at **http://esl.college.hmco.com/students**

As doctors continue to *searching* **WF** for the cure for the common cold, they have found some things that make **WF** people more vulnerable to *catch* a cold.

11

Gerunds and Infinitives

Two verb forms in English are used as nouns: gerunds and infinitives. Gerunds are verbs ending in *-ing* and infinitives are *to* + VERB. How do you know when to use an infinitive and when to use a gerund? This chapter will answer that question.

11.1 Forming Gerunds and Gerund Phrases and Infinitives and Infinitive Phrases

Here are the basic forms of gerunds and infinitives.

Gerund	Infinitive
VERB + -ing	to + VERB
swimming	to swim
laughing	to laugh

A gerund phrase includes the gerund and its related information.

Driving *a car* is something I learned to do just last year.

An infinitive phrase includes the infinitive and its related information.

To drive *a car* is something I would like to learn how to do.

Exercise 1 Read the following diary entry. It contains 10 gerunds and infinitives. Underline all the gerunds and infinitives in the paragraph.

Monday, April 11
4:20 p.m.

Dear Diary,

It's been a while since I've written. I've been very busy. Yesterday I tried out for the school play. I've always wanted <u>to become</u> an actor, but my parents aren't crazy about the idea. Still, it was really fun trying out for the play "Dance Days." I got really scared when the director asked me to sing, but I actually think I did a good job. The dancing, however, was another story. The most difficult part was jumping to the rhythm of the music. I have never been so embarrassed in my life! Can you believe it? I fell down (on my you-know-what!) after attempting a jump. The director ran up to me to ask if I was okay, then we all started laughing. Believe it or not, they've asked me to return

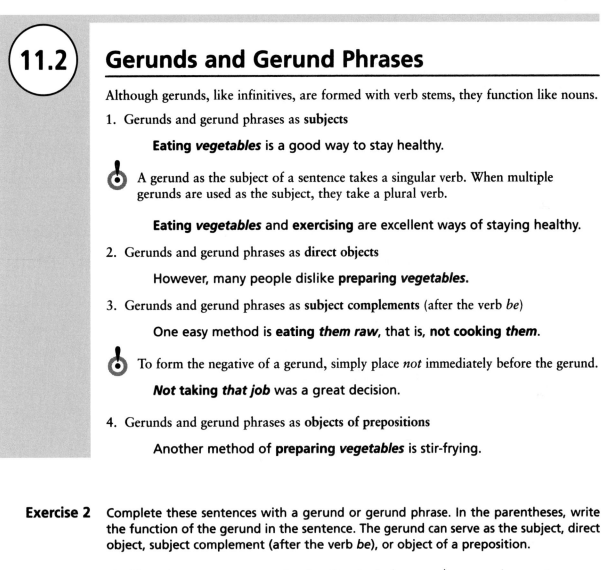

> *this Friday for more practice. I'm going to spend every spare moment till then trying to land on my feet during jumps! I'll let you know what happens.*

(11.2) Gerunds and Gerund Phrases

Although gerunds, like infinitives, are formed with verb stems, they function like nouns.

1. Gerunds and gerund phrases as **subjects**

   Eating *vegetables* is a good way to stay healthy.

   🎯 A gerund as the subject of a sentence takes a singular verb. When multiple gerunds are used as the subject, they take a plural verb.

   Eating *vegetables* and exercising are excellent ways of staying healthy.

2. Gerunds and gerund phrases as **direct objects**

   However, many people dislike preparing *vegetables*.

3. Gerunds and gerund phrases as **subject complements** (after the verb *be*)

   One easy method is eating *them raw*, that is, not cooking *them*.

   🎯 To form the negative of a gerund, simply place *not* immediately before the gerund.

   Not taking *that job* was a great decision.

4. Gerunds and gerund phrases as **objects of prepositions**

   Another method of preparing *vegetables* is stir-frying.

Exercise 2 Complete these sentences with a gerund or gerund phrase. In the parentheses, write the function of the gerund in the sentence. The gerund can serve as the subject, direct object, subject complement (after the verb *be*), or object of a preposition.

1. I buy the newspaper every day, but I'm tired of ___*reading*___ only negative news.

   (*object of preposition*)

2. Lisa's favorite hobby is _____. (_____)

3. _____ is one of the rights given to all citizens.

   (_____)

4. It's almost impossible to set up your own business without _____ .

   (_____)

5. While some people enjoy _____ , I think it's a boring activity.

   (_____)

6. My mother is great at _____ , but I'm not so good at it.

   (_____)

7. I don't mind _____ , but I am tired of _____ every

   week! (_____) (_____)

11.2.1   Verbs Commonly Followed by Gerunds

These verbs frequently have a gerund or a gerund phrase following them.

appreciate	avoid	consider	delay	detest	discuss
dislike	enjoy	finish	involve	miss	postpone
practice	quit	recommend	risk	stop	suggest

My mother **appreciated** getting a puppy for her birthday.

Exercise 3   Complete each sentence with a verb from the list and add an appropriate gerund or gerund phrase.

1. In order to pass the last exam, you should have <u>*considered*</u>   <u>*studying*</u> the

   lecture notes.

2. In order to lose weight, my doctor _____ _____ a

   gym or a sports club.

3. After their big fight, Hector _____ _____ his

   girlfriend.

4. The new art exhibit was excellent! We really _____

   _____ the sculptures and paintings.

5. Participating in extreme sports can be dangerous. These athletes

   _____ _____ their bones and sometimes even

   _____!

6. I could tell by her face that Isabelle _____ _____

   her grades.

(11.3) Infinitives and Infinitive Phrases

Infinitives and infinitive phrases are also used as nouns.

1. Infinitives and infinitive phrases as subjects

   To live *in a large city* requires a lot of patience and nerve.   (less common)

Compare with the gerund as the subject paired with the same verb. (Infinitives can be subjects, but gerunds are much more common as subjects.)

   Living *in a large city* requires a lot of patience and nerve.
   (more common)

2. Infinitives and infinitive phrases as direct objects

   Mario wanted **to stay** *at the beach,* but it began **to rain**.

3. Infinitives and infinitive phrases after phrases beginning with *it*
   (*it* + *be* + ADJECTIVE or NOUN + INFINITIVE)

   It is impossible to get *a cheap apartment* in a large city.   (+ ADJECTIVE)

   Many people say that **it is a good idea** to save **money for the future.**
   (+ NOUN)

Here are more adjectives and nouns commonly used after *it* + *be*:

bad	dangerous	difficult	easy
fun	hard	important	impossible
interesting	necessary	relaxing	a good idea
a bad idea	a pity	a shame	a waste

(*it* + *take* + NOUN + INFINITIVE)

It takes a lot of **energy to find** *the perfect job.*

4. Infinitives and infinitive phrases as a reduction of the phrase *in order to* (showing purpose)

Malik decided to become a flight attendant [in order] **to travel** *the world.*

5. Infinitives and infinitive phrases after certain adjectives

Habiba was **happy** **to learn** *that she'd been accepted to graduate school.*

 To form the negative of an infinitive, simply place *not* immediately before the infinitive.

You should be **careful** **not to strain** *your eyes* in front of the computer.

Here are some common adjectives followed by infinitives.

afraid	ashamed	careful	glad	happy
lucky	proud	relieved	reluctant	sad
shocked	sorry	surprised	sure	willing

Exercise 4 Complete the sentences with an infinitive phrase. In the parentheses, write the function of the infinitive in the sentence. Choose from: *direct object, after a phrase with* it + *ADJECTIVE, to show purpose,* or *after certain adjectives.*

1. Margaret and her sister went to college <u>to become their family's first college</u>

   <u>graduates</u> . (<u>to show purpose</u>)

2. The children were afraid _____

   _____ . (_____)

3. We wanted _____ ,

   but it was too expensive. (_____)

4. I couldn't believe that my boss was willing _____

   _____ . (_____)

5. It's impossible _____

   _____ . (_____)

6. They went to the Bahamas _____

_____ . (_____)

7. It wasn't easy for Jenna _____ .

However, she agreed _____ . (_____)

(_____)

11.3.1   Verbs Commonly Followed by Infinitives

These verbs frequently have an infinitive or an infinitive phrase following them.

afford	agree	ask	decide	demand	deserve
expect	hesitate	hope	learn	need	offer
plan	pretend	promise	refuse	wait	want

When no one else volunteered, Manny **offered** to go.

The students **demanded** to see **the program director** when the course was cancelled.

Editing

∧ **Exercise 5**   The following paragraph contains seven errors in gerund and infinitive use. Find and correct the errors.

As doctors continue to ~~searching~~ for the cure for the common cold, they have found some things that make people more vulnerable to catching a cold. One negative influence is to argue. People who argue are more likely to get colds than those who do not. Another characteristic is be a "loner." People who have strong social networks tend to be happier and therefore more resistant to colds. Finally, to stress over a job can lead to colds. There are many workers who do not feel confident enough to get their job done right. Some researchers believe that this lack of self-confidence can lead to lowered immune systems. To resisting colds, people should look at the quality of their lives. While patients wait for a cure for the common cold, they can begin bolster their bodies by to deal with the treatable issues mentioned above.

11.3.2 Verbs That Need Nouns or Pronouns Before the Infinitive

These verbs often need either a noun or a pronoun before the infinitive.

advise	allow	cause	convince	forbid	force
invite	permit	remind	teach	tell	warn

We all **warned Jason to stop** eating all that junk food.
(noun before infinitive)

My father **taught me to play** tennis when I was young.
(pronoun before infinitive)

Exercise 6 Complete each sentence with the correct forms of the words in parentheses.

When I was a child, my mother (advise / me / study) <u>advised me to study</u> hard
1

every day. She (not want / me / lose out) _____
2

on a quality education. For this reason, she (forbid / me / watch) _____
3

_____ too much television. Instead, she would (tell / me / practice)

_____ the piano. I absolutely hated my
4

mother's forcing (me / play) _____,
5

but I always did what I was told. She would (invite / her friends / listen) _____
6

_____ to my home concerts, and it always made

me so nervous! Well, today I must thank her. As a well-known pianist who travels around

the world, I am happy that she (convince / me / appreciate) _____
7

_____ hard work. I would never have gotten where I am

today without her focus on education and practice.

(**11.4**) # Verbs Commonly Followed by Either Gerunds or Infinitives

These verbs often have either a gerund or an infinitive following them. The meaning is similiar for both.

begin	admire	continue	hate	like
love	prefer	regret	start	try

Jeanne prefers **carrying** her own luggage.   (gerund)

Jeanne prefers **to carry** her own luggage.   (infinitive)

The verbs *forget, remember, stop,* and *try* are also followed by either a gerund or infinitive. However, the meaning is different for each usage.

forget   I forgot **taking** this picture of the Eiffel Tower. In fact, I took several.   (the gerund refers to an earlier action)

I forgot **to take** a picture of the Eiffel Tower. Maybe I'll do it on my next trip.   (the infinitive refers to an action at the same or later time)

remember   Now I remember **taking** this picture. It was on May 8th. (*remember* + GERUND refers to an earlier action)

I remembered **to take** this picture. I did not forget to do this. (*remember* + INFINITIVE refers to an action at the same or later time)

stop   I was driving my car. I stopped **to make** a phone call. (*stop* + INFINITIVE = to interrupt an action to do something else)

My phone bill got too high, so I stopped **making** so many calls. (*stop* + GERUND = to finish an action in progress)

try   You have hiccups? You should try **holding** your breath. (*try* + GERUND = experiment with a solution to a problem)

The doctors tried **to save** her life, but she died. (*try* + INFINITIVE = make an effort to do something that is usually difficult)

Exercise 7   Write two sentences for each verb, one sentence using a gerund and the same sentence using an infinitive instead of a gerund. Note that the meaning of your two sentences will be different.

1. a. forget _____

_____

---

b. forget _____

_____

2. a. stop _____

_____

b. stop _____

_____

Exercise 8   Circle the letter of the correct answer.

1. The doctor asked _____ light ink on the reports because it was hard to read.
   a. the nurse to avoid using
   b. to the nurse avoid using
   c. to avoid using the nurse
   d. the nurse using to avoid

2. I stopped _____ fried foods because my doctor told _____ .
   a. eating; me to stop
   b. to eat; to stop
   c. to eat; me stop
   d. eating; me stopping

3. _____ vegetables is a good way to stay healthy, but many people dislike _____ them.
   a. To eat; to prepare
   b. Eating; to prepare
   c. To eat; preparing
   d. Eating; preparing

4. Because of their difficult schedules, they _____ taking the trip.
   a. wanted
   b. postponed
   c. were reluctant
   d. to hesitate

5. Do you _____ to go there alone?
   a. prefer
   b. suggest
   c. enjoy
   d. appreciate

Original Writing

Exercise 9   Write a paragraph about something special that you have achieved in your life. Give some background that includes how old you were during this time and why it was important for you to achieve this goal. Explain the events that led to this success. How did you feel after this achievement?

Review the uses of gerunds and infinitives in this chapter. Try to include at least four infinitives or infinitive phrases and four gerunds or gerund phrases in your paragraph. Exchange paragraphs with a partner. Review your partner's paper, circling all the gerunds and infinitives and checking for their correct use.

> If you need help with the steps of writing a paragraph, see Appendix 5.
>
> **www**   You will find additional exercises for the grammar in this chapter on the Top 20 website at **http://esl.college.hmco.com/students**

These specialized programs design *VOICE* to provide the current training that is needed in today's changing business environment.

12

Passive Voice and Participial Adjectives

Passive voice can be difficult to understand. Before you study this chapter, it would be a good idea to review the verb tenses in Chapter 1. This will help you understand passive voice better.

Passive versus Active

When a verb is in the active voice, the subject is the actor. In other words, the subject is doing the action.

The dog bit the man. (Who did the biting? The dog.)

In contrast, when a verb is in the passive voice, the subject is the receiver of the action of the verb. The actor may (or may not) be expressed by a *by* + ACTOR expression.

The man was bitten by the dog. (Who did the biting? The dog.)

In the first example (active voice), the speaker emphasizes the dog. In the second example (passive voice), the speaker emphasizes the man. The noun in the subject position is the one that the speaker emphasizes. When should you use the passive voice? Use it when the receiver of the action is more important than the one who did the action.

(12.2) Form of Passive Voice

Passive voice always consists of a form of the verb be followed by the past participle of the action verb: *be* + PAST PARTICIPLE.

Penicillin was discovered in 1928.

The following chart gives you an overview of the passive voice in English verb tenses.

Tense	Active Voice	Passive Voice
Present:	I write it	It is written
Present progressive:	I am writing it	It is being written
Present perfect:	I have written it	It has been written
Past:	I wrote it	It was written
Past progressive:	I was writing it	It was being written
Past perfect:	I had written it	It had been written
Future:	I will write it	It will be written
Future perfect:	I will have written it	It will have been written
Present modal:	I can write it I should write it	It can be written It should be written
Past modal:	I couldn't have written it I may have written it	It couldn't have been written It may have been written

The progressive forms are almost never used in passive voice.

An easy thing to remember about forming the passive voice is that the verb always has one more word (**+1**) than the active voice verb.

Active	Passive + 1
They **answer** their mail immediately.	Their mail **is answered** immediately.
They **have not called** Jack.	Jack **has not been called**.
They **could have sent** the package.	The package **could have been sent**.

Exercise 1   Put a check mark (✓) by the passive verb forms.

___✓___ 1. have been eaten   _____ 6. were taken   _____ 11. should be needed

_____ 2. have been eating   _____ 7. were taking   _____ 12. should be needing

_____ 3. cannot fly   _____ 8. will be taking   _____ 13. hadn't been sliced

_____ 4. cannot be flying   _____ 9. will be taken   _____ 14. weren't sliced

_____ 5. cannot be flown   _____ 10. can be taking   _____ 15. haven't been slicing

Exercise 2   Underline the five passive verb forms in this news report.

In today's news, Prime Minister Clark gave a speech at the graduation ceremony at Dover University. The prime minister <u>was introduced</u> by the president of the university, who was visibly moved by the prime minister's attendance at today's event. Prime Minister Clark received his degree from Dover University in 1979. Today's trip to the university was his first trip back to the area since then. When Clark's name was announced to the audience, a loud cheer could be heard for the lost son who had finally returned to Dover University. In his speech at this event, the prime minister noted the important role that today's graduates will play in shaping the future of our country. "A country is only as strong as its educated. You are our educated; thus, you are our strength. We are counting on you for leadership as we enter a new era." Some thought that the possibility of war with neighboring countries might come up, but serious topics such as this were not mentioned at all.

12.3 How to Change Active Voice to Passive Voice

To change the active voice to passive voice in a sentence with SUBJECT / VERB / OBJECT word order, follow these four easy steps.

1. Begin with a sentence that has an active verb.

    > Mark Twain wrote *The Adventures of Tom Sawyer* in 1876.

    Identify the receiver of the action—*The Adventures of Tom Sawyer.* Move this receiver to the subject position in a new sentence.

    > *The Adventures of Tom Sawyer* ...

2. Identify the verb—"wrote"—and its tense (simple past). After the subject, put the verb *be* in the same verb tense.

    > *The Adventures of Tom Sawyer* **was** ...

3. Next, add the past participle of the verb you identified in Step 2.

    > *The Adventures of Tom Sawyer* **was written** ...

4. Finally, include the original person or thing that did the action (the agent) in a *by* phrase.

    > *The Adventures of Tom Sawyer* **was written** by Mark Twain . . .

    Then add the rest of the information (if there is any) from the original sentence.

    > *The Adventures of Tom Sawyer* **was written** by Mark Twain in 1876.

    In some cases, you may want to omit the agent if the main emphasis is on the receiver (the new subject) or if the agent or actor is obvious.

Exercise 3   Underline the complete verb in each sentence and identify it as *active* or *passive*. Then rewrite the sentence by changing the voice of the verb, either active to passive or passive to active. Remember that when you change active to passive, you may not necessarily include the agent in a *by* phrase.

1. _____*active*_____ In Unit 12, students must use a range of written sources to understand the causes of World War I.

    In Unit 12, a range of written sources must be used to understand the causes of World War I.

2. _____ Han Corporation facilitates the development and growth of the high technology industry in Alaska.

    _____

    _____

3. _____ In this book, the constantly changing nature of theater over several eras and in several countries has been emphasized in great detail by both authors.

_____

_____

4. _____ All native snakes in Ohio are protected by the Nongame and Endangered Species Conservation Act of 1991.

_____

_____

5. _____ The first plastic was unveiled by Alexander Parkes at the 1862 Great International Exhibition in London.

_____

_____

(12.4) Three Common Errors with Passive Voice

Writers tend to make three mistakes with passive voice: in form, in use, and with intransitive verbs (verbs that do not take an object).

1. Error with past participle form

Remember that the verb *be* must be followed by the past participle of the action verb.

> The book **was writing** in 1998.   (incorrect past participle)

> The book **was written** in 1998.   (correct past participle)

2. Error with use

Remember that passive voice is used when the receiver of the action is more important than the agent (doer of the action). You should mention the agent only if it is important to the meaning or if it is not obvious.

> Arabic **is written** [by Arabic speakers] from right to left.   (*by Arabic speakers* is not necessary information)

Some writers use passive voice too often, especially just after they have learned it. Active voice is much more common than passive voice. Use passive voice only when you want the receiver of the action to be the main topic of your words.

The following two examples describe the same event, but the writer's emphasis is different in each.

Active voice: **The dog** bit the thief.   (The writer's focus is *the dog*.)

The thief quietly opened the window of the house. He climbed into the residence as carefully as possible so that he would not make any noise. He did not know, however, that there was a vicious dog watching over the house. The dog heard the noise of the intruder and reacted quickly. Like a bolt of lightning, the dog jumped up and barked ferociously. Then the dog lunged at the man. In a split second, **the dog bit the thief,** which ended the robbery.

Passive voice: **The thief** was bitten by the dog.   (The writer's focus is *the thief*.)

The thief quietly opened the window of the house. He climbed into the residence as carefully as possible so that he would not make any noise. He did not know, however, that there was a vicious dog watching over the house. The thief heard the loud clicking of claws on the floor. The thief could not escape. **He was bitten by the dog,** which ended the robbery.

3. Error with intransitive verbs

English has two kinds of verbs: transitive and intransitive. Transitive verbs are followed by an object.

announce (an engagement)   buy (a gift) discover (a cure)   find (a good deal)   take (a nap)

Intransitive verbs are not followed by an object.

come   die   go   happen   seem   occur

Intransitive verbs do not have grammatical voice, so they cannot be changed from active to passive voice. Study these examples.

Transitive Verb, Active Voice	⇨	**Transitive Verb, Passive Voice**
They discovered a cure ...	⇨	A cure **was discovered** ...
The machine accepts coins ...	⇨	Coins **are accepted** ...

Intransitive Verb, Active Voice	⇨	**No Passive Possible**
The accident happened ...	⇨	~~was happened~~
The man died ...	⇨	~~was died~~

Exercise 4   Identify each of the 20 verbs in this paragraph as *active voice* (A), *passive voice* (P), or *intransitive verb* (I).

1. _____   5. _____   9. _____   13. _____   17. _____

2. _____   6. _____   10. _____   14. _____   18. _____

3. _____   7. _____   11. _____   15. _____   19. _____

4. _____   8. _____   12. _____   16. _____   20. _____

A good presentation **1** <u>can have</u> significant and long-lasting effects on an audience. What **2** <u>happens</u> between speakers and their presentation and the audience **3** <u>involves</u> many factors. Like any tool, a presentation **4** <u>can be applied</u> with skill to **5** <u>achieve</u>* a useful purpose or it **6** <u>can be used</u> to **7** <u>damage</u> and **8** <u>destroy</u>. Although a hammer **9** <u>can be used</u> to **10** <u>build</u> a home, it also **11** <u>can be used</u> to **12** <u>punch</u> holes in a wall. One unethical presentation **13** <u>can affect</u> the way that an audience **14** <u>sees</u> you in all future encounters. Thus, we **15** <u>believe</u> that a good speaker **16** <u>must ask</u> and **17** <u>answer</u> important ethical questions at every point in the speechmaking process. Ethical decision-making **18** <u>is</u> more than a means of **19** <u>improving</u>* speaker credibility; it **20** <u>remains</u> a moral obligation of every good speaker.

---

*Some of the underlined verbs are not main verbs. *Achieve* is an infinitive and *improving* is a gerund. However, these verb forms may still be transitive (active or passive) or intransitive.

Editing

∧ **Exercise 5**   Read this paragraph from a business textbook. If the underlined verb phrase is incorrect, write your corrected edit on the line. If it is correct, write *correct* on the line.

1. _____   5. _____   9. _____

2. _____   6. _____   10. _____

3. _____   7. _____

4. _____   8. _____

Most accounting firms **1** <u>are included</u> on their staffs at least one certified public accountant, or CPA, an individual who **2** <u>has met</u> state requirements for accounting education and experience and **3** <u>has been passed</u> a rigorous two-day accounting examination. The examination **4** <u>is prepared</u> by the American Institute of Certified Public Accountants and covers accounting practice, accounting theory, auditing, taxation, and business law. State requirements usually **5** <u>are included</u> a college degree in accounting and from one to three years of on-the-job experience. Once an individual becomes a CPA, he or she **6** <u>must be attended</u> continuing-education programs to maintain state certification. These specialized programs **7** <u>design</u> to provide the current training that **8** <u>is needed</u> in today's changing business environment. In addition, CPAs **9** <u>must be taken</u> an ethics course to satisfy the continuing-education requirement. Details regarding specific state requirements for practice as a CPA **10** <u>can obtain</u> by contacting the state's board of accountancy.

Editing
∧ Exercise 6   Read these two paragraphs from an education textbook. If the underlined verb phrase is incorrect, write your corrected edit on the line. If it is correct, write *correct* on the line.

1. _____   5. _____   9. _____

2. _____   6. _____   10. _____

3. _____   7. _____

4. _____   8. _____

Education **1** <u>has changed</u> drastically since colonial days. In the 1600s, some girls received elementary instruction, but formal colonial education was mainly for boys, particularly those of the middle and upper classes. Both girls and boys **2** <u>might have had</u> some preliminary training in the four Rs—reading, 'riting [writing], 'rithmetic [arithmetic], and religion—at home. Sometimes, for a small fee, a housewife **3** <u>was offered</u> some training to children in her own home. In these cases, she **4** <u>would be taught</u> a little reading and writing, basic prayers, and religious beliefs. In these dame schools, girls also **5** <u>learned</u> some basic household skills, such as cooking and sewing. The dame schools often **6** <u>are provided</u> all the formal education that some children, especially girls, ever received.

Throughout the colonies, poor children **7** <u>were often apprenticed</u> or indentured to local tradesmen or housewives. Apprenticeships **8** <u>lasted</u> for three to ten years, generally ending around age twenty-one for boys and eighteen for girls. During that time, an apprentice **9** <u>would learn</u> the basic skills of a trade and **10** <u>might also teach</u> basic reading and writing, and perhaps arithmetic, as part of the contractual agreement.

Exercise 7   For each topic below, select a paragraph from a newspaper, magazine, or web source about the topic. Bring a copy of each paragraph to class. Working with a partner, identify the active verbs, passive verbs, and intransitive verbs. Write the verbs in the correct columns. Then answer the questions below.

TOPIC / Source	Active Voice	Passive Voice	Intransitive
a current event			
sports			
an advertisement			

1. Which source had the most passive voice verbs? What was the percentage? (To calculate this, divide the number of passive voice examples by the total number of verbs.) _____

2. Why do you think this source had so many passive voice examples?

_____

_____

_____

_____

3. What is the percentage of verbs that are in passive voice for all three sources
combined? (To calculate this, divide the total number of passive voice verbs by the
total number of all verb occurrences.) _____

(12.5) Participial Adjectives

The past participle is a necessary part of forming passive voice. The past participle can
also act as an adjective with a passive meaning.

> The car was **stolen** by two young men.   (past participle in passive voice)

> The police found the **stolen** car a week later.   (past participle as adjective)

The present participle is part of progressive tenses. The present participle can also act as
an adjective with an active meaning.

> The baby was **crying** loudly.   (present participle in progressive tense)

> The mother sang to the **crying** baby.   (present participle as adjective)

Present participles are verb forms that end in -*ing*.

| interesting | confusing | surprising | annoying | losing |

Past participles are verb forms that end in -*ed* or an irregular form.

| interested | confused | surprised | annoyed | lost |

Example 1: The audience heard the results. The audience did not expect the results.

- The audience was **surprised**. The **surprised** audience was silent.
- The results were **surprising**. No one could believe the **surprising** results.

Example 2: The teacher explained the lesson. The students did not understand anything.

- The explanation was **confusing**. The **confusing** explanation did not help.
- The students were **confused**. The **confused** students need more help now.

Exercise 8 Fill in the blank with the correct adjective or participial adjective form of the verb in parentheses.

Art Show Attracts Crowds

Locals and visitors alike who were (interest) _____ in impressionist

1

paintings flocked to the art museum yesterday. The occasion was the opening day of an

exhibit of twenty-seven paintings on loan from the Orangerie Museum in Paris. Museum

officials here were (surprise) _____ at the (amaze) _____ number

2   *3*

of art patrons who came out to see the (visit) _____ art exhibit. People in the

4

(crowd) _____ rooms were (not disappoint) _____ by the (thrill)

5   *6*

_____ paintings. The impressionist works included those by (interest)

7

_____ and (know) well-_____ painters such as Monet and Degas.

8   *9*

Though the lines were long and they had to wait much more than usual, the (tire)

_____ visitors said that this was certainly a (satisfy) _____

10   *11*

experience. Some were so (thrill) _____ by what they saw that they tried to

12

buy tickets to come again. Unfortunately, tickets for subsequent days are already (sell)

_____ out, so those without tickets in hand will be (disappoint)

13

_____ by the news.

14

At the end of this long day, museum officials were (exhaust) _____ but

15

happy because of the successful opening day.

Exercise 9 Identify each of your answers from Exercise 8 as an adjective (ADJ) or as a participial adjective that is part of passive voice (PV).

1. _____   4. _____   7. _____   10. _____   13. _____

2. _____   5. _____   8. _____   11. _____   14. _____

3. _____   6. _____   9. _____   12. _____   15. _____

Exercise 10 Look in a magazine, journal, encyclopedia, or web article to find three sentences that have past participle forms in them. Write the three sentences here. Circle the past participle forms. By each, write ADJ if it is used as an adjective or PV if it is part of a passive voice construction.

Sentence 1: _____

_____

Sentence 2: _____

_____

Sentence 3: _____

_____

Exercise 11 Circle the letter of the correct answer.

1. The first parts of the test _____ to see if students understand gerunds and articles.
   a. are designing   c. is designing
   b. are designed   d. is designed

2. An improvement in the second edition of the text is the inclusion of lively and _____ material.
   a. can be interesting   c. can be interested
   b. interesting   d. interested

3. In order to _____ an apple pie well, it is imperative to start with fresh ingredients.
   a. making   c. make
   b. be making   d. be made

4. Before Hightacks employees begin working behind the cash register, they _____ thirty-five hours of training, which ends up costing the company more than $1,000 per employee.
   a. are receiving   c. receiving
   b. are received   d. receive

5. Only _____ pilots and flight attendants can understand the reactions of _____ passengers during actual aircraft emergencies.
   a. experiencing, terrifying   c. experienced, terrified
   b. experiencing, terrified   d. experienced, terrifying

6. To keep up with changes and trends in not only hardware but especially software, information systems managers must routinely _____ computer publications and websites that discuss new products.
   a. scan   c. scanned
   b. be scanned   d. have been scanning

∧ **Exercise 12** One of the four underlined words or phrases is not correct. Circle the letter of the error and write a correction above the error.

1. EPS, or earnings per share, <u>is calculating</u> by <u>dividing</u> net income <u>after taxes</u> by
                   A   **B**   **C**

   <u>the existing number of</u> shares of common stock.
         D

2. For many reasons, <u>it is</u> important to ensure that plans <u>are being</u> properly
                 A   **B**

   <u>implemented</u> to recover <u>the stole watches</u>.
      C   **D**

3. Simpler <u>than</u> either the median <u>or</u> the mean, the mode is the value that <u>is appeared</u>
          A   **B**   **C**

   the most <u>frequently</u> in a set of data.
         D

4. <u>The</u> Social Security Act of 1935 is <u>provided</u> current benefits for <u>more than</u> 45
   A   **B**   **C**

   million people, <u>almost</u> one out of every six Americans.
           D

⊙riginal Writing

Exercise 13 Write one to three paragraphs that report the news about an event. The event can be real or imagined. Tell what happened, when it happened, and why it happened. Try to give numbers and examples of details of the event. When possible, describe people's reactions to the event. Were they surprised? Terrified? Annoyed?

Try to use passive voice when possible. Underline your passive voice examples. Remember that passive voice is not as common as active voice or intransitive verbs in real English, so make sure that you do not have a disproportionate percentage of passive voice examples in your writing. Exchange paragraphs with a partner. Review your partner's paragraph, checking for correct use of passive voice.

> If you need help with the steps of writing a paragraph, see Appendix 5.
>
> **www** You will find additional exercises for the grammar in this chapter on the Top 20 website at **http://esl.college.hmco.com/students**

The mail was delayed *so*
my credit card payment didn't
arrive at the company on time.

13

Logical Connectors

In this chapter, you will review the use of logical connectors in English writing—coordinating conjunctions, subordinating conjunctions, and transition words and phrases. These connectors signal relationships between ideas and make your writing smooth, understandable, and cohesive. It is your job as a writer to use connectors appropriately to help your reader understand the information being presented.

13.1 Coordinating Conjunctions and Their Uses

The seven common coordinating conjunctions are *for, and, nor, but, or, yet,* and *so.* Coordinating conjunctions connect two independent clauses and show the relationship between the ideas in the clauses. An easy way many native English speakers remember these conjunctions is to take the first letter of each conjunction and form the acronym FANBOYS.

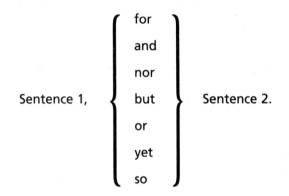

Sentence 1, { for / and / nor / but / or / yet / so } Sentence 2.

Study the meanings of these coordinating conjunctions. Notice in each case that a comma separates the first clause from the conjunction and the second clause. These sentences joined by coordinating conjunctions are called compound sentences.

1. The coordinating conjunction *for* shows reason or cause.

   We went to the park, **for** it was a beautiful day.

2. The coordinating conjunction *and* connects additional information.

   Alice will go to Paris next year, **and** she'll study French language and literature.

 If a compound sentence is short, you can often omit the comma.

   I went to Paris **and** I learned French.

3. The coordinating conjunction *nor* connects additional negative information.

   The football players didn't win the game, **nor** did they score any points.

 When you use *nor*, you must invert the subject and verb (as in question form). The negative element is in the word *nor*, so the verb remains positive.

Incorrect: Larry can't ride a motorcycle, **nor** he can't drive a car.

Correct: Larry can't ride a motorcycle, **nor** *can* he *drive* a car.
(positive verb and inverted word order)

4. The coordinating conjunction *but* contrasts information or shows effect.

The dogs barked all night, but they didn't bother me.

5. The coordinating conjunction *or* gives an alternative.

We can stay home and watch TV, or we can go out to the movies tonight.

6. The coordinating conjunction *yet* contrasts information, similar to *but*, and concedes a point.

All the leaders came to the summit meeting, yet they didn't reach an understanding.

7. The coordinating conjunction *so* connects an action to a result.

Henry inherited some money from his grandmother, so he decided to go on a long trip to Europe.

Exercise 1   Read the paragraph and underline the five connectors.

Many people anxiously await summer, but they aren't always aware of the precautions they should take. One of the best ways to protect the skin from overexposure to the sun is to use a sunscreen lotion. Sunscreens come in all types, and the buyer should look for a few specific ingredients before choosing. Sun protection factors (SPF) are extremely important, for they indicate how long a person can stay in the sun without burning. An SPF of 15 works well for many people, yet it is probably not enough protection for people with fair skin. Sunscreens with an SPF of 15–30 are said to be the most effective, so sunbathers should carefully check the labels of the products to ensure that they are buying the correct type.

13.1.1 Special Uses of *and, but,* and *or*

In addition to connecting independent clauses, the conjunctions *and, but,* and *or* can also connect words or phrases with the same part of speech and syntax in the sentence. Note that a comma is not used to separate two parallel ideas that are not independent clauses.

1. *And* can connect equal items.

> <u>**Larry**</u> and <u>**Billy**</u> study at the same school.
> NOUN   NOUN

2. *But* can contrast two descriptions.

> The new Indian restaurant is <u>**wonderful**</u> but <u>**expensive**</u>.
>   ADJECTIVE   ADJECTIVE

3. *Or* can connect alternative ideas.

> We <u>**can see the new movie**</u> or <u>**visit the museum this weekend**</u>.
>   VERB PHRASE   VERB PHRASE

Exercise 2   In each sentence, circle the coordinating conjunction and underline the parts that it connects.

1. <u>Jeremy</u> (and) <u>his brother</u> are planning a trip to Mexico next year.

2. <u>They want to visit many parts of Mexico,</u> (but) <u>their main goal is to see the coast.</u>

3. They are going to bring along their scuba gear, for their biggest hobby is scuba diving.

4. They've been practicing scuba diving in swimming pools but have never actually swum in open water.

5. It's not an easy trip to plan, so they have asked a travel agent to help.

6. They don't like to fly, yet the easiest way for them to get to Mexico is by plane.

7. They have reluctantly agreed to go directly to the Yucatan Peninsula, for it is the shortest route from their home.

8. The brothers are excited but nervous as the travel date approaches.

9. They plan to take lots of pictures and buy many souvenirs for their family and friends.

10. One problem is the language. They don't speak Spanish, nor do they plan on studying it before their trip.

11. With that in mind, this trip could end up being an excellent experience, or it could be an unfulfilling one for both of them.

12. By this time next year, everyone will know if they were able to overcome the language barrier and enjoy the wonders of Mexico.

Exercise 3 For each item in Exercise 2, write the function of the connector. The possibilities are: *reason* (or *cause*), *additional information*, *additional negative information*, *contrast* (or *effect*), *alternative*, *concession*, or *result*.

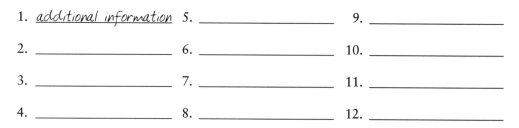

1. _additional information_   5. _____   9. _____

2. _____   6. _____   10. _____

3. _____   7. _____   11. _____

4. _____   8. _____   12. _____

13.1.2   Punctuation with Coordinating Conjunctions

When you write compound sentences with FANBOYS (*for, and, nor, but, or, yet,* and *so*), remember to use a comma before the coordinating conjunction to separate the two clauses.

Incorrect: Jay was the least qualified for the job **yet** he was chosen as the group leader.

Correct: Jay was the least qualified for the job, **yet** he was chosen as the group leader.

Always use a comma with the coordinating conjunctions *so, for,* and *yet,* even if the compound sentences are short.

It snowed yesterday, **so** we are going skiing.

∧ **Exercise 4** Some sentences contain errors in punctuation. If the sentence is correct, put a C in the blank. If the sentence is incorrect, put an X in the blank and make the necessary corrections to punctuation.

  __X__ 1. Joanne ͘and her sister live in New York City.

  _____ 2. All the office furniture and documents must be moved to our new location by next Friday.

  _____ 3. The mail was delayed so my credit card payment didn't arrive at the company on time.

  _____ 4. Bridgette should take up acting for she's got a natural gift.

  _____ 5. The curriculum was revised in early summer and implemented last semester.

  _____ 6. Do you want to go study in the library, or in my living room?

  _____ 7. How many people came to the party? I don't know and I don't care.

  _____ 8. Wendy wanted to come with us on vacation but she was inundated with extra work at her job.

  _____ 9. Derek is interested in becoming an electrical engineer or continuing his studies to eventually become a professor.

  _____ 10. It's not raining outside, nor is it cloudy.

Exercise 5 Complete each sentence with a phrase or phrases to make it sound logical. In some cases, you may choose to write parallel phrases instead of complete sentences. *Hint:* Remember to use a comma if the sentence is compound.

1. I don't like country western music __,__ nor _do I enjoy hiphop._____

2. The hurricane was approaching so_____

  _____

3. Citrus tends to grow best in hot climates and _____

  _____

4. Interest rates continued to rise yet _____

  _____

5. Most people hate cockroaches so _____

  _____

6. We decided to go shopping for _____

_____

7. The children were hungry but _____

_____

8. Most of the world's countries belong to the United Nations yet _____

_____

9. The study of economics is becoming more popular and _____

_____

10. Learning a foreign language is not easy but _____

_____

(13.2) Cause and Effect with Subordinating Conjunctions and Transition Words

In addition to using the coordinating conjunctions *for* and *so* to show cause and effect, you can use the subordinating conjunctions *because* and *since* and the transition words *as a result, consequently, therefore,* and *thus*.

When do you use a subordinating conjunction, and when do you use a transition word to show cause an effect (or contrast and concession—see 13.3)? This choice is a matter of preference and style. Many writers use both to make their writing more varied. Generally, if there is a lot of information, break it into two sentences, using transition words; if there is less information, create a compound sentence with a subordinating conjunction.

1. Subordinating conjunctions that show cause and effect

Use the subordinating conjunctions *because* and *since* when you want to show cause and effect. The conjunction must be at the beginning of a clause, but that clause can come in the middle or at the beginning of the sentence.

> We ate a large lunch **since *we had skipped breakfast.***

> **Since *we had skipped breakfast,*** we ate a large lunch.

When the clause with the subordinating conjunction comes at the beginning of the sentence, it is followed by a comma.

We ate a large lunch **because *we had skipped breakfast*.**

Because *we had skipped breakfast*, we ate a large lunch.

2. Transition words that show cause and effect

Use the transition words *as a result, consequently, therefore,* and *thus* when you want to show cause and effect.

Marco has been going to the gym. **As a result,** he has lost a few pounds.

Marco has been going to the gym. **Consequently,** he has lost a few pounds.

You must use a semicolon before and a comma after the transition word to join it and its clause to another independent clause if you write one long sentence instead of two shorter ones.

Marco has been going to the gym; **therefore,** he has lost a few pounds.

Exercise 6 Complete the paragraph with information that shows cause or effect. Be sure to add punctuation where needed.

I was running to school because _____
                                                            1
Since class had already begun when I arrived _____
                                                            2
_____. The teacher saw me trying to enter the room

without disturbing anyone. As a result, she _____
                                                            3
_____. She told me she wanted to talk to me after

class, so I _____.
            4
I apologized for being late and told her it wouldn't happen again. Consequently, _____
                                                            5
_____.

(13.3) Contrast and Concession in Subordinating Conjunctions and Transition Words

In addition to using the coordinating conjunctions *but* and *yet* to show contrast and concession, you can use the subordinating conjunctions *while* and *although* and the transition words *in contrast, however,* and *on the other hand.*

1. Subordinating conjunctions that show contrast and concession

Use the subordinating conjunctions *while* and *although / even though* when you want to show contrast or concede a point.

> Robert wanted to study at Harvard **while** his parents preferred Yale.

 When the clause with the subordinating conjunction comes at the beginning of the sentence, put a comma after it.

> **Although / even though** Robert's parents preferred Yale, Robert wanted to study at Harvard.

2. Transition words that show contrast

Use the transition words *in contrast, however,* and *on the other hand* when you want to show contrast.

 The transition word most commonly appears at the beginning of a sentence.

> Robert wanted to study at Harvard. **In contrast,** his parents preferred Yale.

 When the transition word appears at the end of the sentence, put a comma before it.

> Robert wanted to study at Harvard. His parents preferred Yale, **however.**

 You must use a semicolon before and a comma after the transition word to join it and its clause to another independent clause.

> Robert wanted to study at Harvard; **however,** his parents preferred Yale.

 When the transition word appears in the middle of a sentence, set it off with commas.

> Robert wanted to study at Harvard. His parents, **on the other hand,** preferred Yale.

3. Transition words that show concession

Use the transition words *nevertheless, even so,* and *despite this* when you want to show concession.

 Put a comma after these transition words when they begin sentences.

He's from Switzerland. **Nevertheless,** he doesn't speak German very well.

He's from Switzerland. **Even so,** he doesn't speak German very well.

He's from Switzerland. **Despite this,** he doesn't speak German very well.

Exercise 7 These sentences are missing transition words or subordinating conjunctions. Fill in each blank with the appropriate word or phrase. *Note:* More than one answer is possible.

1. The economy was in recession last year. _____Nevertheless_____, people continued to invest in the stock market.

2. _____ he's a wonderful student, he doesn't have much common sense.

3. I wanted to remain in my hometown to work. My job promotion will force me to relocate, _____.

4. Alaska is so cold in the winter. _____, the natural beauty of its parks makes it a wonderful place to live.

5. Soccer is fun because it's a team sport. _____, tennis can be a challenge because it's often one against one.

6. Lola asked to be a teacher's aide. The principal, _____, had already chosen someone for the position.

Exercise 8   Circle the coordinating conjunction in each sentence. Then rewrite the sentence, changing the coordinating conjunction to a transition word or a subordinating conjunction. Be sure to change punctuation where necessary.

1. I was hungry, (so) I decided to eat a sandwich.

    Because I was hungry, I decided to eat a sandwich.

2. The restaurant was very expensive, but the food was delicious.

    _____

    _____

3. Elizabeth went to the mountains, but she stayed away from the dangerous trails.

    _____

    _____

4. Henry got a promotion, for he had been working extra hard on weekends.

    _____

    _____

5. We traveled around Italy for more than a month, yet we never got to see Florence.

    _____

    _____

6. The soup was too salty, so very few people ate it.

    _____

    _____

7. The computer specialist claimed that installing the new software would be easy, yet it took over three hours.

    _____

    _____

8. I bought five new bottles of perfume, for the drug store around the corner was having a huge clearance sale.

    _____

    _____

Transition Words That Give Additional Information and Examples

1. Transition words that give additional information

Use the transition words *in addition*, *moreover*, and *furthermore* when you want to give additional information.

 Put a comma after these transition words when they begin sentences.

> Louisa loves to play the piano. **In addition,** she enjoys strumming the guitar.

> Dogs can make great pets. **Moreover,** they can protect the household.

 When the transition word comes at the end of the sentence, put a comma before it.

> Dogs can make great pets. They can protect the household, **moreover.**

2. Transition words that give examples

Use the transition words *for example*, *for instance*, *to illustrate*, and *specifically* when you want to give an example.

> People have become more health conscious these days. **For example,** I see a lot more people jogging these days than I did ten years ago.

> People have become more health conscious these days. **To illustrate,** I see a lot more people jogging these days than I did ten years ago.

> People have become more health conscious these days. **Specifically,** I see a lot more people jogging these days than I did ten years ago.

Put a comma after these transition words when they begin sentences. When the transition word comes in the middle of the sentence, set it off with commas.

> There are many ways you can stay in shape. You can, **for instance,** begin an exercise program.

> There are many ways you can stay in shape. You can begin an exercise program, **for instance.**

Exercise 9   Using the clues given below, write original sentences using transitions for examples or additional information.

1. Brazil   soccer   beaches   (additional information)

   Brazil is famous for soccer. In addition, it has some of the most
   popular beaches in the world.

2. universities   professional training   engineering   (example)

   _____

   _____

3. motorcycles   fun   exciting   (additional information)

   _____

   _____

4. war   economic hardships   social unrest   (additional information)

   _____

   _____

5. Italian pasta   many types   lasagna   (example)

   _____

   _____

6. love   joy   wedding day   (example)

   _____

   _____

13.5 Time Relationships in Subordinating Conjunctions and Transition Words

1. Subordinating conjunctions that show time relationships

Use the subordinating conjunctions *after, before, when,* and *as soon as* when you want to show time relationships.

> **After** I came home, I went directly to bed.

> **Before** I went to bed, I called my daughter.

 Put a comma after the subordinating clause when it comes at the beginning of the sentence.

> I went directly to bed **as soon as** *I came home.*

> **As soon as** *I came home,* I went directly to bed.

2. Transition words that show time relationships

Use the transition words *first, second, next, then,* and *finally* when you want to show time relationships, specifically, a sequence.

> **First,** the young man applied for the job.

 Most of these transition words are followed by a comma if they come at the beginning of the sentence.

> He went to the interview **next.**

> **Then** he waited for an offer.   (*Then* is not followed by a comma if it comes at the beginning of the sentence.)

> He **finally** began his new job.

 Firstly, secondly, and *thirdly* are common in British English but not in Standard American English.

Exercise 10   Complete the paragraph with the missing conjunctions or transition words. *Hint:* The punctuation may help you.

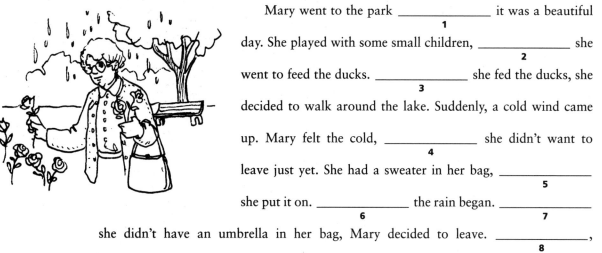

Mary went to the park _____ it was a beautiful
1

day. She played with some small children, _____ she
2

went to feed the ducks. _____ she fed the ducks, she
3

decided to walk around the lake. Suddenly, a cold wind came

up. Mary felt the cold, _____ she didn't want to
4

leave just yet. She had a sweater in her bag, _____
5

she put it on. _____ the rain began. _____
6   7

she didn't have an umbrella in her bag, Mary decided to leave. _____,
8

something caught her eye. It was a beautiful rose bush. She knew it was wrong to pick

the roses. _____, she decided to take a few home with her. With her roses in
9

hand, Mary hailed a taxi, _____ she ventured home.
10

Exercise 11   Circle the letter of the correct answer.

1. I didn't understand the general meaning of the text, _____ the specific details.
   a. and I not   c. nor I got
   b. nor didn't I get   d. nor did I get

2. Lorna refused to come to the staff meeting. _____, she was reprimanded by the manager.
   a. After   c. Even so
   b. As a result   d. Despite this

3. Teddy and his roommate are in the library, _____ studying.
   a. and they are not   c. but they are not
   b. and   d. but not

4. _____ the sun is shining, the temperature is below zero.
   a. Even so,   c. Even though,
   b. Even so   d. Even though

5. The resource center has a number of useful study guides. _____, TOEFL practice books are available to students who want to practice.
   a. For example   c. In addition
   b. Consequently   d. Thus

6. _____ the oven wasn't functioning properly, the cake burned.
   a. For   c. Since
   b. After   d. So

Editing

^ Exercise 12 One of the four underlined words or phrases is not correct. Circle the letter representing the error and write a correction above it.

1. <u>While the media</u> are becoming <u>more and more</u> powerful in many parts of the
   A   **B**

   world, but some countries <u>still</u> impose strict <u>limitations</u> on news coverage.
                              C   **D**

2. <u>As soon as</u> she found a <u>job she</u> rented a small <u>apartment</u> in the center of town. As a
   A   **B**   **C**

   result, <u>she finally</u> felt like an adult.
            D

3. Pollution is <u>increasing</u>; therefore<u>, steps</u> must be taken to prevent the further decline
                 A   **B**

   of air quality. <u>Therefore, there</u> are no guarantees that the environment <u>will improve</u>.
                    C   **D**

4. Maria decided to change her major, <u>for she</u> was not doing <u>well</u> in her coursework.
                                        A   **B**

   Her <u>parents; however</u>, were not happy with her decision.
       C   **D**

Original Writing

Exercise 13 Write a paragraph or short essay about one of your favorite books or movies. Give descriptions of the actions and scenes. Try to use at least five connectors showing reason, result, cause, extra information, and so on. Use the following list to help you, or refer to the full list of connectors in this chapter.

for	in addition	therefore
because	finally	yet
then	however	in contrast
for example	next	nevertheless

Exchange paragraphs with a partner. Review your partner's paragraph, circling all the connectors and checking for their correct use.

> If you need help with the steps of writing a paragraph, see Appendix 5.
>
> **www** You will find additional exercises for the grammar in this chapter on the Top 20 website at **http://esl.college.hmco.com/students**

On Friday night I reward myself by relaxing. I might watch a movie or go out with my friends. Or even stay home and read a book.

FRAG

14

Sentence Matters:

Variety, Common Problems (Run-ons, Comma Splices, Fragments), and Punctuation

This chapter reviews three sentence types: simple, compound, and complex. You can learn and practice ways to add variety to your sentences by varying sentence beginnings as well as sentence structure and length. You can also review and practice editing common sentence errors such as run-ons, comma splices, fragments, and incorrect punctuation.

(14.1) Sentence Types

English sentences come in three basic types: simple, compound, and complex.

Simple Sentences

- Contain one independent clause
- May have more than one subject or verb

> **The Mississippi River** **flows** from northern Minnesota to the Gulf of
>   SUBJECT   VERB
> Mexico.

> **The Mississippi River** **begins** in Minnesota and **ends** in Louisiana
>   SUBJECT   VERB   VERB
> at the Gulf.

Compound Sentences

- Contain two or more independent clauses joined by a coordinating conjunction (*and, or, but, so, for, nor, yet*)
- Have at least two subjects and two verbs
- Have clauses equal in importance

> **The water pipes** in the building **broke**, **so** **the offices were closed**
>   INDEPENDENT CLAUSE   INDEPENDENT CLAUSE
> for the day.

Complex Sentences

- Have one independent clause and one dependent clause joined by a subordinating conjunction (for example, *although, because, before, whose*)
- Have an independent clause that has more importance than the dependent clause

> Although **it was drizzling**, **the city held** the parade as scheduled.
>   DEPENDENT CLAUSE   INDEPENDENT CLAUSE

Exercise 1   Read the sentences below and expand them by adding the parts of speech indicated.

Simple Sentences
1. The tree cast a shadow.
   a. add a subject (house) and change "a shadow" to "shadows"

   The tree and the house cast shadows.

   b. add two adjectives (enormous, old)

   The enormous tree and the old house cast shadows.

c. add a prepositional phrase (over the lawn)

<u>The enormous tree and the old house cast shadows over the lawn.</u>

2. The car turned.

 a. add a verb (sped away) _____

 _____

 b. add two adverbs (sharply, quickly) _____

 _____

 c. add a prepositional phrase (down the highway) _____

 _____

Compound Sentences
 3. We loved the movie.

 a. add a sentence (They hated it.), joined by *but* _____

 _____

 b. add two adverbs (absolutely, simply) _____

 _____

 c. add an adjective (new) _____

 _____

 4. Jimena mowed the lawn.

 a. add a sentence (Ted washed the cars.), joined by *and* _____

 _____

 b. add a prepositional phrase (in the driveway) _____

 _____

 c. add an adjective (overgrown) _____

 _____

Complex Sentences
 5. Whenever she hears him play the guitar, she feels weak.

 a. add a prepositional phrase (in the knees) _____

 _____

b. add an adverb (always) _____

_____

c. add an adjective (dizzy) _____

_____

6. I showered before I ate a breakfast of toast and coffee.

a. add an adverb (quickly) _____

_____

b. add two adjectives (simple, black) _____

_____

Exercise 2   Part 1   Create two simple sentences, two compound sentences, and two complex sentences. You may use the phrases and clauses below or think of your own.

Subjects
the screaming toddler
all of the waiters and
   waitresses
my neighbor Jerry
an elderly woman
the door-to-door
   salesman
you
the judge and her
   husband
the frustrated babysitter

Prepositional Phrases
with toys
in the afternoon
for their trip to Europe
on the playground
onto my front porch
at the border

Verbs
asked (him) to leave
earned
drove
tried to deny
need to renew
spent
entered and won
worked
fined
wouldn't listen to
won
hasn't worked

Nouns
my refusal
$50
late model Cadillac
money
vacation
driver's license
fishing contest

Adjectives/Adverbs
firmly
young
diligently
enough
hard

Connectors
and
but
although
or
nor
ever since

Simple: _____

_____

Simple: _____

_____

Compound: _____

_____

Compound: _____

_____

Complex: _____

_____

Complex: _____

_____

Part 2   Change one simple sentence in Part 1 to a compound sentence and one compound sentence in Part 1 to a complex sentence.

Simple to compound: _____

_____

_____

Compound to complex: _____

_____

_____

14.2 Sentence Variety

Good English writers strive for clarity, but clear writing does not have to be boring or monotonous. Sentence variety is the key to conveying your message in an interesting way.

14.2.1 Vary Sentence Structure and Length

One way to add interest to your writing and increase its effectiveness is to vary the structure and length of your sentences.

- Use a combination of simple, compound, and complex sentences.

- Intersperse short, simple sentences with longer, more complex ones.

- Use modifiers or appositives in simple sentences. An appositive is a word that identifies or explains the meaning of another word in that same sentence. An appositive is usually set off by commas.

George Washington, the first U.S. president, was born in 1732.
APPOSITIVE

- Convert compound sentences into complex ones.

- Use phrases in simple sentences.

Compare these two paragraphs. Which one has variety in sentence structure and length?

A. I had a great weekend. On Saturday, my friend came over. Her name is Linda. We went to the beach. It was hot. We swam all afternoon. We watched the sun set. We ate dinner at a restaurant. We got home late. We were tired. I slept all day Sunday.

B. I had a great weekend. On Saturday, my friend Linda came over, and we went to the beach. It was hot, so we swam all afternoon. Later we watched the sun set and ate dinner at a restaurant. When we got home, it was late and we were tired. I slept all day Sunday.

Editing
∧ Exercise 3   Rewrite each sentence according to the directions in parentheses. You can rewrite in more than one way; for example, you might delete information or break a long sentence into two shorter ones.

1. (Make shorter) She assembled all of her baking supplies, and she found her favorite cookie recipe, and she baked cookies, and she offered them to her family for dessert.

   _____

   _____

2. (Make shorter) This small convertible is easy to drive, and it's easy to park.

   _____

   _____

3. (Use appositive) George Lucas is the director of the *Star Wars* series of movies, and he was interviewed on "Entertainment Tonight," which is a television news entertainment show.

   _____

   _____

4. (Convert to complex; use *although* or *even though*) Computers are an important part of many people's lives, but some people in the world have never seen one.

   _____

   _____

5. (Convert to complex; use *because)* It was cold and rainy, and we had to cancel the planned outdoor activities.

   _____

   _____

Editing
∧ Exercise 4   Rewrite each sentence according to the directions in parentheses. Remember to use variety in structure and length. Then write the sentences as a paragraph in the space provided. Remember to indent your paragraph.

1. (Combine into one sentence) The city was on the Atlantic Ocean. The city was hit by a hurricane. The city was almost entirely destroyed.

   _____

   _____

2. (Separate into two or more sentences) Electrical power to the city was cut off, and the water was contaminated, and many trees were uprooted after the hurricane, and people were very worried about their homes.

_____

_____

3. (Combine into one sentence) Mr. Heldon was the mayor of the city. He appealed to the citizens. He asked them to remain calm, and he asked them to wait for rescue teams.

_____

_____

4. (Separate into two or more sentences) The Red Cross is an international relief organization, and it set up tents for homeless people, and it delivered food and clothing to the residents, and it fed the workers who rescued people from their homes.

_____

_____

_____

Paragraph:

_____

_____

_____

_____

_____

_____

_____

14.2.2 Vary Sentence Beginnings

Another way to add interest to your writing is to avoid beginning all of your sentences the same way. Instead of starting each sentence with the subject, begin some sentences with an adverb or adverb clause, a prepositional or participial phrase, or a conjunction. Be careful not to overuse this technique. Study the following pairs of sentences for variety at the beginning.

His view of the world changed **immediately.**

Immediately, his view of the world changed.

Her interest in fashion surfaced **after she visited Europe.**

After she visited Europe, her interest in fashion surfaced.

The child's cat sat **on the roof** and meowed plaintively.

On the roof, the child's cat sat and meowed plaintively.   *or*

Meowing plaintively, the child's cat sat on the roof.

She was well-aware of the risks involved in plagiarizing a paper; **however,** she was desperate.

She was well-aware of the risks involved in plagiarizing a paper. **Yet** she was desperate.

 The purpose of beginning a sentence with a conjunction is to add emphasis.

Editing

∧ **Exercise 5** As you rewrite each sentence, vary the beginning to add interest or emphasis. Begin your new sentence with the underlined word. Make changes as necessary.

1. The carjacker took control of the car <u>forcefully</u> yet quietly.

   Forcefully yet quietly, the carjacker took control of the car.

2. Carla and Bob moved to the city to be closer to cultural attractions <u>despite</u> the poor housing market and high crime rate in the area.

   _____

   _____

3. The conductor <u>shouted</u> at the top of his voice and ordered all passengers to board the train immediately.

   _____

   _____

4. Residents have formed a neighborhood watch group <u>in</u> an all-out effort to discourage crime.

_____

_____

5. The newly engaged couple sat and drank lemonade <u>under</u> a slowly spinning fan on the porch.

_____

_____

14.2.3   Vary Subject–Verb Sequence

Just as varying the beginning of some sentences adds variety and interest, so does varying the SUBJECT–VERB sequence. Add an exclamation (*Yes!*) or question (*How?*) or command (*Think.*) to your paragraph or essay to break up a succession of declarative statements. Be sure not to overuse this technique.

The new ice cream store is **a block from the park, and it's** having its grand opening today.

The new ice cream store, **a block from the park,** is having its grand opening today.

Winning the lottery is many people's dream **because** they imagine the financial freedom gained will result in automatic happiness.

Winning the lottery is many people's dream. **Why?** They imagine the financial freedom gained will result in automatic happiness.

Ineffective due to overuse:

Winning the lottery is many people's dream. **Why?** They imagine the financial freedom gained will result in automatic happiness. This is not true. **Why?** Happiness is not measured in dollars. **Why not?** Happiness is generated from within, not from without.

Editing

∧ **Exercise 6**   Read the following short essay. Rewrite the sentences on separate paper, using what you have learned and practiced in Sections 14.2.1–14.2.3 to add variety. Use the suggestions in parentheses, or choose another way to rewrite for variety.

Telemarketers, <u>who sell</u> (vary beginning) products and services many people don't need, cause much of the stress people experience today <u>because</u> (question) telemarketers call at all hours of the day and night.

I assume a friend or family member is calling to share some important news <u>whenever</u> (vary beginning) my phone rings. A voice that mispronounces my name and wants to know if I am home is, <u>however,</u> (vary beginning) often on the other end. I generally invite the voice to call back another time.

Thankfully, telemarketers never leave a message on my answering machine. I am tired (make shorter) and I am hungry, and I am crabby <u>after</u> (vary beginning) a day at work and a long traffic commute. I just want to watch the evening news, and (convert to simple sentence) I want to relax with a cup of coffee in my hand. It's not possible. (exclamation)

The phone rings and, like a puppet, I dance to its jingle. I reach for the receiver, and hear yet another unfamiliar voice, asking to speak to the "decision-maker of the household."

Telemarketers <u>are</u> (appositive) the bane of my existence and have caused me to speak sometimes rudely and oftentimes abruptly to people <u>who are probably very much like me</u> (separate subject and verb) in their off-work hours. I wonder if they dislike getting calls from other telemarketers when they get home at night.

(14.3) Common Sentence Problems and Challenges

If your writing contains errors in sentence structure, it is difficult for readers to understand your ideas clearly. This section addresses the most common types of sentence-structure errors: run-on sentences, comma splices, fragments, and punctuation.

14.3.1 Run-on (fused) Sentences and Comma Splices

Run-on Sentence

It's easy to mistakenly connect two sentences when you add sentence variety to your paragraphs, especially in the form of compound and complex sentences. If you don't add a connector or punctuation correctly, the result can be a run-on, or fused, sentence. Here are two simple ways to fix run-ons:

1. Separate the two independent clauses with a period. Do this if the sentence is too long or if the clauses are not closely related.

> We need to make a decision soon our choices are to either refinance our mortgage or take out a home equity loan.   (sentence too long)

Correction: We need to make a decision soon. Our choices are to either refinance our mortgage or take out a home equity loan.

> We need to make a decision soon the Stones have decided to refinance their mortgage.   (clauses unrelated)

Correction: We need to make a decision soon. The Stones have decided to refinance their mortgage.

2. Separate the two independent clauses with a semicolon. Do this if the sentences are not too long or if they are closely related.

> An adjustable rate mortgage is one option a fixed rate mortgage is another.

Correction: An adjustable rate mortgage is one option; a fixed rate mortgage is another.

Comma Splice

Another problem is connecting two sentences with only a comma. This type of error is called a comma splice.

> An adjustable rate mortgage is one option, a fixed rate mortgage is another.

To fix a comma splice, connect the two sentences with a coordinating conjunction, a subordinating conjunction, or a transition.

> An adjustable rate mortgage is one option, **and** a fixed rate mortgage is another.   (coordinating conjunction)

> An adjustable rate mortgage is one option **while** a fixed rate mortgage is another.   (subordinating conjunction)

> An adjustable rate mortgage is one option; **however,** a fixed rate mortgage is another.   (transition)

 The punctuation in the examples changes, depending on the kind of connector.

Editing

∧ Exercise 7   Read each sentence. Put a *C* if the sentence is correct and an *I* if it is incorrect. On a separate sheet of paper, correct each sentence that is incorrect.

_____ 1. Taking a course online has some disadvantages, for example if you have a question, you can't get an immediate answer.

_____ 2. Discussion boards are forums for posting thoughts and opinions; however, as in a classroom, you must monitor what you say in order not to offend your classmates.

_____ 3. Students in some online courses participate from countries all over the world and it's interesting to exchange ideas and information with them.

_____ 4. Online courses require students to be self-disciplined it's easy to put off doing assignments.

_____ 5. In some respects, online classes are similar to those held in a classroom in other respects they are very dissimilar.

_____ 6. Assignments are graded in an online course; therefore, it's important to allow yourself enough time to do them well.

Editing

∧ **Exercise 8** On a separate sheet of paper, edit the following paragraphs. Correct run-on sentences and comma splices. Convert long sentences to shorter, more interesting sentences. Use conjunctions, transitions, and simple sentences to add variety.

1. It was a difficult decision for the Brenner family to make but they decided to leave Michigan where they had lived for almost 20 years and move to Florida because Mr. Brenner was offered a job working as a consultant for a small, progressive engineering company.

    Although they were used to the cold, snowy winters of the north and they were avid snow skiers and ice skaters the entire family was ready for a change they had visions of going to the beach every weekend and swimming in the beautiful blue waters of the Gulf of Mexico.

    Now, after almost ten years in Florida the family realizes it made the right decision for the right reason, everyone is content to stay and not to move back up north.

2. There are many ways to reduce stress in your life one of the best ways I have found is through baking, it takes your mind off your everyday problems and redirects your energy and you become creative and productive.

    The benefits of baking include the pleasure you derive from being creative and the gratitude you receive from the people who are the recipients of your efforts. Like cookies, praise is never hard to swallow.

    Baking also has a down side it often happens that once people discover that stress for you equals baked goods for them they begin to find ways to increase your stress, for example you are assigned to many committees suddenly. The solution? I haven't had time to figure it out yet, I'm too busy baking.

14.3.2 Fragments

Have you ever tried to be concise and put end punctuation after a phrase or dependent clause, creating an incomplete sentence? These incomplete sentences, known as fragments, may have a subject and a verb, but they cannot stand alone as complete thoughts or sentences. You can correct sentence fragments in two ways.

1. Connect the fragment to an independent clause.

I had a hard time getting up this morning. Although I slept well last night.

Correction: I had a hard time getting up this morning although I slept well last night.

2. Change the fragment to an independent clause.

> She was born in Northwoods. A small town with no stoplights on Main Street.

Correction: She was born in Northwoods. It is a small town with no stoplights on Main Street.

∧ **Exercise 9** Read the following short essay and underline the nine fragments. Then rewrite the essay on a separate sheet of paper. Correct the fragments by connecting them to independent clauses or by changing them to independent clauses.

"To Do"

I start off every weekend with a long "To Do" list. And lots of energy. On Friday night I reward myself by relaxing. I might watch a movie or go out with my friends. Or even stay home and read a book.

When Saturday morning rolls around, I take advantage of the opportunity to sleep in. By noon I'm up and ready to tackle the items on my list. I do a load of laundry and then head for the grocery store. Where I spend time looking at all the luscious tropical fruits and choosing some for my Sunday breakfast.

During the late afternoon. I finish the laundry and usually discover my energy level has dropped. I'm going out later, so I take a quick nap. Although I haven't finished my chores.

Suddenly, it's Sunday. Before I know it. I read the paper and enjoy a leisurely breakfast. I check my "To Do" list to see what else I can accomplish. But I'm always shocked. Here it is, mid-afternoon on a Sunday. Too late to start a new project. I might as well finish reading the paper. And think about writing a new list again next week. Where does weekend time go?

14.3.3 Sentence Punctuation

Sentence punctuation helps you create the meaning you want. It also tells readers how to read a sentence, so learning how to use punctuation correctly is essential. Listed here are six of the major punctuation marks that you will need to write correct sentences— period, comma, semicolon, colon, apostrophe, and quotation marks. If you want more detailed information than you find here, it's a good idea to consult an in-depth style and writing guide or grammar reference.

1. Period

   - Indicates a full stop at the end of a sentence

     I'm thinking about going to graduate school next year.

   - Used at the end of an abbreviation

     Dr. Ballard has a Ph.D. in Linguistics.

2. Comma

   - Separates items in a series

     We have meat, cheese, and bread for lunch.

   - Separates independent clauses connected by a coordinating conjunction

     The car needs gas, but it doesn't need any windshield wiper fluid.

   - Separates phrases or dependent clauses before independent clauses

     Even though they have two biological daughters, they are adopting another daughter.

   - Sets off nonrestrictive elements

     Mr. Lantern, owner of the corner bakery, just sold his shop and retired.

   - Sets off direct quotations

     "Dan," she said, "please don't forget to mail these letters."

3. Semicolon

   - Separates two independent clauses with related information

     Joey came on Saturday; Bobby will come tomorrow.

   - Separates two independent clauses connected by transition words

     Last week they bought a plane ticket to Los Angeles; however, today they changed their minds and decided to drive there instead.

   - Separates items in a list whose items contain commas

     Please be sure to bring your passport, if it's current; your inoculation card, if you have one; and your admission letter, stamped and signed by the school official.

4. Colon

- Introduces information in a list

  The cost of the trip includes: round trip airfare, hotel accommodations, transportation charges, and all meals.

- Introduces an explanation of the first clause

  Most of the students share a common goal: they want to improve their writing.

5. Apostrophe

- Indicates omissions in contracted forms

  He's coming, but we've heard that before, haven't we?

- Shows possession

  Would you please return Juan's book to him?

6. Quotation Marks

- Indicate the beginning and end of a direct quote

  Patrick Henry said, "Give me liberty or give me death."

- Indicate the title of a short work

  Have you ever read Franz Kafka's short story "Metamorphosis"?

∧ **Exercise 10**   Insert the correct punctuation needed in the sentences below and change the incorrect punctuation. When you insert a period, be sure to capitalize the first word of the next sentence. There may be more than one way to punctuate some sentences.

I have just finished reading an article called Living in a Dream World by Dr. Carl Young in *Psychology: It's All in Your Mind* magazine. This article explains a great deal about dreams for example it explains that all dreams are not equal in importance. Dreams that have importance will remain in a persons memory for years dreams that have little or no importance are easily forgotten.

In order to analyze one's dreams, it helps to recall the following the people, animals, or objects in the dream, the mood; the atmosphere; and any color in the dream it was surprising to discover that not all people dream in color.

Dreams and their meanings differ from person to person however, there are common themes. A dream about a bird may represent freedom a dream about insects may represent the dreamers hard work; a dream about floating down a river may refer to the passage of time in the dreamer's life.

After I finished reading the article I realized that a person's dreams are an emotional barometer of sorts that should be explored in order to learn what messages the unconscious mind is sending the conscious one.

Exercise 11   For each item, read the first sentence and determine whether it contains any errors. Then read the four choices and circle the letters of all the correct answers.

1. Whenever Emily sees a shopping mall, she has to stop and go in.
   a. Emily sees a shopping mall, she has to stop and go in.
   b. Whenever Emily sees a shopping mall; she has to stop and go in.
   c. However Emily sees a shopping mall, she has to stop and go in.
   d. No changes

2. Harrison Ford is a movie star, he is also a private pilot.
   a. Harrison Ford is a movie star; and he is also a private pilot.
   b. Harrison Ford, a movie star, is also a private pilot.
   c. Harrison Ford is a movie star and a pilot.
   d. No changes

3. People need to safeguard their ATM cards and Social Security numbers. Because identity theft is becoming more widespread.
   a. People need to safeguard their ATM cards and Social Security numbers; because identity theft is becoming more widespread.
   b. Because identity theft is becoming more widespread, people need to safeguard their ATM cards and Social Security numbers.
   c. Because identity theft is becoming more widespread people need to safeguard their ATM cards and Social Security numbers.
   d. No changes

4. I cry. Every time I see a sad movie.
   a. I cry every time I see a sad movie.
   b. Every time I see a sad movie; I cry.
   c. Every time I see a sad movie, I cry.
   d. No changes

5. You are the perfect person for this job you have all the qualifications.
   a. You are the perfect person for this job; you have all the qualifications.
   b. You are the perfect person for this job, you have all the qualifications.
   c. You are the perfect person for this job because you have all the qualifications.
   d. No changes

Original Writing

Exercise 12 Write a paragraph describing one of your dreams. (If you can't remember one, dream one up!) Before you begin writing, review the sentence types you will try to use and the ways you will add variety to your writing. When you finish, edit your writing for correct punctuation. Exchange paragraphs with a partner and check each other's work for correct sentence types and sentence variety.

If you need help with the steps of writing a paragraph, see Appendix 5.

www You will find additional exercises for the grammar in this chapter on the Top 20 website at **http://esl.college.hmco.com/students**

Eating a diet of unhealthy foods containing high amounts of refined carbohydrates leads to weight gain and increased risk of heart disease, diabetes, and getting cancer.

Parallel Structure

In this chapter, you will review and practice using grammatical structures to make your writing balanced. Balancing the grammatical structures of words, phrases, clauses, or sentences in your writing is called parallel structure. It gives coherence to your writing, and you can use it to link ideas. Structures that are connected with coordinating conjunctions or correlative conjunctions are written in parallel form, and writers often emphasize parallel structure through comparisons and repetition. This chapter offers practice that will improve your writing through the use of parallelism.

15.1 Parallel Words

Good English writers make these elements parallel:

• Words that are paired (*tall* and *slim*)

• Items of equal rank (*animal, vegetable,* and *mineral*)

• Items in a series (*bike, swim,* and *run*)

In parallel structure, you balance nouns with nouns, verbs with verbs, adjectives with adjectives, etc. Here are some examples.

1. Connected with coordinating conjunctions:

    My favorite subjects are **history, psychology, *and* math**.   (nouns)

    The dentist did not let me **eat *or* drink** anything for at least an hour. (verbs)

    Their wedding day dawned **bright *and* sunny**.   (adjectives)

    The ambassador spoke **quietly *yet* forcefully**.   (adverbs)

2. Connected with correlative conjunctions:

    I like *both* **Vivaldi *and* Mozart**.   (nouns)

    To succeed in this job, you must *both* **learn fast *and* work hard**.   (verbs)

    The morning dawned *not* **foggy *but* clear**, *not* **humid *but* dry**. (adjectives)

 Two subjects connected by *both ... and* take a plural verb.

Both my plane ticket ***and*** my passport **were** lost.

Editing

∧ **Exercise 1**   As you read the paragraph, find and correct the four errors in parallel structure.

Choosing a career is both an excitement and frightening at the same time. It's exciting because there are so many professions and fields from which you can choose. It's frightening because if you make a mistake and decide on the wrong career, you may be unhappy or have frustration for your entire working life. It's important to consider your options completely and be thorough before making the final decision. Both researching your field of interest and talk to a career counselor can help you make the right choice the first time.

15.2 **Parallel Phrases**

Phrases, as well as words, must be balanced in your writing. Be sure to balance like elements: prepositional phrases with prepositional phrases, infinitive phrases with infinitive phrases, and gerund phrases with gerund phrases. Phrases may be joined with coordinating conjunctions or correlative conjunctions. Here are some examples.

1. Connected with coordinating conjunctions:

The cat climbed **over the fence**, **up the tree**, *and* **onto the roof** of the house next door. (prepositional phrases)

The judge told her **to take the stand** *and* **to tell the truth**. (infinitive phrases)

They usually spend their weekends **entertaining their friends** *or* **fixing up their house**. (gerund phrases)

2. Connected with correlative conjunctions:

His satisfaction lies *not* **in his title** *but* **in his daily work**. (prepositional phrases)

They can't decide *whether* **to take a cruise** *or* **to go on a safari**. (infinitive phrases)

His idea of a relaxing evening is *either* **biking around the island** *or* **watching the sun set over the lake**. (gerund phrases)

As you read the paragraph, underline the parallel words and phrases. Then locate and correct the three errors.

How much do you know about the clouds you see in the sky every day? Clouds are defined by their general appearance and by their altitude in the atmosphere. Cloud types include cirrus, stratus, and cumulus. There are three basic cloud levels: under 10,000 ft., between 10,000 and 20,000 ft., and higher than 20,000 ft. Nimbus clouds produce precipitation and can tower up to 60,000 ft. Learning these few terms and to gaze at the sky are all that you will need to begin impressing your friends and family. Once you have learned the cloud classification system and the weather associated with specific cloud types, you can begin to predict the weather and matching skills with your local TV meteorologist!

15.3 Parallel Clauses

In your writing, be sure to balance noun, adjective, and adverb clauses to give them equal weight. Use coordinating and correlative conjunctions to join your clauses. Study the examples below.

1. Connected with coordinating conjunctions:

    What she says *and* **what she does** are very often two different things! (noun clauses)

    I'm a person **who works hard** *and* **who gets along well with others**. (adjective clauses)

    Are you staying home **because you're tired** *or* **because it's a school night**? (adverb clauses)

2. Connected with correlative conjunctions:

    He appreciated *neither* **what she said** *nor* **how she said it**. (noun clauses)

    She's asking *not* **where he went** *but* **when he went**.   (noun clauses)

    They won the contract *either* **because they bid low** *or* **because they knew someone on the committee**.   (adverb clauses)

For the following paired conjunctions, the subject closer to the verb determines whether the verb is singular or plural.

Not only my parents **but also** my brother **visits** Colorado every winter.

Either my brother **or** my parents **are coming** to Colorado to visit this winter.

Neither my sister **nor** her son **has ever been** to Colorado.

Editing
∧ Exercise 3   As you read the paragraph, study the underlined words, phrases, and clauses. Then locate and correct the five errors in parallel structure.

What people eat and how much they are exercising are two factors that determine their overall health. Eating a diet of foods that supply inadequate nutrients and that contain high amounts of refined carbohydrates leads to weight gain and increased risk of heart disease, diabetes, and getting cancer. Thus, it is important to eat not only a wide variety of fresh fruit and vegetables every day but also grains, proteins, and so-called healthy fats. Many people also suffer poor health because they fail to exercise or to be active. Failing to exercise because they don't have enough time or that they find it boring is probably the biggest problem they face. However, time and being bored are not reasons to give up but hurdles that they have to overcome.

15.4 Parallel Sentences

Finally, balancing sentences with sentences adds parallelism to your writing. Just like words, phrases, and clauses, sentences can be joined with coordinating or correlative conjunctions.

1. Connected with coordinating conjunctions:

    One day he was there, *and* the next day he was gone.   (simple)

    He was tired, and he looked ill, *so* I urged him to see a doctor, *and* he saw one the next day.   (compound)

    If you leave now, you can still catch a bus, *but* if you stay, you'll have to take a cab home.   (complex)

2. Connected with correlative conjunctions (often sounds formal):

    ***Not only* does she hold a full-time job Monday through Friday, *but* she *also* volunteers at a hospice on weekends.**

    ***Either* he turns in his report tomorrow *or* he starts looking for a new job.**

 Nor is most commonly used with *neither* as a correlative conjunction.

    Neither he nor I can come to the party.

For as a coordinating conjunction means *because* and is considered formal usage.

    We decided to abandon the idea of buying a house, **for** the prices had risen dramatically and were now out of our range.

Exercise 4   Add a clause to each of the incomplete structures below in order to make each structure parallel.

1. The first exercise in the unit was easy, but ___*the rest were hard*_____ .

2. The idea of parallel structure makes sense, and it's almost formulaic, so _____

    _____ .

3. Either the grammatical structures are balanced or _____

    _____ .

4. Not only do instructors mark down for errors in parallelism, but _____

    _____ .

5. If you proofread your work, you'll catch your mistakes, but _____

    _____ .

∧ **Exercise 5**   Rewrite these sentences to make their elements parallel.

1. The day I bought my red and white Fiat convertible turned out to be cold with a lot of wind, and it rained.

   _____

   _____

2. Your keys have to be here somewhere! Let's check the sofa cushions and then check the kitchen counter. You can look in your purse, too.

   _____

   _____

3. It takes time to brainstorm ideas, writing a first draft, and for revisions.

   _____

   _____

4. While working at your desk, you can do isometric exercises. You can do the same if you're sitting at a traffic light.

   _____

   _____

5. She was disappointed that she had not been chosen to receive the scholarship, yet that she had been considered by the committee pleased her.

   _____

   _____

∧ **Exercise 6**   Edit and then rewrite the following sentences. Use correlative conjunctions to make the grammatical structures in each sentence parallel.

1. Almost half of the students in Section 003 of Freshman Composition neither showed up for the final nor did they turn in their five required essays.

    _____

    _____

2. She was not only a gracious winner but also humble.

    _____

    _____

3. It would be best if you included sources for your topic both from the Internet and used the university library.

    _____

    _____

4. The bank president was indicted for embezzling not $1 million but for embezzling $2 million.

    _____

    _____

5. They need to either make a bid on the house or they should keep looking.

    _____

    _____

6. Both the time of the flight and how much it costs are important considerations when booking a trip.

    _____

    _____

(15.5) Parallel Comparisons

When you make comparisons using parallel structures, use these expressions:

-er / more / less … than	as … as	the same as	similar to

Remember that the items you are comparing must have the same grammatical structure.

Incorrect: Going to a movie is more expensive than to rent a video.

Correct: **Going to a movie** is *more* expensive *than* **renting a video**.

Incorrect: Investing in his company is the same as to throw your money away.

Correct: **Investing in his company** is *the same as* **throwing your money away**.

When you use parallelism in comparisons, the comparisons must follow these rules.

1. Comparisons should be complete. Repeat the whole parallel structure in each item and include all the comparison words.

Incorrect: I am happier at my new job.

Correct: I am happier **at my new job** *than* **at my old one**.
I am happier **at my new job** *than* **I was at my old one**.

Incorrect: I can't believe you lost. You played as well, if not better than your opponent.

Correct: I can't believe you lost. **You** played *as* well *as*, if not better *than* **your opponent**.

Incorrect: Michael Jordan is taller than anyone on the team.   (He is on the team, so he can't be taller than anyone on the team.)

Correct: **Michael Jordan** is taller *than* **anyone else** on the team.
Michael Jordan is taller *than* **any other player** on the team.

2. Comparisons should be clear. Make sure the meaning of your comparison is obvious.

Incorrect: I think your boss likes Angela more than you.   (Does this mean more than you like Angela or more than your boss likes you? The meaning is unclear.)

Correct: I think **your boss likes Angela** *more than* **you like Angela**.
I think **your boss likes Angela** *more than* **your boss likes you**.

3. Comparisons should be between similar items. The comparison must make sense.

Incorrect: The cost of a house in Mississippi is less than Texas.   (*House* and *Texas* are not similar.)

Correct: The cost of **a house in Mississippi** is *less than* **one in Texas.**

Incorrect: Popular music in the United States is similar to your country. (*Music* and *your country* are not similar.)

Correct: **Popular music in the United States** is *similar to* **music in your country.**

Editing

∧ **Exercise 7**   Edit and then rewrite the comparisons in the following sentences to make each sentence parallel.

1. Some students are better at following directions.

_____

_____

2. Writing in a second language is more difficult than to speak.

_____

_____

3. The dress that you wore to my wedding is similar to Sharon's wedding.

_____

_____

4. The soup tastes as good today as yesterday.

_____

_____

5. I think I prefer listening to reggae music more than you.

_____

_____

6. The rules for using semi-colons in English are almost the same as Spanish.

_____

_____

Exercise 8   Use the phrases below to write sentences containing comparisons. Have a partner check your sentences for parallel form.

1. my interests

   _____

   _____

2. environmentally safe

   _____

   _____

3. writing comparisons

   _____

   _____

4. community colleges

   _____

   _____

5. winter driving

   _____

   _____

6. her personality

   _____

   _____

(15.6) Parallel Repetition

Parallel repetition means repeating articles, prepositions, *to* before a verb, or other words to emphasize parallel structure. This repetition can help make the parallel items clear and eliminate omissions or awkwardness from your writing. When you repeat articles or prepositions, you add clarity to a series of items. The repeated word must appear with each item, not just two of three items.

At the same time, parallel structure makes repeating some words unnecessary. In general, avoid repetition when it makes your writing too wordy. Compare the examples below.

Articles

For the first time in his life he had **a good job, a home,** and **a family.** (repeated article in a series adds clarity)

Employees received **a raise** and **bonus** this year. (no need to repeat the article before *bonus* for clarity)

to before a verb

Now is the time **to organize, to plan,** and **to act.** (repeated *to* before a verb adds emphasis)

It's important **to choose a career, get the necessary training,** and **find satisfying work.** (repeated *to* before a verb not necessary for clarity)

Prepositions

Uncle Bill stashed money not only **in the kitchen** and **in the bedroom,** but also **in the attic** and **in the garage.** (repeated preposition adds emphasis)

She told her son to play ball not **in the living room** but **the yard.** (repeated preposition not necessary for clarity)

Relative Pronouns

The candidate believes **that this country is ready for change, that the people are willing to sacrifice,** and **that there can be no change without sacrifice.** (repeated *that* necessary for clarity)

He wants a job **that pays well** or **leads to more responsibility.** (repeated relative pronoun not necessary for clarity)

Subjects

In her mind, **life was an adventure** or **life wasn't worth living.** (repeated subject necessary for clarity)

She **opened** the door and **welcomed** us to her home. (repeated subject not necessary for clarity)

Wordiness

My editor is good at **researching** background facts, **researching** hard-to-find material, and **researching** information just published. (repeating *researching* causes wordiness)

My editor is good at **researching** background facts, hard-to-find material, and information just published. (more concise and still clear)

When you write a paragraph, especially one of comparison/contrast, repeating parallel structures can help you develop the main idea. You may use parallel structure in all or in only some sentences of your paragraph. Study the examples of parallel structure in the following paragraph.

There are several differences between **living in an** apartment *and* **living in a** house. One **difference is** privacy. **Living in a** house offers a person more privacy than **living in an** apartment does. Another **difference is** maintenance. **Living in a** house requires the tenant to make all repairs and upkeep, *but* **living in an** apartment puts responsibility for upkeep on the landlord. A third **difference is** cost. *Not only* is **living in a** house usually more expensive than **living in an** apartment in terms of rent, *but* it *also* costs more **to furnish** *and* **to keep up** a house than it does an apartment.

Editing

∧ **Exercise 9**   Edit the following sentences, adding or eliminating repetition, to improve the parallel structure.

1. We were relieved to learn that he had come, that he had signed the agreement, and had left without incident.

   _____

   _____

2. She set out a plate of cookies, bowl of fruit, and pitcher of lemonade for her guests.

   _____

   _____

3. Mr. Owens went to the travel agency, and Mr. Owens booked a trip to Greece for both himself and his wife.

_____

_____

4. She's amazing—look at the way she handles the responsibility of home, the responsibility of work, and the responsibility of school.

_____

_____

5. They told us that they couldn't come and they had reasons.

_____

_____

6. You lost the relay race, not because you weren't fit but your teammates weren't.

_____

_____

Editing
∧ **Exercise 10** Read the following excerpts from famous speeches, noting the underlined structures. Locate the nine errors in parallelism and correct them by rewriting the structures, adding or deleting words as necessary.

1. **Patrick Henry to the Second Virginia Convention on March 23, 1775:**

"… Sir, we have done everything that could be done to avert the storm that is now coming on. We have petitioned; we remonstrated; we have supplicated; we have prostrated ourselves before the throne and have implored its interposition to arrest the tyrannical hands of the Ministry and Parliament.

… The battle, sir, is not to the strong alone; it is to the vigilant, the active, the brave. I know not what course others may take, but as for me—give me liberty or you can give me death!"

2. **Abraham Lincoln at the dedication of a cemetery in Gettysburg, Pennsylvania, on November 19, 1863:**

"…We have come to dedicate a portion of that field as a final resting-place for those who here gave their lives that that nation might live. … But in a larger sense, we cannot dedicate, <u>we cannot consecrate</u>, this ground <u>cannot be hallowed by us</u>. ... It is rather for us to be here dedicated to the great task remaining before us ... that we here highly resolve <u>that these dead</u> shall not have died in vain, <u>that this nation</u> under God will have a new birth of freedom, and <u>government of the people</u>, <u>by the people</u>, <u>for people</u> shall not perish from the earth."

3. **John F. Kennedy at his inauguration in Washington, D.C., on January 20, 1961:**

"We observe today not a victory of party but a celebration of freedom. ... <u>Let us</u> never negotiate out of fear, but <u>let us</u> never fear to negotiate.

<u>Let both sides</u> explore what problems unite us instead of belaboring those problems which divide us. <u>Let both sides</u> seek to invoke the wonders of science instead of its terrors. ... <u>The energy</u>, <u>the faith</u>, <u>devotion</u> which we bring to this endeavor will light our country and all who serve it, and <u>the glow</u> from that fire can truly light the world.

And so, my fellow Americans, <u>ask not what your country can do for you</u>; <u>ask what you are able to do for the country</u>."

4. **Robert F. Kennedy at a rally informing the audience that Martin Luther King, Jr., had been assassinated on April 4, 1968:**

"... <u>What we need in the United States is not division</u>; <u>what we need in the United States is not hatred</u>; <u>what the United States needs is not violence or lawlessness</u>; but <u>love</u> and <u>wisdom</u>, and <u>compassion</u> toward one another, and a feeling of justice toward those who still suffer within our country, whether <u>they be white</u> or <u>they are black</u>."

Exercise 11   Read each sentence and circle the letter of the correct answer.

1. I have no idea where she lives _____.
   a. and works
   b. or where she works
   c. but where she works
   d. nor works

2. _____ the bank _____ the post office was closed for the holiday.
   a. Not only ... but also
   b. Not ... but
   c. Both ... or
   d. Either ... or

3. My three favorite ways to relax are _____.
   a. reading, napping, and to cook
   b. to read, to nap, or to cook
   c. to read, to nap, and to cook
   d. reading, napping, or cooking

4. _____ Erica Marie's _____ Mark's names were included on the list of guests.
   a. Neither ... nor
   b. Not ... but
   c. Either ... or
   d. Both ... and

5. The book was _____, if not more exciting than, the movie was.
   a. exciting as
   b. the same exciting as
   c. as exciting
   d. as exciting as

6. We have _____ time, _____ money, and _____ people to make this project succeed.
   a. the, the, the
   b. ∅, ∅, the
   c. the, ∅, the
   d. ∅, the, ∅

Original Writing

Exercise 12   Imagine you are a speechwriter for a political or educational leader. Write a speech presenting the leader's view of an issue or offering solutions to an issue. Examples of issues are raising taxes to improve schools or making efforts to lower high school dropout rates. Before you begin, make a list of some parallel structures you want to include in the speech. In your speech, underline the parallel structures you were able to use from your list. Exchange paragraphs with a partner and check each other's work for correct parallel structure.

> If you need help with the steps of writing a paragraph, see Appendix 5.
>
> **WWW** You will find additional exercises for the grammar in this chapter on the Top 20 website at **http://esl.college.hmco.com/students**

Every generation has a special name. For example, people ^ were born between 1946 and 1960 in the United States are called "Baby Boomers."

Adjective Clauses

This chapter reviews everything you need to know about adjective clauses and their reduced forms. First, a definition:

An adjective clause is a group of words with a subject and a verb that modifies or describes a noun or a pronoun.

The firefighters tried to save the **old** house.   *(The adjective describes house.)*

The firefighters tried to save the old house **that was burning**.   *(The adjective clause describes house.)*

16.1 Adjective Clauses and Relative Pronouns

You will recognize adjective clauses by these relative pronouns, which come at the beginning of the clause.

who	whom	that	which	whose

who   The boy **who lives down the street** is my friend.

This sentence combines these two simple sentences:

> The boy is my friend.
>
> He lives down the street.

which   Two news articles **which appeared in the latest edition of *Nova*** were written by my science professor.

This sentence combines these two simple sentences:

> Two news articles were written by my science professor.
>
> They appeared in the latest edition of *Nova*.

that   The Japanese food **that Keith likes best** is sashimi.

This sentence combines these two simple sentences:

> The Japanese food is sashimi.
>
> Keith likes it best.

whom   The people **whom Maria works for** are very interesting.

This sentence combines these two simple sentences:

> The people are very interesting.
>
> Maria works for them.

whose   The TV newscaster **whose opinions I trust most** is on channel 7.

This sentence combines these two simple sentences:

> The TV newscaster is on channel 7.
>
> I trust her opinions most.

Who and *whom* are used only for people. *Which* is used only for things. *That* is used for both people and things (less formal than *who(m)* and *which*). *Whose* is the possessive and is used for both people and things.

Exercise 1 Read the paragraph and underline the six adjective clauses.

One of the most common types of cars is the SUV (Sport Utility Vehicle). SUVs are machines <u>that were originally used in the military or in rugged terrain</u>. These cars, which normally have four-wheel drive, are better able to maneuver in rough road conditions. Jeeps, which have been popular around the world for many years, originated with the U.S. military. Similarly, Land Rovers are vehicles that the British military has utilized extensively. SUVs are vehicles that have many advantages, but the amount of gas that they use is extremely high.

Editing
∧ **Exercise 2** Read the following sentences. If the sentence is correct, put a C in the blank. If it is incorrect, put an X in the blank and make the correction.

_____ 1. I wish I had pictures of all the places that I have visited.

_____ 2. Perhaps the best memories of my trips are the people which I have met.

_____ 3. Of all the wonderful places I have been, the one that I remember the most is Cape Breton, Canada.

_____ 4. Even though they will probably never have the chance to visit me, I keep in contact with many of these foreign friends which I have made over the years.

_____ 5. Nowadays, however, it is the Internet who helps me maintain my contacts.

_____ 6. Without this tool, I would be unable to keep up with my friends, whose lives change as much as mine does.

16.2 Non-restrictive and Restrictive Adjective Clauses

Adjective clauses come in two types: non-restrictive and restrictive. Non-restrictive clauses are separated from the rest of the sentence by a comma. Restrictive clauses are not.

16.2.1 Non-restrictive Adjective Clauses

When the information in the adjective clause is not essential to the meaning of the sentence, set it off with a comma or commas.

> My sister, **who lives in California**, is a doctor.
> (The adjective clause gives extra information. You can take out the information between the commas and not change the meaning of the sentence.)

> The Eiffel Tower has an elevator, **which I rode to the top.**

 Non-restrictive clauses always use a comma.

16.2.2 Restrictive Adjective Clauses

When the information in the adjective clause is essential to the meaning of the sentence, do not set it off with a comma or commas. If you take a restrictive clause out of the sentence, either the sentence will not make sense or the meaning will not be correct.

> My sister **who lives in California** is a doctor.
> (The adjective clause gives essential information if you have more than one sister. If you take out the information, it's not clear which sister you mean.)

> The car **that has a broken headlight** belongs to my brother.
> (The adjective clause specifies a particular car.)

Exercise 3   Use the extra information in the second sentence to create a non-restrictive adjective clause that you add to the first sentence. To begin the clause, use the relative pronoun in parentheses. Be sure to use commas to set off the clause.

1. Tashkent is experiencing economic growth these days.
   Tashkent is the capital of Uzbekistan. (which)

   <u>Tashkent, which is the capital of</u>

   <u>Uzbekistan, is experiencing economic</u>

   <u>growth these days.</u>

2. My boss is planning to transfer to Uzbekistan.
   My boss has been working for the company for 10 years. (who)

   _____

   _____

3. His consulting firm is opening a new Central Asian office.
   The firm is one of the most successful in the country. (which)

   _____

   _____

4. The consulting firm's financial advisors were happy with the expansion.
   The advisors routinely analyze economic trends abroad. (who)

   _____

   _____

Editing

∧ **Exercise 4**   Read the following sentences and underline the adjective clause. If the sentence is punctuated correctly, put a C in the blank. If it is not punctuated correctly, put an X in the blank and make the correction.

   __C__ 1. My parents, <u>who are now retired</u>, live in a suburb of London.

   __X__ 2. Their youngest son , <u>who is a student at London's School of Economics</u> , lives

   there.

   _____ 3. This university which is one of the most prestigious in all of Europe caters to

   some of the brightest young minds of today.

   _____ 4. The students who study there can be assured that they will get a quality

   education.

_____ 5. High-paying jobs will certainly be available for the students who graduate from the London School of Economics.

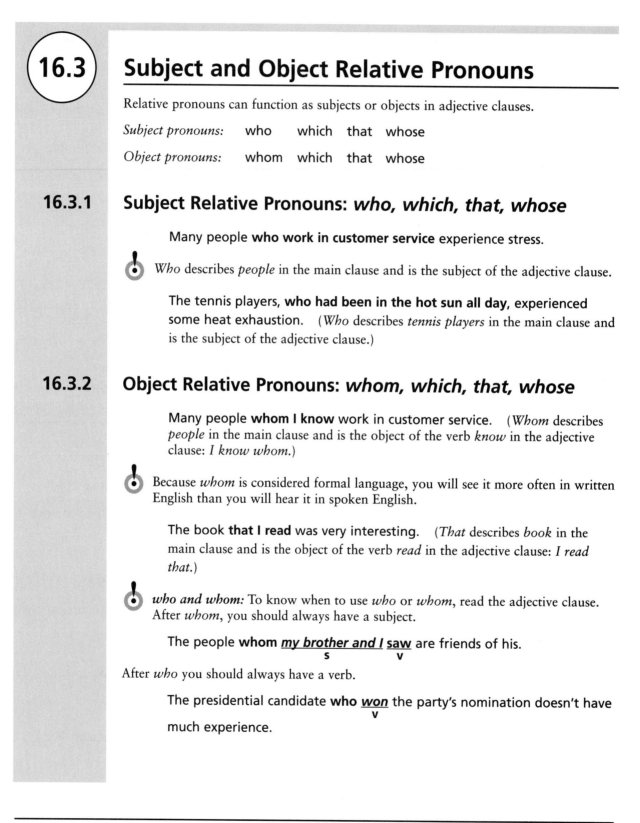

16.3   Subject and Object Relative Pronouns

Relative pronouns can function as subjects or objects in adjective clauses.

Subject pronouns: who   which   that   whose

Object pronouns: whom   which   that   whose

16.3.1   Subject Relative Pronouns: *who, which, that, whose*

Many people **who work in customer service** experience stress.

Who describes *people* in the main clause and is the subject of the adjective clause.

The tennis players, **who had been in the hot sun all day**, experienced some heat exhaustion.   (*Who* describes *tennis players* in the main clause and is the subject of the adjective clause.)

16.3.2   Object Relative Pronouns: *whom, which, that, whose*

Many people **whom I know** work in customer service.   (*Whom* describes *people* in the main clause and is the object of the verb *know* in the adjective clause: *I know whom.*)

Because *whom* is considered formal language, you will see it more often in written English than you will hear it in spoken English.

The book **that I read** was very interesting.   (*That* describes *book* in the main clause and is the object of the verb *read* in the adjective clause: *I read that.*)

who and whom: To know when to use *who* or *whom*, read the adjective clause. After *whom*, you should always have a subject.

The people **whom <u>*my brother and I*</u> <u>saw</u>** are friends of his.
                                    s   v

After *who* you should always have a verb.

The presidential candidate **who <u>won</u>** the party's nomination doesn't have
                                                       v

much experience.

Exercise 5 Read the paragraph and insert the correct relative pronouns in the blanks. Sometimes more than one answer is possible.

International travel has changed dramatically in the past 50 years. In the mid-twentieth century, people ___who/that___ wanted to travel to exotic destinations often
                                   1
went by ship. Such famous vessels as the *Queen Mary* were commonly used by travelers

_____ ventured abroad. However, since the invention and modernization of
        2
the jet plane, _____ has continued to grow in popularity, transatlantic ocean
                        3
liners have become less popular. One reason is the speed of the journey. Ocean liners,

_____ often take more than one week to get from the United States to Europe,
        4
are not practical for businesspeople. For example, a person _____ a company
                                                                    5
sends to Europe for a convention cannot spare such a long time traveling. This person's

objective, _____ is standard procedure for most businesses, is to go to the
                6
convention, do business, then come home. Some people, however, are tired of the "faster

is better" mentality _____ modern airlines are advertising. They are now
                            7
looking for alternative, more exotic modes of travel. For these people, _____
                                                                                8
are anticipating the "journey" as much as visiting the destination, high-priced ocean liner

trips are just the ticket!

Subject and Object Relative Pronouns

16.3.2 Omitting the Object Relative Pronoun

When the relative pronoun is the object of the adjective clause, native English speakers often omit the relative pronoun.*

> The women **whom I regularly see on Sundays** are my mother's friends.

> The women **I regularly see on Sundays** are my mother's friends.

> The job advertisement **that the company provided to the newspaper** appeared last week.

> The job advertisement **the company provided to the newspaper** appeared last week.

🛇 It is incorrect to omit the relative pronoun when it refers to the subject of the adjective clause.

Incorrect: The girl is sitting in the park looks nervous.

Correct: The girl **who is sitting in the park** looks nervous.

_____

*(See also Section 16.7 about adjective clause reductions.)

Editing

∧ **Exercise 6**   Read the diary entry and circle the six relative pronouns. If a relative pronoun can be eliminated, draw a line through it.

Dear Diary,

Today was a very exciting day for me. It was my first day in high school, and I was extremely excited. I signed up for the Spanish class ~~which~~ I had wanted for a long time. Surprise! I got into the class! The teacher, who is from Malaga, Spain, is very nice. I also got into a chemistry class. The lab, which is filled with all sorts of scientific equipment, is a bit scary, but I think it will be interesting. Lunch time was great because I got to see all the friends that I hadn't seen all summer long. Overall, I think this will be a wonderful year. There are so many interesting extracurricular activities that I want to participate in, as well. Overall, I think this is a year that will keep me busy and happy!

16.4 Relative Pronouns as Objects of Prepositions in Adjective Clauses

In addition to functioning as subjects or as objects, relative pronouns can also begin adjective clauses that function as objects of prepositions. Here are some examples with the prepositions *to* and *for*.

> The fitness club **to *which* I belong** is co-ed.   (*Which* is the object of the preposition *to* and refers to *club* in the main clause.)

Other variations are possible when there is a preposition in the adjective clause:

> The fitness club ***which* I belong *to*** is co-ed.

> The fitness club ***that* I belong *to*** is co-ed.

Incorrect: The fitness club ***that* I belong** is co-ed.   (Be careful not to forget the preposition if it is necessary.)

Incorrect: The fitness club **to *that* I belong** is co-ed.   (Don't put a preposition before the relative pronoun *that*.)

Correct: The fitness club **I belong *to*** is co-ed.   (relative pronoun omitted)

Incorrect: The woman **for *who* you bought the flowers** was very happy. (Don't put a preposition before the relative pronoun *who*.)

Correct: The woman **for *whom* you bought the flowers** was very happy to receive them.

Exercise 7   In each pair of sentences, change the second sentence to an adjective clause. Add a relative pronoun and commas where they are needed.

1. a. The college has a professional development office.
   b. George just graduated from the college.

   The college from which George just graduated has a professional development office.

2. a. The woman works in the university's professional development office.
   b. George spoke to the woman.

   _____

   _____

3. a. The Student Services Building is near the center of campus.
   b. This office is located in the Student Services Building.

   _____

   _____

4. a. The university students are recent graduates.
   b. These services are most beneficial for university students.

   _____

   _____

5. a. Some of the employment tests took two hours to complete.
   b. George paid a small fee for some of these tests.

   _____

   _____

6. a. A private employment agency would be his last resort.
   b. George has heard good things about this agency.

   _____

   _____

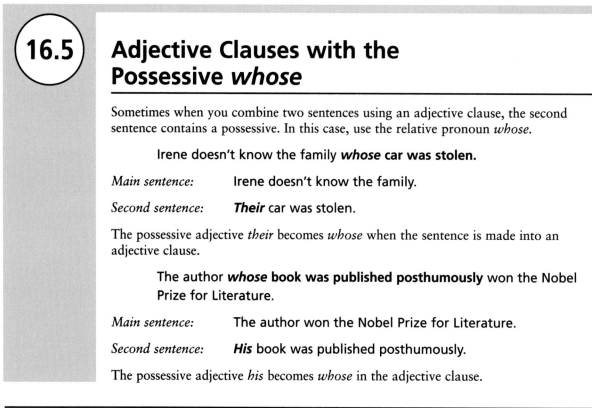

(16.5) Adjective Clauses with the Possessive *whose*

Sometimes when you combine two sentences using an adjective clause, the second sentence contains a possessive. In this case, use the relative pronoun *whose*.

Irene doesn't know the family **whose car was stolen.**

Main sentence:　　Irene doesn't know the family.

Second sentence:　**Their** car was stolen.

The possessive adjective *their* becomes *whose* when the sentence is made into an adjective clause.

The author **whose book was published posthumously** won the Nobel Prize for Literature.

Main sentence:　　The author won the Nobel Prize for Literature.

Second sentence:　**His** book was published posthumously.

The possessive adjective *his* becomes *whose* in the adjective clause.

Exercise 8   Study the picture and write an original sentence about each student. Use an adjective clause with the relative pronoun *whose*.

1.   *The boy whose glasses are on his head is Charles.*

2.   _____

     _____

3.   _____

     _____

4.   _____

     _____

5.   _____

     _____

16.6   Adjective Clauses That Describe Place, Time, and Reason

An adjective clause can describe a place, a time, or a reason. These clauses begin with the relative adverbs *where*, *when*, and *why*.

16.6.1   Adjective Clauses That Express Place: *where*

Use the relative adverb *where* to describe a place.

> The city **where I was born** is an ancient Roman site.

> The rooms **where George Washington slept** are now famous landmarks.

 When we talk about places, we often use the prepositions *in* and *at*.

> **in** Singapore   **at** the beach

In adjective clauses the relative adverb *where* often replaces the phrase *in which* or *at which*.

> The city **where I was born** = The city **in which I was born**

> The rooms **where George Washington slept** = The rooms **which George Washington slept in**

16.6.2   Adjective Clauses That Express Time: *when*

Use the relative adverb *when* to express time and time relationships.

> The exact moment **when I won the Spanish poetry contest** was last Friday afternoon at 3:15 p.m.

> Do you recall the day **when we got married?**

 In adjective clauses, *when* can replace *in which* or *on which*.

> The exact moment **when I won the Spanish poetry contest** = The exact moment **in which I won the Spanish poetry contest**

> The day **when we got married** = The day **on which we got married**

16.6.3   Adjective Clauses That Give Reasons: *why*

To give reasons, you can use *for which* or *that* to begin the adjective clause.

> The reason **for which Dr. Hughes won the hospital award** was his hard work.

> The reason **that Dr. Hughes won the hospital award** was his hard work.

Exercise 9 Complete the dialogue using the words from the box. You may use some of the words more than once.

who(m)	which	that	whose	where	when

John: Hey, Pablo! What's new?

Pablo: Not much. My professor just returned the exams _____ we took
                     1

last week.

John: Oh yeah? How'd you do?

Pablo: Not as well as I had hoped, unfortunately. I misunderstood two questions

_____ were in part 2 of the test, and they were worth 20 points each!
     2

John: That's a bummer. Maybe you can do some extra work. Is the professor

_____ teaches the class flexible?
     3

Pablo: I think so. I just can't believe that the reason _____ I missed those
                     4

questions was because I read the directions too quickly.

John: Hey, that happens. I remember one time _____ I thought I had done
                     5

so well on a test, and later I found out that all my answers were supposed to be

the opposite! You know how sometimes questions ask for the negative? So, I

understand.

Pablo: I don't know. Maybe I *should* talk to my professor. This exam grade

_____ I got will ruin my grade point average.
     6

John: Look, it's noon. Why don't you go to the place _____ your professor
                     7

has lunch and talk to him? It can't hurt.

Pablo: You're right, John. I'm going to go right now. And I'll let you know what

happens. If nothing else, I've learned that this is a professor _____
                     8

directions are tricky!

John: Good luck.

Pablo: Thanks …

(16.7) Adjective Clause Reductions

Sometimes a clause, which contains a subject and a verb, can be reduced or shortened to a phrase. To do this you usually omit the relative pronouns and alter the verb. Here are some rules about clause reductions.

1. If the adjective clause contains the verb *be* (in any form), you can omit the relative pronoun and the verb *be*.

> The man *who is* next to me must be a diplomat of some kind.
>
> ⇩
>
> The man next to me must be a diplomat of some kind.

> People *who were* born before 1960 in the United States are called "Baby Boomers."
>
> ⇩
>
> People born before 1960 in the United States are called "Baby Boomers."

> Shakespeare, *who is* the most well-known British author of all time, continues to fascinate readers today.
>
> ⇩
>
> Shakespeare, the most well-known British author of all time, continues to fascinate readers today.

❗ This particular reduction is called an *appositive*. It is a noun phrase that gives a definition or explanation of the previously mentioned noun.

2. You can sometimes reduce adjective clauses without the verb *be*. In this case, omit the relative pronoun and change the verb to the *-ing* or present participle form.

> We study in a university *which consists* of six separate colleges.
>
> ⇩
>
> We study in a university **consisting** of six separate colleges.

> People *who live* in cities generally don't get as much exercise as those *who live* in rural areas.
>
> ⇩
>
> People **living** in cities generally don't get as much exercise as those **living** in rural areas.

Editing

∧ **Exercise 10**   Underline the adjective clauses in these sentences. If an adjective clause can be reduced to a phrase, make those changes above the clause.

1. More than two hundred craftspeople were present at the art fair.

2. Some of the people who presented their crafts came from Asian countries.

3. Many of the pottery samples which were on hand were hundreds of years old.

4. Some spectators who could afford it bought some special items.

5. Most people, however, were content to just look at the fine arts and crafts that were being shown.

6. Khalimov and Sons, who are well-known artisans from Kazakstan, had particularly interesting vases and bowls.

7. Their studio, which is located in Almaty, has been around for almost 300 years.

8. It was a pleasure to see so many people who learned about ethnic arts and crafts.

Exercise 11   Circle the letter of the correct answer. Watch out for punctuation!

1. The car _____ I was riding in broke down last night.
   a. who
   b. in which
   c. that
   d. whom

2. How many people _____ vote oppose the election process?
   a. which
   b. that
   c. ∅
   d. whom

3. The Great Wall of China _____ is the world's largest man-made structure.
   a. which can be seen from space
   b. who can be viewed from space
   c. , that can be viewed from space,
   d. , which can be viewed from space,

Adjective Clause Reductions   **229**

4. The dog _____ tail you pulled is hiding behind the chair.
   a. that
   b. which
   c. whose
   d. of whom

5. Can you tell me how to get to the bank _____ the student discounts?
   a. where offers
   b. in which offers
   c. offering
   d. whose offering

6. My car, _____, is not worth anything anymore!
   a. whose engine is falling apart
   b. that engine is falling apart
   c. in which engine is falling apart
   d. for which engine is falling apart

Editing

∧ **Exercise 12**   In each sentence one of the four underlined words or phrases is not correct. Circle the letter of the error and write the correction above the error.

1. The <u>music in which</u> you were used to <u>listening</u> to when you <u>were younger</u> is no
        A   B   C

   longer in <u>fashion</u>.
        D

2. Can someone <u>who</u> works here <u>help me</u> find the <u>room where</u> I need to be in, <u>please</u>?
           A   B   C   D

3. The city <u>where</u> Shakespeare <u>was born</u> is a national British Treasure, and thousands
          A   B

   of people visit <u>Stratford which is</u> a small town on the Avon <u>River, every year</u>.
               C   D

4. People <u>trying</u> to advance in business too quickly often lose <u>their sense</u> of self; this
         A   B

   can lead to problems for <u>which</u> there are no solutions <u>for</u>.
                 C   D

⊚riginal Writing

Exercise 13   Write a paragraph or short essay about your school. Give descriptions of some of your classmates, the classrooms, your instructors, or the textbooks. Use at least five adjective clauses in your writing. Try to use some restrictive clauses (no commas) and non-restrictive clauses (commas). Use as many of the following relative pronouns as you can: *who(m)*, *where*, *which*, *when*, *that*, *why*, and *whose*. Include some adjective clauses with prepositions. Exchange your writing with a partner. Review your partner's paragraph, underlining all the adjective clauses and checking for their correct use.

> If you need help with the steps of writing a paragraph, see Appendix 5.
>
> **www**   You will find additional exercises for the grammar in this chapter on the Top 20 website at **http://esl.college.hmco.com/students**

The small dish on the sidewalk was extremely old, and the antique dealer knew at once

WC

<u>*what*</u> *it was very valuable.*

Noun Clauses

This chapter reviews everything you need to know about noun clauses. First, a definition:

A noun clause is a group of words with a subject and a verb that can be a subject, an object, or an object of a preposition.

My roommate told me **that** *he signed up for the course yesterday.* *(The noun clause is the object of the verb* told.*)*

(17.1) Forms of Noun Clauses

A noun clause usually consists of three key components:

- A relative pronoun or adverb—many of the same ones that begin adjective clauses (see Chapter 16)
- A subject
- A verb

These are the words that commonly begin noun clauses.

who	whom	what	when	where	why
which	how	how (adjective)	whether	if	that

-*ever* Words

whoever	whomever	whatever	whenever
whichever	wherever	however	however (adjective)

> ***Why* the accident happened** is a mystery.

> No one knows ***whether* the meeting is on the first floor or the second floor.**

> The witnesses said ***that* the man entered the bank around 9 a.m.**

> You can talk to ***whomever* you choose.**

> It is important ***that* all of the passengers arrive at the airport early.**

In sentences with the previous structure:

It + *be* + ADJECTIVE + (NOUN CLAUSE: *that* + S + V)

remember to include the word *It* as the subject. Every sentence needs a subject!

Incorrect: Is necessary ***that* all the students take both English and science.**

Correct: **It** is necessary ***that* all the students take both English and science.**

Incorrect: Is obligatory ***that* people be at least eighteen years old to vote?**

Correct: Is **it** obligatory ***that* people be at least eighteen years old to vote?**

Sometimes the relative pronoun that begins the noun clause is also the subject of the clause. This may happen with *who, what,* or *which.*

SUBJECT   VERB   OBJECT (noun clause)
No one understands **what** first ***causes* this chemical reaction.**
SUBJECT   VERB

SUBJECT (noun clause)   VERB   OBJECT
What first ***causes* this chemical reaction** is the addition of oxygen.
SUBJECT   VERB

Exercise 1   Read this essay and underline the seven noun clauses.

Translating Leadership Styles

From country to country and even from culture to culture, styles of what people consider good leadership vary. In the United States, leadership means getting things done. CEOs generally have a great deal of authority and are expected to use it. Qualities that make an effective leader in Chicago or Dallas, however, might not be valued in England or Japan. What experts in the global marketplace are coming to understand is that no two cultures view leadership in the same way.

According to analysts, effective Japanese leaders make employees feel secure, they expect compliance, and they display a "harmonious personality." Japanese leaders assume that employees have a family-like loyalty to the company. In effect, they act as "parents" in the family, supporting individuals and demonstrating understanding but maintaining firm control over information and operations.

In German and Austrian organizations, a style called "Towards a Common Goal" is prevalent. Each department has a clear chain of command, and information and instruction are passed down from top to bottom. Leaders, who are primarily autocratic, base their authority on their place in the organization's hierarchy. Thus, in Germany and Austria, which position a leader occupies within a company is crucial.

Accord and compromise characterize leadership in Sweden and Finland, where leaders motivate employees through communication and consensual decision making. Aptly called "Consensus," this leadership style requires that the company maintain open communication. In fact, Swedish law mandates that management discuss important decisions with all employees before implementation.

Regardless of the country or culture, experts list three skills that are a *must* for good global leaders. Whoever has good interpersonal skills and financial discipline and gives employees minimal rules and maximum trust will be a good leader anywhere.

Functions of Noun Clauses

A noun clause functions in a sentence just like a noun—as a subject, object of the verb, or object of a preposition. Remember that you can recognize a noun clause by one of the relative pronouns or adverbs that begins the clause (see Section 17.1 for a list of these words).

Don't confuse noun clauses with noun phrases.

Noun Phrase	Noun Clause
The cause of the hotel fire is a mystery.	*How* the fire began is a mystery.
The government is investigating **the cause of the hotel fire.**	The government is investigating *how* the hotel fire began.

17.2.1 Noun Clause as Subject

A noun clause can be the subject in a sentence. It is important to keep in mind that a noun clause as a unit is singular, so it requires a singular verb.

SUBJECT (noun clause) VERB OBJECT
<u>**What** really *causes* this skin reaction</u> consumes millions of research dollars.
SUBJECT VERB
(relative pronoun)

17.2.2 Noun Clause as Object of the Verb

A noun clause can be the object of a verb in a sentence. Remember to use the correct word order in the clause.

SUBJECT VERB OBJECT (noun clause)
An allergy to wheat limits <u>**how** a patient's body *can fight* back</u>.
ADVERB SUBJECT VERB

17.2.3 Noun Clause as Object of the Preposition

A noun clause can be the object of a preposition in a sentence.

PREPOSITION OBJECT (noun clause)
According to <u>**what** the doctor's report *said*</u>, an allergy may be the cause.
SUBJECT VERB
(relative pronoun)

PREPOSITION OBJECT (noun clause)
The doctor gave allergy medicine to <u>**whoever** *wanted* it</u>.
SUBJECT VERB
(relative pronoun)

In *that* clauses functioning as subjects of sentences, the word *that* is necessary. In all other cases, the word *that* is optional when it begins noun clauses. However, in formal speaking and in writing, we strongly recommend that you include the word that rather than omit it whenever it can occur.

Speaking (informal):

The report says six million people came to the U.S. between 1990 and 2000.

Writing (also formal speaking):

The report says **that** six million people came to the U.S. between 1990 and 2000.

Exercise 2 Read this joke about an antique collector and a cat. Write *NP* (noun phrase) or *NC* (noun clause) above each underlined group of words. Identify its function as *S* (subject), *OV* (object of the verb), or *OP* (object of the preposition).

An Antique Cat

1 NP S

1 An antique collector with lots of money was walking in the downtown area of a city one day. He saw **2** a small skinny cat on the sidewalk. The cat was drinking some milk from a small dish. The art collector looked again at the dish. **3** What the antique collector saw shocked him. **4** The small dish on the sidewalk was extremely old, and the antique dealer knew at once **5** that it was very valuable. He was so interested in **6** what he had just seen that he immediately walked into the store to talk to the owner about buying the valuable antique dish. The man did not want the owner to suspect **7** <u>that the dish was so valuable,</u> so he offered the owner some money for the cat. He said **8** <u>that he would pay $10 for the cat,</u> but the owner refused. The man was getting desperate, so he offered the owner **9** <u>a crisp fifty-dollar bill from his wallet.</u> At this point, the owner could no longer refuse **10** <u>what the man was offering.</u> Then the man quickly added, "You know … how about including the dish, too? That cat is probably used to eating from that dish." The owner replied, "No, sir, I'm sorry. You may be right about the cat and the dish, but that dish is not for sale. "Why not?" asked the man. The owner answered, "Well, I'll tell you **11** <u>why it's not for sale.</u> You see, it's my lucky dish. So far this week, I've sold **12** <u>fifteen skinny cats!"</u>

Editing
∧ **Exercise 3**   Some of the underlined groups of words in this paragraph contain an error. Circle the errors and write corrections above them.

The Art of Telling a Joke

We all know people who tell great jokes at parties and other gatherings. Perhaps you have wondered whether **1** <u>could you ever</u> be such a good joke teller. If so, there is good news for you. The skills needed to become a good joke teller can be practiced and learned. While it is true **2** <u>than</u> some people are naturally good at telling jokes, there are a good number of people who have become good joke tellers through practice. Good joke tellers completely understand **3** <u>what is their joke</u> before they start telling it. Good joke tellers can add **4** <u>whatever want</u> to the joke as they tell it, but they clearly know the details of the beginning, middle, and ending of the joke. **5** <u>Is also important</u> to consider **6** <u>who the audience is.</u> Perhaps you have learned through experience **7** <u>that</u> not all jokes are appropriate for all audiences. Finally, for a joke to be successful, it is imperative that the **8** <u>joke has</u> a good punch line. Do you wonder **9** <u>that you can learn these skills</u> for telling jokes? They are not so difficult. With the right amount of practice, **10** <u>is certain</u> that you can become a great joke teller.

∧ Exercise 4 Read this joke about who is in charge of the jungle. On the lines, write a correction for the errors in the corresponding underlined sections.

1. _____   5. _____

2. _____   6. _____

3. _____   7. _____

4. _____   8. _____

Who Is the Real King of the Jungle?

One day a lion woke up in a cranky mood. As he walked out from the bushes where he had been sleeping, he found a small monkey. The lion roared loudly and asked, "Do you know **1** <u>who is the king of the jungle</u>?"

The tiny, scared monkey quickly replied that **2** <u>was the king of the jungle the lion.</u> **3** <u>The monkey had given the anticipated answer</u> pleased the lion greatly. Feeling very satisfied, the lion walked slowly away from the little monkey.

Just minutes later, the lion ran into a rabbit. The rabbit realized **4** <u>that had</u> nowhere to hide, so it just sat there trembling. Again, the lion roared loudly and shouted, "Tell me **5** <u>who is the king of the jungle</u>."

The little rabbit answered as clearly as it could, "You are the king of the jungle." Feeling even better and more arrogant than before, the lion walked slowly away from the rabbit.

A few minutes later, the lion found himself in front of an old elephant. Once again, the lion roared and shouted, **6** <u>"Who the king of the jungle is?"</u>

The old elephant did not hesitate a second. He grabbed the lion with his trunk and threw the lion against a huge tree. The elephant did this three more times until the lion lay on the ground, exhausted and bruised. The lion was confused by **7** <u>that had just</u> happened.

"I don't know **8** <u>why did you do this</u>," said the lion. "If you don't know the answer to my question, there is no reason to get angry about it."

17.3 Common Problems with Noun Clauses

1. Wrong Word Order

Remember that the word order for noun clauses is

>   RELATIVE PRONOUN or ADVERB / SUBJECT / VERB

or, if the relative pronoun or adverb is also the subject,

>   SUBJECT (RELATIVE PRONOUN or ADVERB) / VERB

Incorrect: I don't know **when happened the accident.**

Correct: I don't know **when the accident happened.**

Incorrect: Can you remember **who is she?**

Correct: Can you remember **who she is?**

2. Omitting the Verb

Don't forget the verb in the main sentence!

Incorrect: **Why the pilot didn't show up** a mystery.

Correct: **Why the pilot didn't show up** *remains* a mystery.

Incorrect: **That teachers need more pay** a simple fact.

Correct: **That teachers need more pay** *is* a simple fact.

3. Wrong Verb Form After Certain Expressions

For certain expressions that mean "importance," you must always use the base form of the verb in the noun clause—not future tense, past tense, or even the added -*s* in third-person singular. Here are the expressions.

It is important that ...	suggest that ...	request that ...
It is imperative that ...	recommend that ...	insist that ...
It is necessary that ...	demand that ...	propose that ...

Incorrect: It is important that **Mr. Thompson is here at 9 a.m.**

Correct: It is important that **Mr. Thompson** *be* **here at 9 a.m.**

Incorrect: The airline recommended **that Kate arrives two hours early.**

Correct: The airline recommended **that Kate** *arrive* **two hours early.**

4. Wrong Verb Tense with Reported Speech

In reported speech, the verb in a noun clause is one tense "older" than the same verb in a sentence without a noun clause. In other words, *present* changes to *past*, *past* changes to *past perfect*, and *will* changes to *would*.

Quoted Speech	⇨	Reported Speech
Present tense: He said, "I **work** at IBM."	⇨	*Past tense:* He said **that he** *worked* **at IBM.**
Present progressive: He said, "I **am working** at IBM."	⇨	*Past progressive:* He said **that he** *was working* **at IBM.**
Past tense: He said, "I **worked** at IBM."	⇨	*Past perfect:* He said **that he** *had worked* **at IBM.**
Present perfect: He said, "I **have worked** at IBM."	⇨	*Past perfect:* He said **that he** *had worked* **at IBM.**

Incorrect: The 1990 report said **that the U.S. has 200 million people.**

Correct: The 1990 report said **that the U.S.** *had* **200 million people.**

Exercise 5   Change these questions to sentences with noun clauses.

1. When was Lincoln born?

   Nobody in my class can remember when Lincoln was born.

2. Why is it important to wear sunscreen in the summer?

   The nurse explained _____

   _____

3. Does Pepsi have more calories than Coca-Cola?

   I'm not sure _____

   _____

4. How far is Dallas from Denver?

   If you want to know_____

   _____, check the Internet.

5. Which websites have the best prices for T-shirts?

   This newspaper article discusses _____

   _____ .

6. When do geese migrate?

_____

_____ is related to the climate and seasons of the year.

7. Sammy said, "I'm hungry."

Sammy said _____

_____.

8. Why did the explosion occur?

The television reporters are talking about _____

_____.

Exercise 6   Complete these sentences to make true statements. Pay attention to the verb forms that you use in the noun clauses.

Topic: Traveling to a Foreign Country

1. It is important that a traveler _____

_____

2. Some governments require that travelers _____

_____

3. Some doctors suggest that a traveler to underdeveloped countries _____

_____

4. Airports can be crowded, so airlines recommend that an international traveler

_____

5. It is recommended that travelers with young children _____

_____

Exercise 7   Circle the letter of the correct answer. Be prepared to explain your answers.

1. _____ is certainly an interesting topic for discussion.
   a. That cats have whiskers   c. Why do cats have whiskers
   b. Why cats have whiskers   d. The whiskers that cats have

2. _____ the answer to that extremely difficult question.
   a. Does anyone know   c. Nobody knows
   b. Does no one know   d. Why nobody knows

3. The city's election report from 2002 stated that _____ errors.
   a. the election had   c. had the election
   b. the election has   d. has the election

4. It is important that each traveler _____ a visa if the country that he or she is
   visiting requires this.
   a. obtain   c. obtains
   b. must obtain   d. is obtaining

5. Although I studied for the test for over a week, I cannot recall _____.
   a. what is the capital of Ecuador   c. which city is built on a pyramid
   b. how many moons does Mars have   d. how many angles has a pentagon

6. How the accident _____ unknown.
   a. did it happen   c. is happened
   b. happened   d. happened is

∧ **Exercise 8**   In each sentence one of the four underlined words or phrases is not correct. Circle the letter of the error and write a correction above it.

Economic Problems

1. Due to the severe problems <u>that have</u> resulted from the banking scandal and the
   A

   subsequent failure of the government to <u>take the necessary measures</u> to avoid
   B

   <u>such a problem</u> again, most economists are predicting <u>if</u> the national economy will
   C   D

   suffer a period of hyperinflation.

2. Exactly <u>which step the government leaders should take</u> next <u>are</u> among the many
   A   B

   topics <u>that</u> Congress <u>will discuss in its meeting next week.</u>
   C   D

3. <u>Both economists and politicians</u> note <u>that</u> very few <u>individuals really understand</u>
   A   B   C

   how devastating <u>can be a long period of hyperinflation.</u>
   D

4. The good news for any country that <u>is facing</u> hyperinflation is <u>which</u> several
   A   B

   countries <u>have had</u> this problem and were <u>able to solve it.</u>
   C   D

⊙riginal Writing

Exercise 9   Write a joke in your own words that is appropriate to share in class. There are two ways to work on this assignment. 1) Find a joke in English from an English-speaking friend, from a magazine, or from the Internet; or 2) translate a joke from another language. In either case, be sure to write the joke in your own words. Do not plagiarize. Include three to six noun clauses in your joke in different functions in the sentences. Then exchange your writing with a partner, underlining all the noun clauses and checking for their correct use.

> If you need help with the steps of writing a paragraph, see Appendix 5.
>
> **www**   You will find additional exercises for the grammar in this chapter on the Top 20 website at **http://esl.college.hmco.com/students**

While I was in the middle of making dinner last night ∧ᴾ, a serious car accident occurred outside my apartment.

Adverb Clauses

This chapter reviews everything you need to know about adverb clauses. First, a definition:

An adverb clause is a group of words with a subject and a verb that modifies a verb, an adjective, or another adverb.

My roommate *will go* home to visit her parents **when** she finishes her research paper.   *(The adverb clause modifies, or tells more about, the verb* will go.*)*

Adverb Clauses and Subordinating Conjunctions

You will recognize adverb clauses by the following subordinating conjunctions, most of which come at the beginning of the clause.

Reason/Cause:	**because since**
Condition:	**if even if unless when in case in the event that**
Contrast:	**while although**
Concession:	**although though even though**
Result:	**so so that** *(not used to begin sentences)*
Time relationship:	**after as soon as before when while until whenever as**

> Hee-Jon went to the park *because* **the weather was fine.**   (reason)
>
> *Because* **the weather was fine,** Hee-Jon went to the park.

Here is the rule for punctuating an adverb clause: Put a comma after the clause if the clause begins the sentence. If the adverb clause comes after the main clause, no punctuation is needed.

> *Although* **the movie was well advertised,** it didn't make a lot of money at the box office.
>
> *Until* **we get money to buy a car,** we're going to take the bus to work.

Exercise 1   In each sentence, underline the subordinating conjunction and write its function on the line.

1. <u>Whenever</u> Irene looks for a new job, she gets nervous. _____*time*_____

2. This happens because she doesn't have a lot of experience in interviewing.

   _____

3. If she took a course in job hunting, she would probably be more confident.

   _____

4. She will appear more motivated and ready to start a new career after doing

   this. _____

5. While the course is not free, the benefits will help her in the long run.

_____

∧ **Exercise 2**   Read the following sentences. Some contain errors in punctuation or syntax. If the sentence is correct, put a C in the blank. If the sentence is incorrect, put an X in the blank and make the correction.

Trouble in the Steel Industry

    __X__   1. While they are theoretically beneficial, global trade agreements do not always work to the benefit of everyone. An example of this is the international steel industry.

    _____ 2. As the U.S. steel industry began losing more and more money, its steelworkers worried about losing their jobs

    _____ 3. The domestic situation deteriorated steadily as cheaper steel imports began to flood the U.S. market.

    _____ 4. Because the president wanted to protect the domestic steel industry he decided to levy a heavy tax on steel imports.

    _____ 5. Importers of steel from abroad began to question the lawfulness of this action, after it was decided upon.

    _____ 6. So that it could prevent this from happening again the European Union called on the World Trade Organization (WTO) to investigate.

    _____ 7. While this situation can be remedied by using external forces such as the WTO, it is unlikely that the import/export battles between the United States and the rest of the world will end soon.

Exercise 3   Some clauses in this paragraph are incomplete. Read the paragraph once. Then go back and fill in the missing information.

A Productive Day

After I _____,
1
I immediately went to my room. It was extremely dirty, so _____
2
_____. My family hates it when

_____. This
3
process took about two hours, but it was not unpleasant. I listened to my favorite CD

while _____.
4
When I finished cleaning, I _____.
5
After that, I called my best friend Joey. We like to play basketball together if _____
6
_____. As soon as we finished talking,

_____. We
7
played one on one for a few hours, then I went home. Because I didn't have any

homework, _____.
8
All in all, it was a productive day.

18.2 Adverb Clauses and Verb Tense

In sentences with adverb clauses, use the same verb tense in both parts of the sentence—the main clause and the adverb clause.

> Whenever the manager **calls** a meeting, the employees **get** nervous. (present tense)

> Because the manager **called** a meeting, the employees **got** nervous. (past tense)

Exercise 4   Complete each sentence with information that makes sense. Be sure to pay attention to the verb tense in both clauses.

1. When dot.com companies first appeared, many business people _____

   _____

2. This economic boom began to drop as _____

   _____

3. Many investors lost money after _____

   _____

4. While dot.coms struggle to hold on to their profits, other respectable companies ___

   _____

5. Because investors are showing less interest in risky ventures, they _____

   _____

Exercise 5 Use the introductory information in column 1 and the subordinating conjunctions in column 2 to create sentences with adverbial clauses. Draw a line from each main sentence to a subordinating conjunction that makes sense, then complete the adverb clause. Remember, an adverb clause takes the form: SUBORDINATING CONJUNCTION + S + V. More than one match is correct.

Main Sentence

1. The students were happy

2. My little brother is crying

3. The flowers have bloomed

4. Nodira is going to buy a new car

5. The rainforest will disappear

6. People continue to smoke

7. Sheila has become a doctor

8. Paris is a beloved tourist destination

Adverb Clause

although _____

_____

because *they finished their exams*

if _____

_____

even though _____

_____

after_____

_____

while_____

_____

before _____

_____

unless _____

_____

Exercise 6 Choose six sentences from Exercise 5 and rewrite them using the adverb clause at the beginning of the sentence. Be sure to use appropriate punctuation.

1. *Because they finished their exams, the students were happy.*

2. _____

_____

3. _____

_____

4. _____

_____

5. _____

_____

6. _____

_____

18.3 Adverb Clause Reductions—Forming Adverb Phrases

Sometimes a clause, which contains a subject and a verb, can be reduced or shortened to a phrase. To reduce an adverb clause to an adverb phrase, you usually omit the subject and sometimes alter or omit the verb. The following subordinating conjunctions begin adverb clauses that can be reduced.

if	even if	unless	when	while	although
though	after	before	until	whenever	even though

There are two ways to form an adverb phrase from an adverb clause.

1. Delete the subject and the *be* verb.

   When John is tired, *he* usually goes home to take a nap.

   When tired, *John* usually goes home to take a nap.

 Sometimes you need to change the pronoun in the main clause to the specific noun. *John* replaces the pronoun *he* in the main clause.

2. If the adverb clause contains a verb that is not a *be* verb, you can sometimes delete the subject and change the verb to the progressive form.

   While Karen ate the pizza, *she* watched a horror movie on TV.

   While eating the pizza, *Karen* watched a horror movie on TV.

18.3.1 Dangling Modifiers

If you're not careful when you reduce adverb clauses, it's easy to create a dangling modifier. First, make sure that the subject of the adverb clause is the same as the subject of the independent clause. If the subjects are different, reducing the adverb clause to an adverb phrase creates a dangling modifier.

Correct: While Irene was studying, the dog began to bark.

Incorrect: While studying, the dog began to bark.   (The dog was not studying, so *studying* is a dangling modifier. It doesn't have anything to modify that makes sense.)

Another way to check that your adverb phrase is correct is to take the subject of the main clause, put it in front of the adverb clause, and see if it makes sense.

The dog, while studying ...   (You can stop there because the dog can't study.)

Editing

∧ **Exercise 7**   Underline the adverb clauses in the following paragraph. If an adverb clause can be reduced to an adverb phrase, make the changes above the clause.

Lisa

While ~~Lisa was~~ hiking through the Andes Mountains, ~~she~~ had a very bad scare. She had seen a rocky hill not too far away and decided to try to climb it. When Lisa was half-way up the hill, the rocky surface began to crumble. She was terrified, and she didn't know what to do. She held on to the rocks and tried to adjust her footing. After she got a good foothold, she attempted to resume climbing. Thirty minutes later, an exhausted and frightened Lisa reached the top of the hill. Nowadays Lisa stays away from rocky mountains. Even if she is invited by her closest friends to go hiking, she'll politely refuse.

Editing

∧ Exercise 8   In some of the following sentences, the underlined part contains an error. If the sentence is correct, put a C in the blank. If the sentence is incorrect, identify the error in the blank as *P* (punctuation), *IR* (incorrect reduction), or *DM* (dangling modifier). Then make corrections above the original sentence.

<u>IR</u>   1. <u>Before ∧̲ ̲became a famous inventor</u>, Thomas Edison was known by his teachers
       he
       as a lazy student.

_____ 2. The military operation was not supported by <u>the public, although</u> the
       president ordered the mission.

_____ 3. <u>Even though it was raining</u>, the Olympic competition was carried out as it had
       been scheduled.

_____ 4. <u>Because the educational policy was amended</u>, the business school students had
       to take an exit examination prior to graduation.

_____ 5. The delegates returned to their <u>hotel after the presentations ended</u>.

_____ 6. <u>While making dinner last night</u>, a serious car accident occurred outside my
       apartment.

_____ 7. <u>Unless the workers unite</u>, the company will not prosper in the global
       marketplace.

_____ 8. <u>After hearing the government's latest pollution statistics</u> many scientific
       experts commented on the validity of the numbers.

18.4 | *Because* versus *because of*

Because and *because of* take different grammatical structures, and it is important to know the difference.

Adverb clauses can begin with *because*.

> **Because it was raining,** we decided to cancel our trip to the mountains.

Adverb phrases can begin with *because of*.

> **Because of the rain,** we decided to cancel our trip to the mountains.

 The two sentences have the same meaning, but note that in the second sentence, *because of* must be followed by a noun.

Exercise 9 In each sentence, change the adverb clause to an adverb phrase or change the adverb phrase to an adverb clause.

1. Because of his accounting mistake, the company lost thousands of dollars.

   Because he made an accounting mistake, the company lost thousands of dollars.

2. Because the driver was reckless, his car ran into a ditch.

   _____

   _____

3. We didn't get to see the concert because the tickets were too expensive.

   _____

   _____

4. Because of the difficulty level of the exam, the majority of the students failed.

   _____

   _____

5. Greece's agriculture production declined because of the drought.

   _____

   _____

6. Because the fans got too rowdy, the soccer match was cancelled.

_____

_____

Exercise 10   Circle the letter of the correct answer.

1. After the man _____ his bonus, he took his family out to celebrate.
   a. got   c. will get
   b. is getting   d. gets

2. _____ in the military, many people decide to become commercial pilots.
   a. After serve   c. After they serves
   b. After be serve   d. After serving

3. Henry received a full scholarship to Stanford University _____ excellent grades.
   a. because his   c. because of his
   b. because he   d. because

4. Whenever Joanne _____, she brews some natural tea and meditates.
   a. gets a headache   c. got a headache
   b. will get a headache   d. gets a headache

5. _____ she had no professional dance experience, Phoebe became a famous folk dancer.
   a. Because   c. Although
   b. Unless   d. If

6. While the soup was simmering on the stove, Allie _____ her homework.
   a. does   c. has done
   b. was doing   d. is doing

Editing
∧ **Exercise 11**   In each sentence one of the four underlined words or phrases is not correct. Circle the letter of the error and write the correction above the error.

1. <u>Although it beautiful</u>, the <u>5-star hotel</u> was <u>too</u> expensive for <u>me to enjoy</u>.
        A   **B**   **C**   **D**

2. <u>After Ned</u> returned from <u>work</u>, he <u>puts on</u> his favorite music <u>to relax</u>.
     A   **B**   **C**   **D**

3. Stem cell research <u>will certainly remain</u> a controversial <u>issue if</u> conservatives <u>and</u>
                    A   **B**   **C**

   liberals <u>not come</u> to a consensus very soon.
       D

4. <u>Though</u> <u>boring</u>, the spectators <u>decided</u> to stay and watch the <u>remaining portion</u> of
    A   **B**   **C**   **D**

   the Broadway musical.

Original Writing

Exercise 12   Write a paragraph or short essay about something that you did as a child that you were punished for or something that you were praised for. Include some of the following information.

- What you did

- Whom you were with

- How it happened

- Why you did it

- How you got caught or how someone found out

- What kind of punishment or praise you received

- If you ever did it again

Use at least five adverb clauses or adverb phrases in your writing. Refer to the list of subordinating conjunctions on page 244 to help you. Exchange your writing with a partner. Review your partner's paragraph, underlining all the adverb clauses or adverb phrases and checking for their correct use.

If you need help with the steps of writing a paragraph, see Appendix 5.

www   You will find additional exercises for the grammar in this chapter on the Top 20 website at **http://esl.college.hmco.com/students**

The runner ran so hard in the race that she was out of breathe before the third mile.
WC

19

Confusing Pairs of Words:
Verbs and Nouns

In this chapter you will review and practice pairs of verbs and nouns that often confuse writers and speakers of English. (Chapter 20 covers confusing pairs of pronouns, adjectives, adverbs, and prepositions.)

Verbs and Nouns

The following verbs and nouns sound similar and can be easily confused. Study their meanings and the examples.

affect   verb; to influence

> The words of that speech always **affect** me deeply.

effect   noun; the result

> His speech had an **effect** on my way of thinking about the issue.

effect   verb; to produce a change (less commonly used)

> The government **effected** changes in the law to guarantee its citizens' rights.

advise   verb; to recommend

> The arresting officer has to **advise** you of your right to remain silent.

advice   noun; recommendation

> The lawyer's **advice** to her client was to plead not guilty.

breathe   verb; to inhale and exhale air

> It's so hot and stuffy in here I can hardly **breathe**.

breath   noun; the air you take in or let out

> How long can you hold your **breath** under water?

desert   verb; to leave or abandon

> They **deserted** the building after a fire destroyed it.

desert   noun; a dry place with sand and little vegetation

> The Mojave **Desert** lies in southern California.

dessert   noun; the last course of a meal

> They offered cake, pie, and ice cream for **dessert**.

Editing
∧ **Exercise 1**   Read the passage below. Find the five errors in verb and noun usage and correct them.

Work-related stress affects more people today than ever before. Psychologists who have studied the overall effect of stress on humans have discovered that it is possible to reverse the negative affects work-related stress can cause.

Often helpful in reducing head, neck, lower back, and shoulder pain, which affect people most often, is yoga. Yoga is a system of poses used to control one's body and mind. Learning to breath correctly and to coordinate the breath with movement is an important part of yoga. A shallow breath will not allow you to relax enough to attain needed physical flexibility. Taking deeper breathes improves oxygenation of the blood, just as aerobic exercise does.

To get started, experts advice you first see your doctor for a physical exam. Next, enroll in a yoga class to learn the correct postures from a teacher. With that advice and after practicing the postures as you breathe deeply, in time you will begin to experience the benefits of a relaxed nervous system and stronger immune system.

Once you begin a program of yoga or any other regimen to help deal with the effects of stress, it is important not to desert it. On the contrary, one of the additional benefits of undergoing regular exercise is that you are able to indulge in a favorite desert from time to time without worrying about the extra calories. Even the experts advise rewarding yourself for successfully sticking to an exercise program.

Exercise 2   Write your own sentences using the following words.

1. effect _____

_____

2. advise _____

_____

3. desert (verb) _____

_____

4. breath _____

_____

5. advice _____

_____

6. affect _____

_____

19.2 Verb Pairs

Verb pairs can be confusing. Take some time to study and review these pairs. Then do the exercises that follow.

come   to move towards something

My parents are **coming** to visit me from Idaho.

Why don't you **come** over to my house this weekend?

come back   to leave the original location and then later return there

I need to talk to you, but I can **come back** later.

She's visiting her parents in Peru, but she'll **come back** after the holidays.

go   to move away from something

My parents **go** to New Mexico every summer.

Let's **go** to the video store and get a movie to watch later.

go back   to return to a previous location

After this semester, I'll **go** back to my country.

I forgot to get the eggs, so I'm **going back** to the store.

fall, fell, fallen   to collapse, drop, or go down

She **fell** off a ladder while she was trimming the trees in her yard.

Before the leaves had **fallen**, it snowed.

feel, felt, felt   to sense or touch; to believe; to be affected by

She **felt** a sharp pain in her ankle when she hit the ground.

They **feel** they are learning a lot in that class.

hear   to be aware of sound (involuntary action)

Did you **hear** all that noise from the neighbor's party last night?

I **heard** the news about your promotion!

listen   to choose to hear (voluntary action)

I could **listen** to this music all night long.

You need to **listen** to good advice when it's given.

borrow   to ask for temporary use of something from someone; to take

Can I **borrow** your car this weekend?

I **borrowed** $20 from him until next Tuesday.

lend   to allow temporary use of something by someone; to give

She **lent** me her car for the entire weekend.

Could you **lend** me $20 until next Tuesday?

lie, lay, lain   intransitive verb (does not take an object); to recline

He **lay** on the ground after being hit by an opposing team member.

I'm tired. I'm going to **lie** down and take a short nap.

lay, laid, laid   transitive verb (takes an object); to place or put

Every night, he **lays** his clothes out for the next day.

I know I **laid** my keys on the counter when I came in. Where are they?

make   to build or construct; to create or produce; to change something

>   To **make** you happy, I **made** you a sandwich.

>   We need to **make** plans for our new business if we intend to **make** any money.

do   to perform or accomplish something; to talk about actions or work

>   Could you **do** me a favor and **do** the shopping for me this weekend?

>   What does he **do** for a living? I think he **does** interior decorating.

must   to be obligated or required   **must not**   to be prohibited

>   You **must** have a visa to enter the country.

>   You **must not** let your passport expire.

have to   to be obligated or required   **don't have to**   to be optional or unnecessary

>   You **have to** have a visa to enter the country.

>   You **don't have to** live on campus when you study, but dorms are available.

raise, raised, raised   transitive verb (takes an object); to increase; to lift or move something to a higher position

>   Gas station owners **raised** the price of gas by 50 cents almost overnight.

>   They play the national anthem whenever they **raise** the flag.

rise, rose, risen   intransitive verb (does not take an object); to increase; something moves to a higher position

>   Gas prices **rose** by 50 cents almost overnight.

>   The sun **rises** a few minutes earlier every day until the summer solstice.

say   to speak (used without an indirect object); does not indicate who the listener was

>   They **said** that they were going to come over about 6:30 tonight.

tell   to speak (used with an indirect object); indicates who was listening; expressions include: *tell a lie, tell the truth, tell the time, tell a story*

>   They **told** me that they were going to come over about 6:30 tonight.

see to use one's eyes (involuntary action)

> I **saw** the accident while I was waiting for the light to change.

look to use one's eyes (voluntary action); focus is on the object; shorter duration than *watch*

> We **looked** at six new houses that were on the market.

> Could you **look** at my paper and correct the errors?

watch to use one's eyes (voluntary action); focus is on what the object is doing; longer duration than *look*

> We **watched** that new TV program last night.

> I don't want the soup to boil over. Could you **watch** it while I answer the phone?

take to carry something to another place (when you go there) away from the speaker

> Don't forget to **take** your umbrella when you leave.

> She never **takes** sunscreen with her when she goes to the beach.

bring to carry something to this place (when you come here) towards the speaker

> Don't forget to **bring** your umbrella when you come.

> He **brings** his daughter here to the office with him once in a while.

teach to instruct (a person) or to give knowledge

> This computer program **teaches** students how to design airports.

learn to acquire or gain knowledge

> If you **learn** some test-taking strategies, you'll feel less anxious at exam time.

> **used to** (+ VERB)   to no longer occur or happen (indicates change)
>
> > We **used to** watch the news on ABC, but now we watch CBS.
> >
> > He didn't **use to** come to work so early. It's 7:15, and he starts at 8:00.
>
> **be/get used to** (+ NOUN or NOUN equivalent)   to become accustomed to or familiar with something
>
> > After living in Florida for 10 years, I'm **used to** hot, humid weather.
> >
> > They arrived here only two weeks ago. They still need to **get used to** hearing English all the time.

> **waste**   to use something unwisely or foolishly
>
> > Please turn off the lights when you're not in the room. You're **wasting** energy by leaving them on.
> >
> > He sat in my office and **wasted** half an hour of my time chatting about his dog.
>
> **lose**   to be unable to find or locate; to not win
>
> > It's easy to **lose** money if you don't invest wisely.
> >
> > They **lost** the game by two points in the last 10 seconds of the final quarter.

Exercise 3   As you read the essay, underline the correct verbs.

Last summer we **1** (did, <u>made</u>) plans for a trip out West to Colorado. We stopped along the way to enjoy all the outdoors had to offer. From our camper in Denver, for example, we could **2** (watch, see) the Rocky Mountains. They were absolutely majestic— **3** (rising, raising) mightily from the land, standing tall and stately, looking powerful against the piercing blue Colorado sky. Looking at them **4** (did, made) me **5** (feel, fell) as though I were experiencing nature for the first time.

It was only then that we discovered we had forgotten to **6** (take, bring) along our camera. I don't know why we forgot—we **7** (were used to traveling, used to travel) more than we have lately, so maybe we just got out of the habit of packing the camera. I thought I had **8** (said, told) my husband Dennis to pack it, but he **9** (said, told) he hadn't **10** (heard, listened to) me **11** (say, tell) anything about it.

I **12** (felt, fell) awful, but we decided not to **13** (lose, waste) time worrying about it.

If we couldn't **14** (borrow, lend) a camera from my sister who lived in nearby Westminster, then we would simply buy a new one. After all, our purpose in **15** (coming, going) to Denver was to capture the natural beauty of one of America's western states.

Our vacation was wonderful and we **16** (watched, saw) many beautiful places besides Colorado. We **17** (looked, watched) the sun set over rivers, valleys, and mountains all across the West and **18** (saw, looked) it **19** (raise, rise) in the early morning stillness that **20** (lay, laid) at the edge of forests and woods. We sat in silence and **21** (listened to, heard) the sounds of nature: water flowing over rocks in a stream, birds calling, and small animals scurrying about unseen, in search of food.

If you ever get the chance to **22** (come, go) camping, you **23** (must not, don't have to) pass it up. Don't **24** (lose, waste) time trying to decide whether it will be a worthwhile opportunity—it will! Camping **25** (learned, taught) us a great deal. What we **26** (took, brought) back with us, along with our pictures and memories, was a renewed interest in nature. We're not **27** (losing, wasting) any time planning our next trip. In fact, once we **28** (came, went) home, we got out the atlas right away!

Exercise 4   Write sentences using the following words and/or phrases.

1. lend money _____

   _____

2. learn _____

   _____

3. prices fell _____

   _____

4. has raised _____

   _____

5. take _____

   _____

6. be used to _____

_____

Exercise 5 Put the following list of words, phrases, and expressions in the correct column below. Then, on separate paper, use three words or phrases from each column in sentences. *Suggestion:* This is not an easy exercise. Consult a dictionary, an English speaker, or a web source for help.

the laundry	well on an exam	plans for tonight	money	a mistake
the dishes	a phone call	a good job	one sick	so much noise
a term paper	the shopping	dinner	up for lost time	new friends
math	some yard work	trouble	angry	coffee
homework	good time	bread	for a living	an enemy
fun of	a face	a favor	a key word search	something over
a salad	housework	time in jail		someone happy

Do	Make
the laundry	

19.3 Other Confusing Verbs

It's easy to confuse some verbs because they are used in idiomatic expressions and thus have multiple meanings. Other verbs cause confusion because they are used in specific structures that you have to learn.

The Verb *get*

arrive   (*get* + PLACE)

> When did you **get** home?

> What time does your plane **get** to Atlanta?

become   (*get* + ADJECTIVE)

> Are you **getting** hungry?

> She **got** so excited about the party.

> (ALSO: *get sick, get sleepy, get angry, get upset, get engaged, get married, get divorced, get busy*)

Special expressions

> I **got up** late today.

> He **got off** the plane at 6:00.

> (ALSO: *get on the bus, get over an illness, get out of the car, get in trouble, get with something, get behind in work, get off work*)

receive   (*get* + NOUN)

> He's **getting** a raise.

> I **got** a letter from Mom today.

> (ALSO: *get a ticket, get a job, get a new car, get some news, get a call*)

cause something to happen   (*get* + PRONOUN + INFINITIVE)

> I **got** them to reduce my taxes.

> We **got** her to reconsider taking the job.

Verbs That Use the Infinitive Without *to*

see   I **saw** him ~~to~~ leave the party.

hear   His mother **heard** him ~~to~~ scream.

watch   The police **watched** him ~~to~~ break into the house.

make   The boss **made** us all ~~to~~ work late.

have   She **had** someone ~~to~~ do her nails for her 80th birthday.

let   I **let** the children ~~to~~ stay up late tonight.

Exercise 6   Answer the questions using verbs from Section 19.3.

Part A   Use *get.*

1. When did they arrive?

   They got here late last night.

2. When did you receive your degree?

   _____

3. When did you become ill?

   _____

4. What time did you finish work last night?

   _____

5. When did you have Alex paint your house?

   _____

Part B   Use the verbs without an infinitive. Make sentences of your own.

1. watched / turn / corner   *I watched the car turn the corner ahead of me.*

2. let / ride / bus / alone _____

   _____

3. made / eat / Brussels sprouts _____

   _____

4. didn't see / deliver / mail _____

_____

5. can hear / ringing _____

_____

6. will help / study / exam _____

_____

19.4 Nouns

When nouns have similar forms or similar meanings, it's easy to get them confused. Understanding the difference between count nouns and noncount nouns will help you use nouns correctly in your writing.

Count nouns can be counted. They have two forms: singular and plural.

> Could you give me **an example** of a past tense verb?

> Could you give me **three examples** of confusing verbs?

Noncount nouns cannot be counted. They have only one form. We don't use noncount nouns with words that indicate singular or plural.

Correct: The **sand** on this beach is unusually dark.

Incorrect: The many **sands** on this beach are unusually dark.

history   (noncount) events that happened in the past

> They say that **history** repeats itself.

story   (count) literature; retelling of something

> Did you read the **story** on the front page?

child   (count, singular) a young person

> They have one **child**, a daughter.

children   (count, plural) young people

> Their two **children** are now in college.

time (noncount) quantity, period, or duration of minutes, hours, months, etc.

There isn't enough **time** to accomplish all the tasks on my list.

time(s) (count) separate occasions, experiences

We had a good **time** at the party last night.

I've asked him for his e-mail address at least three **times**.

news (noncount) information about events

I saw the **news** about the war on TV.

information (noncount) knowledge, facts

Could you give us some **information** about your new restaurant?

work (noncount)

I love my **work** and the people I work with.

works (count) product, creation

They have two **works** of art from Picasso displayed.

homework (noncount)

There's too much **homework** to do in an hour!

a number (plural) many

You have **a number** of options to consider.

the number (singular) the total

The number of people coming is small.

Exercise 7   Complete the sentences using nouns from Section 19.4.

I read an interesting _____*story*_____ in the newspaper this morning. It
1
was about a person who spends most of her _____ working with
2
_____ from a local elementary school.
3

It seems _____ of children in the school are gifted and, thus,
4
are way ahead of their classmates. For example, one gifted _____
5
was known for finishing his _____ so quickly that his teachers
6
couldn't find any _____ to challenge him.
7

Apparently, this _____ reached a local artist who then
8
volunteered to come into the classroom three _____ a week
9
to work with the gifted students. She develops activities to teach them about
the _____ of art and helps them to create their own
10
_____ of art, which they display on the walls throughout the
11
school.

Interestingly, the effect of her working with these gifted students has been to motivate
the other children in the school to work harder. _____ of children
12
participating in the program has grown, and people in the community have begun
lobbying to create a separate art school within the elementary school itself. The article
said to call the school for more _____ about the proposed plan.
13

Exercise 8   On a separate piece of paper, write new sentences using any nouns you wrote incorrectly in Exercise 7.

Exercise 9   Circle the letter of the correct answer.

1. Have you _____ to the news much lately? All you ever seem to _____ about is
   crime and pollution. What's up with that?
   a. heard, hear   c. listened, listen
   b. listened, hear   d. heard, listen

2. I've started taking some new allergy medicine, and I think I'm experiencing some side _____ from it. Should I _____ the doctor about it?
   a. effect, tell
   b. affects, say
   c. affect, tell
   d. effects, tell

3. After I _____ from the dentist, we can _____ to the mall and finish our shopping.
   a. go back, go
   b. go, come back
   c. affect, tell
   d. come back, go back

4. Now, don't take this wrong. You _____ take my _____, but you could stand to _____ a few pounds.
   a. don't have to, advice, lose
   b. must not, advice, lost
   c. must, advise, lose
   d. don't have to, advise, lose

5. We never _____ anything on the weekends. You only want to _____ TV or _____ your CDs. I'm tired of that!
   a. make, look, hear
   b. do, watch, listen to
   c. do, see, listen
   d. make, watch, hear

6. Listen—between us, I think we're _____ our time trying to convince the company to shorten the workweek.
   a. losing
   b. wasting
   c. lost
   d. wasted

7. As a child, I _____ get up about 7:00 a.m., _____ my bed, and then go downstairs into the living room to _____ cartoons on TV every Saturday morning.
   a. was used to, made, see
   b. got used to, do, watch
   c. used to, make, watch
   d. used to, make, look

8. The counselor _____ Julian yesterday that he needed to _____ his GPA in order to qualify for a scholarship. At least that's what Julian _____ to me when I asked him what the counselor _____ him.
   a. said, rise, told, said
   b. told, raise, told, had told
   c. told, raise, said, had told
   d. said, rise, said, had said

⊙riginal Writing

Exercise 10   A friend of yours is having trouble adjusting to life away from home and to the academic demands of studying at a university. Write a short essay in which you offer advice, perhaps including a list of tips or some do's and don'ts, to your friend. Before you begin, make a list of the nouns and verbs from this chapter that you will try to use. In your essay, underline the ones you were able to use. Exchange paragraphs with a partner, checking each other's work for correct nouns and verbs.

If you need help with the steps of writing a paragraph, see Appendix 5.

www   You will find additional exercises for the grammar in this chapter on the Top 20 website at **http://esl.college.hmco.com/students**

WF

*Like most others Consultants,
a good financial planner must
be paid for the services
offered.*

20

Confusing Pairs of Words:
Pronouns, Adjectives, Adverbs, and Prepositions

In this chapter you will review and practice pairs of pronouns, adjectives, adverbs, and prepositions that often confuse writers and speakers of English. (Chapter 19 covers confusing pairs of verbs and nouns.)

20.1 Pronouns

The following pronoun pairs can be easily confused. Study their meanings and the examples.

each   every one person or thing in a group considered individually. The location in the sentence determines whether *each* and the verb are singular or plural.

> **Each** (one) of the employees *has* an office.   (singular)
>
> The employees (they) **each** *have* an office.   (plural)

every   each one in a group; always singular

> **Every** employee *has* an office.
>
> **Every** one of the employees *has* an office.

its   possessive form of *it*; belonging to the thing mentioned

> The dog wagged **its** tail as I approached.

it's   contracted form of *it is* or *it has*

> **It's** true (it is). **It's** (it has) been years since I visited Chicago.

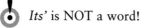 *Its'* is NOT a word!

none   not any (can be used with singular or plural)

> **None** of the cake was eaten.
>
> **None** of the cakes was eaten.   (formal)
>
> **None** of the cakes were eaten.   (informal)

not one   not any (used with singular verb)

> **Not one** of the cakes was eaten.

their   possessive form of *they*

     Have you seen **their** new car?

they're   contracted form of *they are*

     They're coming over for dinner tonight.

there   used as subject of *be* verb in a clause or sentence

     There is another new car dealer in town. **There** are now at least seven dealers to choose from when buying a car.

whose   possessive for *who* or *which*

     Whose car keys are these?

     The dog **whose** collar is missing belongs to my neighbor.

who's   contracted form of *who is* or *who has*

     Who's (who is) going with me? **Who's** (who has) made the list of what we need to get?

your   possessive for *you*

     Please spell **your** last name for me.

you're   contracted form of *you are*

     You're the new secretary, aren't you?

Exercise 1   Circle the correct form of the word in parentheses.

1. (There, They're) is no doubt that (they're, their) the ones responsible for winning the election. (Not one, None) of the others were even remotely involved.

2. I find it amazing that the committee members each (is, are) allowed to conduct a 30-minute interview of the candidates.

3. However, (its, it's) not my decision to make. Besides, once the group makes (its, it's) choice, we can move on to the voters and find out (they're, their) preferences.

4. (Who's, Whose) idea was this anyway? (Who's, Whose) in charge of campaign strategies?

5. Each of the regional advisors (has, have) an opportunity to suggest strategies. (Whose, Who's) the advisor for (you're, your) region?

6. I'm pretty sure (its, it's) Randall Kelly.

7. (You're, Your) lucky (it's, its) not Pat Goodman. Not one of the campaign

volunteers (wants, want) to deal with him. Each of them (run, runs) when he heads

in (there, their) direction! Here he comes now. I'll catch you later.

Exercise 2   Write sentences using the following words.

1. their _____

_____

2. each _____

_____

3. whose _____

_____

4. its _____

_____

5. there _____

_____

6. none (*with count noun*) _____

_____

7. none (*with noncount noun*) _____

_____

20.2 Adjectives and Adverbs

Here's a quick review: Adjectives modify nouns (**windy** city). Adverbs modify verbs, adjectives, or other adverbs (eat **fast**, it is **strongly** encouraged, walk **more slowly**).

20.2.1 Quantifiers, Intensifiers, and Emphasizers

Writers use the adjectives in this section to indicate how many or to intensify or emphasize something.

> **few**   not many or not enough; can have a negative connotation
>
> > **Few** people attended the event. We were disappointed.
> >
> > **Few** people are as nice as he is. He's a great guy to have for a friend!
>
> **a few**   not many; no negative connotation
>
> > **A few** people came to the party.

> **little**   not much or not enough; can have negative connotation
>
> > I have **little** time for a vacation this year. I really need one though.
> >
> > **Little** money was wasted on repairs this year. The board was pleased.
>
> **a little**   not much; some
>
> > He spent **a little** time visiting area orchards.

> **few-fewer-fewest**   used with count nouns
>
> > She has **fewer** clients this year than she had last year.
>
> **little-less-least**   used with noncount nouns

> He has **less** money to spend on home repairs now because he has been working **fewer** hours at work this year than in previous years.

many   used with count nouns

> There are rules, but there are **many** exceptions as well.

much   used with noncount nouns; usually used in negative sentences

> We haven't had **much** time to practice this season.

quite   intensifier; not as strong as *very*

> I got home **quite** late last night.
>
> The test was **quite** hard.

very   intensifier

> I got home **very** late last night.
>
> The test was **very** hard.

too   emphasizer; implies excessiveness and often requires additional information to complete the meaning

> I got home **too** late to watch the news last night.

so (+ ADJECTIVE / ADVERB *that*)   emphasizer; if an explanation is not given, the assumption is that the listener knows the result

> I got home **so** late last night (that I'm tired today).
>
> The test was **so** hard (that I'm sure I failed it).

such (+ *a / an* + ADJECTIVE + NOUN *that*)   emphasizer; if an explanation is not given, the assumption is that listener knows the result

> I got home at **such** a late hour last night (that I'm tired today).
>
> It was **such** a difficult test (that I'm sure I failed it).

Editing

∧ **Exercise 3**   The seven sentences below are out of order. Reorder them by placing a 1 next to the first sentence, a 2 next to the second, etc. Then find and correct the three quantifier, intensifier, or emphasizer errors.

_____ 1. In the past, not very much research had been conducted on the topic of stress and its effects on the body.

_____ 2. Of course, there are many Americans who prefer to take a little vacation than they are allowed.

_____ 3. Three weeks is considered little time to "recharge a person's batteries," although having a little time off is better than having none.

_____ 4. There are fewer of these types of workers today, however, as more attention is paid to the much problems caused by work-related stress.

___I___ 5. In the United States, unfortunately, few employers offer their employees more than three weeks of vacation each year.

_____ 6. Today, however, there has been so an increased interest in the subject that government grants are available for continued research and study on the topic.

_____ 7. A few companies offer four weeks of vacation, but employees usually have to have already worked at least 10 years for the company to qualify for that much time off.

20.2.2 More Pairs and Groups of Adjectives and Adverbs

Many more adjectives and adverbs in English can be difficult to use correctly. Study the following groupings of meanings and examples. (There are a few pronouns in these groupings that can be confused with similar adjectives or adverbs.)

ago   in the past; used with amount of time; reference point is the present time

I worked with him three years **ago**.

before (+ NOUN or clause)   in the past; used with or without amount of time; reference point is past time

I've worked with him **before**.

I worked with him three years **before** I came here.

all   total amount

All of the students worried about the exam.

almost   nearly; not quite

Almost all of the students passed the exam.

most   the largest number or amount

Most students had studied for the exam.

all right   in good condition; satisfactory; correct

Your tires look **all right**.

alright   Though this form is considered wrong by many, it is often used informally; it means the same as *all right*.

all ready   prepared

> I studied for the exam, and I'm **all ready** to take it.

already   before now, previously; earlier than expected; by a specific time

> I've **already** paid my gas bill for April.

> She had **already** eaten when he called to invite her to dinner.

anymore   any longer; from now on

> They don't watch TV **anymore**.

still   up to a specific time (continue)

> Are you **still** awake? It's late!

> I **still** don't understand past perfect tense.

anxious   worried, concerned; eager (commonly used)

> He feels **anxious** about the job interview.

> The kids are **anxious** for summer vacation.   (becoming accepted to mean *eager*)

eager   enthusiastic

> He's **eager** to start his new job.

bad   low standard, poor; not good; incorrect; not in good health; sorry

> The movie we watched last night was **bad**.

> It's **bad** luck to walk under a ladder, right?

> As a result of her smoking, she's in **bad** health.

> I feel **bad** for her—she just had her car stolen for the third time.

badly   poorly, in a bad way or manner

> The team played **badly** in the final quarter and lost the game.

> I did **badly** on the oral presentation for my Public Speaking class.

good   positive, not bad; appropriate; high quality

> I just finished reading a **good** book on sports.

> That was a **good** answer to my question.

> The meal at La Maison was **good** but not too expensive.

well   (ADJECTIVE) in good health

> I was sick last week, but I'm **well** now.

well   (ADVERB) successfully; proficiently; in a good way or manner

> She works **well** with children.

> You handled that awkward situation quite **well**.

ever   at any time

Have you **ever** driven in a stock car race?

She hadn't **ever** planned to open her own business.

never   at no time

No, I have **never** heard of the rock group, Boulder Heads.

like   (PREPOSITION) similar

People say we look **like** sisters, but we aren't.

like   (ADJECTIVE) having the same characteristics; equivalent

Jaguars and **like** cars have high insurance rates.

The radio station will have to raise a **like** amount again next year.

alike   (used after linking verbs) similar

People say we look **alike**.

unlike   (PREPOSITION + NOUN) dissimilar

He is not **unlike** his brother.

another   (ADJECTIVE) additional

I need **another** cup of coffee.

another   (PRONOUN) an additional one

She drank a cup of coffee and then **another**.

other   (ADJECTIVE)

Other students took the same exam.

others   (PRONOUN) additional ones

Others took the same exam.

the other(s)   one of two; the remaining one or ones

I didn't care much for this video. **The other** one I watched was funnier.   (ADJECTIVE)

I didn't care much for this video, but I liked **the other**.   (PRONOUN)

this, that   singular; near / far

> **This** kind of music hurts my ears.
>
> **That** problem is one I just can't solve.

these, those   plural; near / far

> **These** kinds of exams are hard.
>
> **Those** stories are wonderful for kids.

Editing
∧ **Exercise 4**   As you read the passage, find and correct the eight errors in word usage.

How many people each year lose large sums of money through bad investments? How many others aren't even aware that almost their money has been invested badly?

Whether you're already an investor or are already to become one, you can benefit from these six tips. Be sure all your retirement funds will still be there when you need them!

1. Know your financial goals and your "risk-comfort level." If high-risk investments make you anxious, then invest in something that will preserve your capital and offer you less risk. This kinds of funds will obviously yield a lower rate of return than other higher-risk investments, but these lower return is your trade-off for feeling comfortable.

2. Consult a financial planner. Meet with the planner to discuss your personal financial goals and to develop a plan specific to your needs and circumstances. These kinds of meetings should continue to occur with your planner even if your investments are doing well.

3. Like most others investment consultants, your financial planner will be paid for his/her services. Know what fees you will pay and how they are calculated. Ask questions if you are unsure how the fees are assessed.

4. Make sure your investments are diversified. Don't never invest all of your money in alike asset classes. Find out if there is a fee to transfer from one fund to another.

5. Monitor both your investments and account statements. Before investing in a new

fund, read the prospectus. If you do not understand it well enough, ask the other person to read it as well. If you still have questions, consult other sources.

6. Finally, be prepared to invest for the long term. If an investment sounds too good to be true, it probably is. Unlike good investments, scams often promise unusually high rates of return. These promises should be investigated thoroughly before you invest in the fund.

Exercise 5   Write sentences of your own using the following words or phrases.

1. all right _____

_____

2. anymore _____

_____

3. badly _____

_____

4. almost _____

_____

5. others _____

_____

6. other _____

_____

Prepositions link nouns or pronouns to other words in the sentence in order to express relationships. Examples of relationships include time, location, and direction. (See Chapter 6 for more about prepositions.)

Many prepositions are confusing because they are used idiomatically. Study the uses and examples in this section.

between   used for two persons or things

> The inheritance was split **between** the two brothers.

among   used for three or more persons or things

> **Among** the seven children, only three were able to attend college.

in, after   to indicate time

> I'll see you **in** a week **after** final exams.

in, on   to indicate location (stationary)

> She sat **in** the living room **on** the sofa.

into, onto   to indicate action or movement toward a direction

> As she rushed **into** the room to answer the phone, her coffee spilled **onto** the floor.

except   but, excluding

> Everyone came **except** his sister-in-law.

accept   (VERB) to receive

> Everyone wanted to **accept** his invitation.

since   from a time in the past (*since* + name of the time)

> I've known him **since** 1999.

for   amount or duration of time (*for* + length of time)

> I've known him **for** three years.

Editing

∧ **Exercise 6** Read each sentence and mark C for correct or I for incorrect. Then correct the sentences that contain errors.

    accept

___I___ 1. She decided to ~~except~~ the position offered by the Anthropology Department.

_____ 2. Between all the instructors in the English Department, Dr. Harris has taught the longest.

_____ 3. I know the papers were sitting onto the desk when I came in this morning.

_____ 4. They walked into the classroom at least 10 minutes late.

_____ 5. We've been waiting for our test results since a week.

_____ 6. Between you and me, I think we're slated for budget cuts.

_____ 7. He's been chairman of the Chemistry Department since four years ago.

_____ 8. Everyone scored well on the exam accept Ruth.

_____ 9. Ellen has been publishing her research studies for years.

_____ 10. The staff is having a problem accepting him as the new dean.

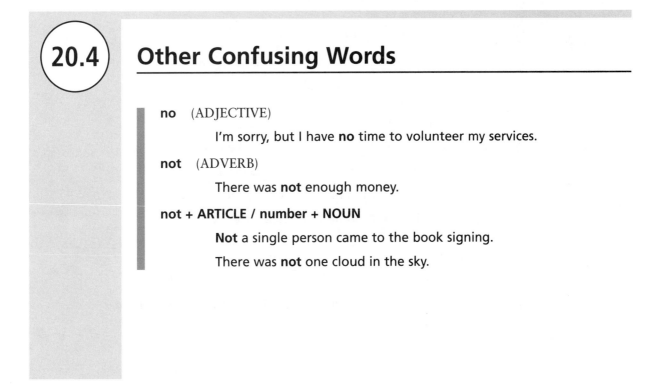

(20.4) Other Confusing Words

no (ADJECTIVE)

    I'm sorry, but I have **no** time to volunteer my services.

not (ADVERB)

    There was **not** enough money.

not + ARTICLE / number + NOUN

    Not a single person came to the book signing.

    There was **not** one cloud in the sky.

than   (CONJUNCTION) use between clauses in a comparison; in comparison with

> You're much better at tennis **than** I am.
>
> She doesn't love anyone more **than** (she loves) him.

then   (ADVERB) at that time; next; that time

> First we'll watch the movie, and **then** we'll study.

then   (NOUN)

> He brought her flowers. From **then** on, everyone knew they would marry.

there is, there are   used as a subject filler; verb agrees with noun after *to be*

> There *is* no *explanation* for his behavior.
>
> *Were* there any *people* injured in the accident?

to + INFINITIVE, in order to + INFINITIVE, for + NOUN   expressions used to show purpose

> I came here **to** fill out an application.
>
> I came here **in order to** fill out an application.
>
> I came here **for** an application.

too, so, either, neither   used to avoid repeating words or phrases

> Julie is confused about all of this. I am **too**.
>
> Julie is confused about all of this. **So** am I.
>
> He didn't turn in his final paper. I didn't **either**.
>
> He didn't turn in his final paper. **Neither** did I.

so, not   used to respond to a question or comment

> Is Liz working today? I think **so**.   I don't think **so**.
>
> How was your interview? Did it go well? I'm afraid **not**.
>
> Will it rain? I hope **so**. I hope **not**.

Exercise 7   Answer the questions with words from Section 20.4.

Part A   Fill in the blank. Use *no, not, too, so, either,* or *neither*.

1. Did you visit the Lincoln Memorial? There was ___*no*___ time for sightseeing.

2. I completely forgot to do the assignment. _____ did I.

3. Does this mean I can get my money back? I'm afraid _____.

4. He's not going to Sherrie's party. I'm not _____.

5. How was flying? Beautiful. _____ a cloud in the sky.

6. Did you get the job? I hope _____.

7. We'll be at the mall by 7:00 p.m. Okay, I will _____.

8. She hasn't seen any movies recently. _____ have I.

Part B   Write sentences of your own using these words.

1. than _____

   _____

2. then _____

   _____

3. there is _____

   _____

4. there are _____

   _____

5. to _____

   _____

6. in order to _____

   _____

Exercise 8   Circle the letter of the correct answer.

1. _____ so funny! That statue is casting _____ shadow directly over those people's heads, and they look as though _____ wearing hats.
   a. It's, its, they're   c. Its, its, their
   b. It's, it's, they're   d. Its, it's, there

2. She ran off to join the circus?! That makes _____ _____ sense. I don't get it. _____ do I.
   a. such, little, So
   b. such, little, Neither
   c. so, few, Neither
   d. so, little, Either

3. _____ all of _____ answers sound _____ to me.
   a. Almost, this, alike
   b. Most, this, like
   c. Almost, these, alike
   d. Almost, these, like

4. How sad ... She has _____ friends and _____ of them is willing to help her out.
   a. few, not one
   b. many, a few
   c. a few, none
   d. a little, not one

5. My kids are _____ making plans for summer vacation. One wants to go to California, but _____ ones want to go to Arizona.
   a. already, the other
   b. already, the others
   c. all ready, the another
   d. all ready, other

6. Did you hear that _____ on the news last night? Some guy got mad at his neighbor, and _____ with _____ warning drove his car through the neighbor's fence.
   a. history, then, no
   b. story, than, not
   c. history, than, not
   d. story, then, no

7. I feel _____ that everyone _____ you knew I was leaving _____ a week.
   a. badly, except, before
   b. badly, except, in
   c. bad, except, in
   d. bad, accept, in

8. How strange ... We talked to him only three weeks _____. At that time he said he'd _____ leave this job for _____ one, even if it paid more.
   a. ago, ever, another
   b. before, ever, the other
   c. before, never, another
   d. ago, never, another

Original Writing

Exercise 9   Write a paragraph either 1) giving advice on staying healthy or 2) giving your opinion on an educational issue you are interested in. Before you begin, make a list of the words from this chapter that you will try to include. In your paragraph, underline the ones from the list you were able to use. Exchange paragraphs with a partner and check each other's work for correct use of confusing words.

If you need help with the steps of writing a paragraph, see Appendix 5.

www   You will find additional exercises for the grammar in this chapter on the Top 20 website at **http://esl.college.hmco.com/students**

Appendixes

(1) Parts of Speech

1. Noun: the name of a person, place, thing, or idea

   - Count nouns: can be counted; can be singular and plural

   - Noncount (mass nouns): cannot be counted; have one singular form

     The **cashier** put the **cans** of **tuna** in a plastic **bag**.
        C   C   NC   C

2. Verb: a word that expresses action or state of being

   - Transitive verbs: have an object

   - Intransitive verbs: do not have an object

     The secretary **called** the travel agency, but the agent **had left**.
               TV   IV

3. Pronoun: a word that can replace a noun

   - Subject pronouns: *I, you, he, she, it, we, you, they, who*

   - Object pronouns: *me, you, him, her, it, us, you, them, whom*

   - Possessive pronouns: *mine, yours, his, hers, ours, yours, theirs*

     He will not fix this problem. According to **him**, this problem is **mine**.
     SP   **OP**   **POSS PRO**

4. Adjective: a word that describes a noun or pronoun

   - Descriptive adjective (an adjective that gives a description or characteristic): *blue, old*

   - Demonstrative adjectives: *this, that, these, those*

   - Possessive adjectives: *my, your, his, her, its, our, your, their, whose*

   - Articles: *a, an, some*

     This green notebook belongs to **a** boy in **my** history class.
     DEM **DESC**   **ART**   **POSS ADJ**

5. Adverb: a word that modifies a verb, an adjective, a whole sentence, or another adverb

   - Manner: tells how (*quickly, slowly*)

   - Place: tells where (*there, here*)

   - Time: tells when (*yesterday, then*)

   - Frequency: tells how often (*always, occasionally*)

   - Degree: tells to what degree (*very, extremely*)

     She **rarely** goes **there** except when it is **very** hot.
         FREQ   **PLACE**   **DEGREE**

6. Preposition: a word (or group of words) that connects nouns or pronouns to a sentence

   According to the paper, the wedding was **at** noon **on** March 25th.
   PREP   **PREP**   **PREP**

7. Conjunction: a word that links two clauses, two phrases, or two words

- Coordinating conjunction: connects two words, phrases, or independent clauses

  FANBOYS: *for, and, nor, but, or, yet, so*

- Subordinating conjunction: introduces a dependent clause (*when, if*)

- Correlative conjunctions: connect equivalent sentence parts (*both ... and ...*)

  When the meeting ended, **neither** Jo **nor** Sue stood up first.
  SUB   CORR   CORR

8. Interjection: a word that expresses strong feelings or emotion

   Wow! Look at how fast that plane is moving!
   INT

② Irregular Verb Forms

Present	Past	Past Participle	Present	Past	Past Participle
arise	arose	arisen	feel	felt	felt
awake	awoke	awoken	fight	fought	fought
be	was/were	been	find	found	found
bear	bore	born / borne	fit	fit	fit
beat	beat	beaten / beat	flee	fled	fled
become	became	become	fling	flung	flung
begin	began	begun	fly	flew	flown
bend	bent	bent	forbid	forbade	forbidden
bet	bet	bet	forecast	forecast	forecast
bid	bid	bid	foresee	foresaw	foreseen
bind	bound	bound	foretell	foretold	foretold
bite	bit	bitten	forget	forgot	forgotten
bleed	bled	bled	forgive	forgave	forgiven
blow	blew	blown	forsake	forsook	forsaken
break	broke	broken	freeze	froze	frozen
bring	brought	brought	get	got	gotten
broadcast	broadcast	broadcast	give	gave	given
build	built	built	go	went	gone
burn	burned	burned	grind	ground	ground
burst	burst	burst	grow	grew	grown
bust	bust	bust	hang	hung	hung
buy	bought	bought	have	had	had
cast	cast	cast	hear	heard	heard
catch	caught	caught	hide	hid	hidden
choose	chose	chosen	hit	hit	hit
cling	clung	clung	hold	held	hold
come	came	come	hurt	hurt	hurt
cost	cost	cost	input	input	input
creep	crept	crept	keep	kept	kept
cut	cut	cut	kneel	knelt	knelt
deal	dealt	dealt	know	knew	known
dig	dug	dug	lay	laid	laid
dive	dove	dived	lead	led	led
do	did	done	leave	left	left
draw	drew	drawn	lend	lent	lent
dream	dreamed / dreamt	dreamed / dreamt	let	let	let
			lie	lay	lain
drink	drank	drunk	light	lit / lighted	lit / lighted
drive	drove	driven	lose	lost	lost
eat	ate	eaten	make	made	made
fall	fell	fallen	mean	meant	meant
feed	fed	fed	meet	met	met

Present	Past	Past Participle	Present	Past	Past Participle
mislead	misled	misled	speak	spoke	spoken
mistake	mistook	mistaken	speed	sped	sped
misunderstand	misunderstood	misunderstood	spend	spent	spent
overcome	overcame	overcome	spin	spun	spun
overdo	overdid	overdone	split	split	split
override	overrode	overridden	spread	spread	spread
oversee	oversaw	overseen	stand	stood	stood
oversleep	overslept	overslept	steal	stole	stolen
overtake	overtook	overtaken	stick	stuck	stuck
overthrow	overthrew	overthrown	stink	stank / stunk	stunk
pay	paid	paid	strike	struck	struck / stricken
prove	proved	proven / proved	string	strung	strung
put	put	put	strive	strove	striven
quit	quit	quit	swear	swore	sworn
read	read	read	sweep	swept	swept
ride	rode	ridden	swell	swelled	swollen
ring	rang	rung	swim	swam	swum
rise	rose	risen	swing	swung	swung
run	ran	run	take	took	taken
say	said	said	teach	taught	taught
see	saw	seen	tear	tore	torn
seek	sought	sought	tell	told	told
sell	sold	sold	think	thought	thought
send	sent	sent	throw	threw	thrown
set	set	set	thrust	thrust	thrust
sew	sewed	sewn / sewed	understand	understood	understood
shake	shook	shaken	undertake	undertook	undertaken
shed	shed	shed	undo	undid	undone
shoot	shot	shot	uphold	upheld	upheld
show	showed	shown / showed	upset	upset	upset
			wake	woke	woken
shrink	shrank	shrunk	wear	wore	worn
shut	shut	shut	weave	wove	woven
sing	sang	sung	weep	wept	wept
sit	sat	sat	wet	wet	wet
sleep	slept	slept	win	won	won
slide	slid	slid	wind	wound	wound
sling	slung	slung	withdraw	withdrew	withdrawn
slit	slit	slit	write	wrote	written

③ Irregular Noun Plurals

Ending	Change	Examples
_____fe	fe ⇨ ve + -s	1 knife / 4 knives
_____f	f ⇨ v + -es	1 loaf / 3 loaves
_____o	+ -es	1 tomato / 3 tomatoes
_____us	us ⇨ -i	a focus / the foci
_____is	is ⇨ -es	1 thesis / their theses
_____on	on ⇨ -a	1 criterion / the real criteria
mixed	mixed	man / men woman / women child / children mouse / mice tooth / teeth person / people
no change	no change	1 fish / 2 fish 1 sheep / 2 sheep

④ Comparative and Superlative Forms of Adjectives and Adverbs

Comparative = used for two people or things
Superlative = used when there are three or more people or items to compare

Syllables	Neutral	Comparative	Superlative
one syllable	tall	taller	the tallest
two syllables ending in -y	hungry	hungrier	the hungriest
others	handsome quickly cheaply	more handsome more quickly more cheaply	the most handsome the most quickly the most cheaply
irregular	good bad far far	better worse farther further	the best the worst the farthest the furthest

⑤ Understanding the Writing Process: The Seven Steps

This section can be read at any time during the course. You will want to refer to these seven steps many times as you write your essays.

The Assignment

Imagine that you have been given the following assignment: *Write an essay in which you discuss the benefits or problems of vegetarianism.* What should you do first? What should you do second, and so on? There are many ways to write, but most good writers follow certain general steps in the writing process. These steps are guidelines that are not always followed in order.

Look at this list of steps. Which ones do you do? Which ones have you never done?

1. Choosing a topic
2. Brainstorming
3. Outline and rough draft
4. Cleaning up the rough draft
5. Peer editing
6. Revising the draft
7. Proofing the final paper

Next you will see how one student, Sean, went through the steps to do the assignment. First, read the final essay that Sean gave his teacher.

Better Living as a Vegetarian

1   The hamburger is an American cultural icon that is known all over the world. Eating meat, especially beef, is an integral part of daily life for a majority of people in the United States. The consumption of large quantities of meat is a major contributing factor toward a great many deaths in this country, including the unnecessarily high number of deaths from heart-related problems. Though it has caught on slowly in this culture, vegetarianism is a way of life that can help improve not only the quality of people's lives but also their longevity.

2   Surprising as it may sound, vegetarianism can have beneficial effects on the environment. Because demand for meat animals is so high, cattle are being raised in areas where rain forests once stood. As rain forest land is cleared in order to make room for cattle ranches, the environmental balance is upset. This could have serious consequences for humans. Studies show that much of the current global warming is due to disturbing the rain forests.

3   More important at an individual level is the question of how eating meat affects a person's health. Meat, unlike vegetables, can contain very large amounts of fat. Eating this fat has been connected in research cases with certain kinds of cancer. If people cut down on the amounts of meat they ate, they would automatically be lowering their risks of disease. Furthermore, eating animal fat can lead to obesity, and obesity can cause numerous health problems. For example,

obesity can cause people to slow down and their heart to have to work harder. This results in high blood pressure. Meat is also high in cholesterol, and this only adds to health problems. With so much fat consumption in this country, it is no wonder that heart disease is a leading killer of Americans.

4   If people followed vegetarian diets, their health would improve. In fact, it could even save someone's life. Eating certain kinds of vegetables, such as broccoli, brussels sprouts, and cauliflower, has been shown to reduce the chance of contracting colon cancer later in life. Vegetables do not contain the "bad" fats that meat does. Vegetables do not contain cholesterol, either. Furthermore, native inhabitants of areas of the world where people eat more vegetables than meat, notably certain areas of the former Soviet Asian republics, routinely live to be over one hundred.

5   Some people argue that, human nature being what it is, it would be unhealthy for humans to not eat meat. They say that humans are naturally carnivores and cannot help wanting to consume a juicy piece of red meat. However, anthropologists have shown that early humans ate meat only when other foods were not abundant. Man is inherently an herbivore, not a carnivore.

6   Numerous scientific studies have shown the benefits of vegetarianism for people in general, and I know firsthand how my life has improved since I decided to give up meat entirely. Though it was difficult at first, I have never regretted my decision to become a vegetarian. I feel better, and my friends tell me that I look better than ever before. More and more people are becoming aware of the risks associated with meat consumption. If you become vegetarian, your life will improve, too.

Steps in the Writing Process

Step 1: Choosing a Topic

For this assignment, the topic was given: the benefits or problems of vegetarianism. As you consider the assignment, you have to decide what kind of essay to write. Will you compare or contrast the benefits of vegetarianism with another type of diet? Will you talk about the causes and effects of vegetarianism? Will you argue that vegetarianism is or is not better than eating animal products?

Sean chose to write an argumentative essay about vegetarianism to try to convince readers of its benefits.

Step 2: Brainstorming

The next step for Sean was to brainstorm.

In this step, you write every idea that pops into your head about your topic. Some of these ideas will be good, and some will be bad; write them all. The main purpose of brainstorming is to write as many ideas as you can think of. If one idea looks especially good, you might circle that idea or put a check next to it. If you write an idea and you know right away that you are not going to use it, you can cross it out.

Brainstorming methods include making lists, clustering, and diagramming. Use whatever method you like best.

Look at Sean's brainstorming diagram on the topic of vegetarianism.

3. ~~More exercising~~
2. Benefits for me
1. Why I changed

My own experience
as a veg.

examples of
benefits of certain
vegetables (broccoli
as anti-cancer?)

Vegetarianism?

environmental
benefits

① animal raising
   costs more
② cutting down
   rain forests
   for cattle farms
   (? global warming)

~~animal
testing
is
barbaric~~

~~types of
vegetarians~~

① no meat
   at all
② only dairy
③ fish/seafood ok

health
benefits

1. Longer life
2. danger of
   too much
   fat
   ⓐ high blood
      pressure
   ⓑ obesity

3. E

4. animals carry
   some parasites
   & disease
4. Longer life
   in some places
   that eat
   little meat

As you can see from the brainstorming diagram, Sean considered many benefits of being a vegetarian. Notice a few items in the diagram. As he organized his brainstorming, Sean wrote "examples of benefits of certain vegetables" as a spoke on the wheel. Then he realized that this point would be a good number 3 in the list of benefits, so he drew an arrow to show that he should move it there. For number 4, Sean wrote "animal testing for cosmetics." Then he decided that this is not related to the topic of the benefits of becoming a vegetarian, so he crossed it out.

Getting the Information
How would you get the information for this brainstorming exercise?

• You might read a book or an article about vegetarianism.

• You could spend time in a library looking for articles on the subject.

• You could also interview an expert on the topic, such as a vegetarian or a nutritionist. This method is not only useful but also fun. You can ask the person specific questions about parts of the topic that are not clear to you.

Step 3: Outline and Rough Draft

This step has two parts: an outline and a rough draft.

Outline

Next, create an outline for the essay. Here is Sean's rough outline that he wrote from his brainstorming notes.

I. Introduction

   a. Define vegetarianism

   b. List different types

   c. Thesis statement: _____

II. Environmental benefits

   a. Rain forests

   b. Global warming

III. Health issues

   a. Too much fat from meat: obesity, diseases, cancer,

   b. High blood pressure and heart disease

   c. Cancer-fighting properties of broccoli and cauliflower, etc.

IV. Counterargument

   a. Man is carnivore?

   b. Not true

V. Conclusion

   Opinion: life will improve

After you have chosen the main points for your essay, you will need to develop some supporting details. You should include examples, reasons, explanations, definitions, or personal experiences. One of the most common techniques in generating these supporting details is asking specific questions about the topic, for example:

Support

- What is it?

- What happened?

- How did this happen?

- What is it like or not like? Why?

Rough Draft

Next, Sean wrote a rough draft. In this step you take information from your brainstorming session and write the essay. This first draft may contain many errors, such as misspellings, incomplete ideas, and comma errors. At this point, don't worry about correcting the errors. The main thing is to put your ideas into sentences.

You may feel that you don't know what you think about the topic yet. In this case, it may be difficult for you to write, but it's important to just write, no matter what comes out. Sometimes writing helps you think, and as soon as you form a new thought, you can write it.

Making changes   As you write the rough draft, you may want to add information or take some out. In some cases, your rough draft may not follow your outline exactly. That is okay. Writers don't always stick with their original plan or follow the steps in the writing process in order. Sometimes they go back and forth between steps. The writing process is much more like a cycle than a line.

Read Sean's rough draft with his teacher's comments.

Better Living as a Vegetarian

Wow – too abrupt? You don't talk about hamburgers anymore??

Do you like hamburgers? Eating meat, especially beef, is an interesting part of the daily
vocabulary?

life in the United States. In addition, this high eating of meat is a major contributing thing/*factor*
word choice?

causes
that makes a great many deaths in this country, including the unnecessarily high number of

deaths from heart-related problems. Vegetarianism has caught on slowly in this culture.
) and it
Vegetarianism is a way of life that can help improve not only the quality of people's lives but

also people's longevity.   → *the quality but also the length of people's lives*

This is not a topic sentence
Because demand for meat animals is so high., Cattle are being raised in areas where the
c

rain forest once stood. As rain forest land is cleared in massive amounts in order to make

room for the cattle ranches, the environmental balance is being upset. This could have

For example,   *transition?*

serious consequences for us in both the near and long term. How much of the current global

warming is due to man's disturbing the rain forest?

You need a more specific topic relating to health.

Meat contains a high amount of fat. Eating this fat has been connected in research

cases with certain kinds of cancer. Furthermore, eating animal fat can lead to obesity, and

obesity can cause many different kinds of diseases, for example, obesity can cause people to

slow down and their heart to have to work harder. This results in high blood pressure.

Meat is high in cholesterol, and this only adds to the health problems. With the high

consumption of animal fat in this country, it is no wonder that heart disease is a leading

killer of Americans.

     On the other hand, eating a vegetarian diet can improve a person's health. And

necessary?

vegetables taste so good. In fact, it can even save someone's life. Eating certain kinds of

vegetables such as broccoli, brussels sprouts, and cauliflower has been shown to reduce the

combine sentences?

chance of having colon cancer later in life. Vegetables do not contain the "bad" fats that

meat does. Vegetables do not contain cholesterol, either. Native inhabitants of areas of the

world where mostly vegetables are consumed, notably certain areas of the former Soviet

Asian republics, routinely live to be over one hundred.

good sentence

     Though numerous scientific studies have shown the benefits of vegetarianism for people

in general, and I know first-hand how my life has improved since I decided to give up meat

entirely. In 1994, I saw a TV program that discussed problems connected to animals that are

raised for food. the program showed how millions of chickens are raised in dirty, crowded

conditions until they are killed. The program also talked about how diseases can be spread

from cow or pig to humans due to unsanitary conditions. Shortly after I saw this show, I

not related to your topic

decided to try life without eating meat. Though it was difficult at first, I have never regretted

my decision to become a vegetarian. I feel better and my friends tell me that I look better

than ever before.

Being a vegetarian has many benefits. Try it.

This is too short! How about making a prediction or suggestion for the reader. The previous paragraph told how the writer became a vegetarian, so doesn't it make sense for the conclusion to say something like "I'm sure your life will be better too if you become a vegetarian?"

I like this essay. You really need to work on the conclusion.

Rough draft tips   Here are some things to remember about the rough draft copy:

- The rough draft is not the final copy. Even native speakers who are good writers do not write an essay only one time. They rewrite as many times as necessary until the essay is the best that it can be.

- It's okay for you to make notes on your drafts, circle words, draw connecting lines, cross out words, write new information. Make notes to yourself about what to change, what to add, or what to reconsider.

- If you can't think of a word or an idea as you write, leave a blank space or circle. Then go back and fill in the space later. If you write a word that you know isn't the right one, circle or underline it so you can fill in the right word later. Don't stop writing. When people read your draft, they can see these areas you are having trouble with and offer comments that may help.

- Don't be afraid to throw some sentences away if they don't sound right. Just as a good housekeeper throws away unnecessary things from the house, so a good writer throws out unnecessary or wrong words or sentences.

Step 4: Cleaning Up the Rough Draft

The handwriting in the first draft is usually not neat. Sometimes it's so messy that only the writer can read it! Use a word processor, if possible, to make writing and revising easier.

After you make notes on your rough draft, put it away for several hours or a few days. You may find it helpful to come back to the paper later when you are fresh and are more likely to see problems. At that time, copy the draft again in a neater hand or type it on a computer, if you have one. If you notice any words or sentences that don't belong, throw them out. At this time you may also want to add ideas that make the paper better.

Step 5: Peer Editing

Sean used a peer editing sheet to get feedback on his essay draft. Peer editing is important in the writing process. You don't always see your own mistakes or places where information is missing because you are too close to the essay that you created. Ask someone to read your draft and give you feedback about your writing. Choose someone that you trust and feel comfortable with. Some people feel uneasy about peer editing, but the result is almost always a better essay. Remember to be polite when you edit another student's paper.

Step 6: Revising the Draft

This step consists of three parts:

1. Reacting to the comments on the peer editing sheet

2. Rereading the essay and making changes

3. Rewriting the essay one more time

Step 7: Proofing the Final Paper

Most of the hard work is over now. In this step, the writer pretends to be a brand-new reader who has never seen the essay before. Proofread your essay for grammar, punctuation, and spelling errors and to see if the sentences flow smoothly.

Of course, the very last step is to turn the paper in to your teacher and hope that you get a good grade!

Writer's Note: **Proofread**

One good way to proofread your essay is to first set it aside for several hours or a day or two. The next time you read your essay, your head will be clearer and you will be more likely to see any problems.

Symbol	Meaning	Example
∧	insert a word or words	The name of ∧ cat is Boots. The U.S. president lives in the ∧ House.
⌐⌐	word order	They bought two books new yesterday.
??	unclear meaning	The dry rain fell from the sky. ??
#	error with number	He is the best of all the student in my class. #
℘	delete	The company president ℘e has a new plan.
→	indent paragraph	→ This report will compare the weather in Brazil with the weather in Canada.
=	parallel structure	This amazing car was designed in Argentina, constructed in Mexico, and it was sold mainly = in Canada.
VT	wrong verb tense	VT Tomorrow I went to the bank. VT She is owning two houses.
WF	wrong word form	WF She is live with her aunt.
MODAL	add a modal; wrong modal	MODAL I'm not sure if I ∧ play tennis tomorrow. MODAL If you have a headache, I think that you may take an aspirin.
VOICE	wrong voice (change active to passive OR passive to active)	VOICE That book wrote in 1964.
TRANS	add a transition or connector	TRANS He studied hard. ∧ He did not pass.

COND	error with conditional	If I were you, <u>I will go</u> there immediately. *COND*
S/V	subject-verb agreement	The <u>customers was</u> angry about the service. *S/V*
ART	article error	If you are hungry, you can buy ˄sandwich. *ART* What is <u>a</u> name of the book that you read? *ART*
WC	error with word choice	I had a bad <u>cool</u>, so I did not go to class. *WC* Unfortunately, we <u>lost</u> our flight. *WC*
CAP	error with capitalization	He went to his aunt's house in <u>boston</u>. *CAP*
FRAG	sentence fragment	When the rain started to fall. *FRAG*
CS	comma splice	It rained all night<u>,</u> the river was full. *CS*
PRO	pronoun error	My sister is here. <u>He</u> arrived here yesterday. *PRO*
REF?	unclear reference	In 1822, the company finally introduced a new product. <u>This</u> was important. *REF?*
RO	run-on	Dallas is in <u>Texas, it</u> is not the capital city. *RO*
SP	spelling	With such a long neck, the <u>girafe</u> is unique. *SP*
IDIOM	error with an idiom	He did not <u>beat around the trees</u>. *IDIOM* He passed the test with <u>flying color</u>. *IDIOM*
P	punctuation	She was not late *P*
PREP	error with preposition	If you look <u>on</u> the sun for a long time, your eyes will hurt. *PREP* When in Los Angeles, he stays <u>in</u> the Hilton Hotel. *PREP*
POSS	error with possessive	The <u>presidents'</u> name is Johnson. *POSS*

Credits

Page 14, Exercise 15
Pauk, Walter and John P. Fiore, *Succeed in College* (Boston: Houghton Mifflin, 2000): 95.

Page 15, Exercise 16
Bulliet, Richard W. and Pamela Kyle Crossley, Daniel R. Headrick, Steven L. Johnson, and David Northrup, *The Earth and Its Peoples: A Global History* (Boston: Houghton Mifflin, 2000): 81–82.

Page 16, Exercise 17
Pride, William H., Robert J. Hughes, and Jack R. Kapoor, *Business* (Boston: Houghton Mifflin, 1999): 391.

Page 17, Exercise 18
Hunt, Douglas, *The Riverside Anthology of Literature, 3rd ed.* (Boston: Houghton Mifflin, 1997): 4–5.

Page 23, Exercise 2
Janda, Kenneth et al., *The Challenge of Democracy Brief, 4th ed.* (Boston: Houghton Mifflin, 2002): 149.

Page 94–95, Exercise 5
Bulliet, Richard W. and Pamela Kyle Crossley, Daniel R. Headrick, Steven L. Johnson, and David Northrup, *The Earth and Its Peoples: A Global History* (Boston: Houghton Mifflin, 2000): 432.

Page 147, Exercise 5
Adapted from "Four Things that Can Make You a Virus Target," *Self*, January 2002.

Page 158, Exercise 4
Daly, John A. and Isa N. Engleberg, *Presentations in Everyday Life: Strategies for Effective Speaking* (Boston: Houghton Mifflin, 2001): 191.

Page 159, Exercise 5
Pride, William H., Robert J. Hughes, and Jack R. Kapoor, *Business* (Boston: Houghton Mifflin, 1999): 454.

Page 159, Exercise 6
Ryan, K. and J. Cooper, *Those Who Can, Teach* (Boston: Houghton Mifflin, 2001): 358–359.

Page 233, Exercise 1
Pride, William H., Robert J. Hughes, and Jack R. Kapoor, *Business* (Boston: Houghton Mifflin, 1999): 154.

Page 293, Appendix 5
Folse, Keith S., A. Muchmore-Vokoun, and E. Vestri Solomon, *Great Essays* (Boston: Houghton Mifflin, 1999): 126–134.